ML

FREEDOM FROM FEAR

Freedom from Fear

The Slave and his Emancipation

◆◆◆◆◆◆◆◆◆◆◆◆◆◆◆◆◆◆◆◆◆◆◆◆

O. A. SHERRARD

GREENWOOD PRESS, PUBLISHERS
WESTPORT, CONNECTICUT

Library of Congress Cataloging in Publication Data

Sherrard, Owen Aubrey, 1887-1962.
    Freedom from fear.

    Reprint of the ed. published by St. Martin's Press,
New York.
    Bibliography: p.
    1. Slave-trade--Great Britain. 2. Slavery in
Great Britain--Anti-slavery movements. 3. Slavery--
Emancipation. I. Title.
[HT1162.S45 1973]   301.44'93   73-10755
ISBN 0-8371-7024-9

First published in 1961 by St. Martin's Press, New York

Reprinted with the permission of St. Martin's Press

Reprinted in 1973 by Greenwood Press,
a division of Williamhouse-Regency Inc.

Library of Congress Catalogue Card Number 73-10755

ISBN 0-8371-7024-9

Printed in the United States of America

CONTENTS

Preface, 7   1774957

PART ONE : THE SLAVE

I.	*The Ancient World*	11
II.	*Las Casas*	24
III.	*Sir John Hawkins*	33
IV.	*The Assiento*	42
V.	*The Trade*	51
VI.	*The Raw Material*	58
VII.	*The Slave at Work*	67
VIII.	*The Slave in the English Colonies*	77
IX.	*Thistlewood*	85

PART TWO : EMANCIPATION

X.	*'The People called Quakers'*	97
XI.	*Granville Sharp and the Law*	102
XII.	*Clarkson writes an Essay*	111
XIII.	*Slave Trade or Slavery?*	120
XIV.	*Wilberforce*	128
XV.	*Conflicting Evidence*	135
XVI.	*The Struggle in Parliament*	145
XVII.	*Patchwork*	164
XVIII.	*Freedom*	170

Postscript, 181

Bibliography, 191

Index, 195

PREFACE

I HAVE TO THANK Mrs. Bellamy of Lyme Regis for permission to quote from Sarah Fox's Diaries; the Librarian of Rhodes House, Oxford, for permission to quote from Ramsay's Papers; the authorities of the Lincoln Archives for permission to quote from the Thistlewood Journals; and the Anti-Slavery Society for much help and encouragement.

For those who are interested I have included a list of the books I have consulted.

PART ONE

•••••••••••••••••••••••••••••••••••••••

THE SLAVE

PART I : THE SLAVE

I. The Ancient World

I

SLAVERY HAS no birthday. In the annals of history the slave is present from the beginning, inglorious and unexplained, as though he had sprung, complete with his manacles and misery, from the serpent's head, when Paradise was lost. He appears often enough in the earliest chronicles, whether on parchment or in stone, but only as the anonymous tool and chattel of his master. Without wealth or power to reward, he had no claim on sculptor or scribe. They were not concerned with his pedigree or with his function in the world; his origin was unknown to them, his end immaterial. Their business was to praise the great king who commanded their services, and their only interest in the slave was to thrust him into the crowd of captives who graced the conqueror's triumph. Enough immortality for him if his tribe's name figured in the scroll of the vanquished. But if slavery had no birthday, and the slaves who were its manifestation no name, they were to exercise an influence on history greater than conqueror, or scribe, or sculptor could ever have conceived—at what cost to the slaves who can tell? Nor, though their influence has ceased, has their story ended, for slavery is not yet dead.

From the broad historical outlook, they have passed through two stages; in the first bearing on their shoulders, like a patient Atlas, the glories of many long dead civilizations; and in the second, more wretched than the first, losing even that vicarious honour, and falling to an abject state in which they contributed solely to private greed. Their condition, especially in their second phase, should have seared the conscience of a nominally Christian world, but left it peculiarly unmoved. The idea of slavery was so deeply ingrained that no one questioned its propriety. All nations either endured or enjoyed it. England participated, though less as a slave-owning than as a slave-trading country; and it was only by degrees and the efforts of devoted men that she awoke to a full realization of its horrors. But having woken, England took action, fighting and winning the battle of emancipation against an incredulous world and an angry phalanx of vested interests. To appreciate the greatness of her task, there is need of some brief knowledge of the growth and progress of slavery. Here is the story.

II

The belief that 'man is born free' was a dream that came to Rousseau in the eighteenth century, and in the same century Congress wrote into the Declaration of Independence the fallacy that 'all men are created equal'. Neither statement found a place in the more realistic views of the ancient world. 'It is allowed', said Aristotle, 'on all hands that in a State which is to enjoy a noble polity the citizens must be relieved from anxiety about the bare necessaries of life. But the means of securing this relief are not easy to apprehend. The natural suggestion is that there should be a large subject population' (Aristotle. *Politics* II, IX).

When he came to the question of finding that population, Aristotle asserted dogmatically that some men were 'naturally slaves for whom the condition of slavery was alike expedient and just'. But perhaps because the supply of natural slaves fell palpably short of the demand or perhaps because he knew of slaves who did not conform to his definition, he added that there might be also legal slaves, men who had fallen to their low estate, not because they had been born with slavish souls, but because they had been overtaken by disaster or defeat. Those were the slaves who gave the greatest cause for anxiety, for the simple reason that while there is 'a mutual helpfulness and friendship of master and slave wherever the relation is in accordance with Nature's ordinance, just the contrary is the case where it is unnatural and depends upon law and force' (ibid. I, VI). Yet the problem of numbers still remained, and so, finally, Aristotle admitted in a hurried scrambling sentence, that 'distinct alike from the science of the slavemaster and of the slave is the science of acquiring slaves which is in a sense a science of war or of the chase' (ibid. I, VII).

Aristotle thus gave up the theory of natural slaves, adopting instead the view that slavery was the penalty of weakness, and that war was its true purveyor. So far as the ancient world was concerned he was not far wrong. The fact gave a special flavour to ancient slavery, for wars are not waged between individuals but communities, and the outcome of war therefore tended to be the enslavement of a complete people or tribe. Of course there were also individual slaves—captives of the spear; and debtors; and those inveterate German gamblers who pledged and lost their own freedom in one last desperate throw (Tacitus. *On Britain and Germany*, p. 121). Of course, too, in a world of limited trade, the slave market made an early appearance, seeing that its merchandise needed no factory and could be acquired who knows how. But history would scarcely notice the individual unless particularly notorious—Samson, for instance, eyeless in Gaza. More memorable, more 'historical' was the descent of a whole people to become 'a large subject population'.

The best known case is that of the Israelites. They sold themselves to Egypt when they were few in numbers and too weak to maintain themselves; but multiplying in course of time, they at last posed for their masters the problem of racial antagonism—a problem not unknown at the present time. When they had won their freedom, they were not forgetful of their past. Recognizing that slaves can be a danger as well as a benefit, their first resolve was to exterminate rather than to enslave the tribes of Canaan. But success soon inflated their ideas; and whether yielding to trickery, as the story goes, or to a growing desire for ease and ostentation, they spared the men of Gibeon, dooming them to perpetual bondage as 'hewers of wood and drawers of water' (Joshua 9; 27). Yet, even so, their memory of Egypt was not obliterated, and because of that memory their laws governing the treatment of slaves were exceptionally humane, as judged by the standards of the time.

Originally, the members of a subject race seem to have been less the property of individual masters than a pool of 'nationalized' labour, providing the workmen for a Pharaoh or a Nebuchadnezzar, for a congregation or a state. In their public aspect they were the instruments by which ambitious kings could build palaces for themselves and temples for their gods without the fear of financial disaster or labour shortage. Slaves, acting the part of modern machinery, produced the wonders of the past—the pyramids, the ancient temples, the fabulous cities which excite our admiration even in their ruins. But in the course of centuries the outward form of slavery changed from the subjugation of whole tribes to the purchase of individuals—in a word from public ownership to private possession; and this change had a marked effect on its nature. The methods of recruitment became increasingly degraded, and slavery itself increasingly abject. The change had begun in Aristotle's time, but was still far from complete.

It is as well to recall that there were two main civilizations in Greece, the intellectual and artistic world of Athens and over against it the military and disciplinarian regime of Sparta. Both needed, or thought they needed, slaves for the realization of their destiny, but they differed considerably in their attitude towards their slaves, and the difference emphasizes certain aspects which are not without importance.

In classical times Athens had slaves in plenty on which to found her 'noble polity'. As the Athenians claimed to be autochthonous, it is not clear whence this servile population came, but in numbers it was many times larger than the free population. Yet, if one must suppose these slaves were purchased rather than conquered, the State did not for that reason wash its hands of them. They were not regarded simply as goods and chattels to be dealt with as the individual owners thought fit; they were a species of poor relation and as such were accorded some small rights and offered some slight protection. Owners could not put their slaves to death, nor could strangers assault them without becoming liable to actions at law. Nor again was cruelty condoned; a slave who felt himself to be brutally treated could compel his master to put him up for sale. In general the lot of slaves in Attica seems to have been reasonably mild, at least milder than elsewhere; many of them were even employed on minor official duties, as for instance the policing of the City.

But then the Athenians were a particularly enlightened people, endowed with that gift of the artistic temperament which gives an insight into the feelings of others. The finer and more exalted characters, men such as Plato, though they accepted the common belief that the perfect flowering of their civilization depended on 'a subject population', yet found a certain embarrassment in the thought and some reluctance to admit it. This incipient understanding with its hint of compassion was no doubt encouraged by the fact that the great Athenian landowners lived, not in the capital, but on their estates, supervising the work of their dependants and no doubt taking a rational interest in their welfare. Such an intercourse would make for sympathy and tend to win the loyalty and affection of the slaves, so that the latent, and often open, antagonism which exists almost universally between a master race and its subject population seems in Attica to have been practically non-existent. The slaves were not continually seeking an opportunity to revolt, nor were they notoriously anxious to act as Quislings. During the Peloponnesian War, which led to the downfall of Athens, they remained loyal until the Spartans, giving up the system of yearly inroads into Attica, entered instead into permanent occupation of Decelea, driving off the landowners and living themselves on the produce of the country. Thereafter, in their masters' absence, the slaves had little option but to work for the Spartan invaders, and it is not surprising that some twenty thousand in all deserted to the enemy. But it is to be noted that twenty thousand was a mere five per cent of the slave population, and the movement was obviously a matter of compulsion.

Athens was *sui generis*. She treated her slaves well, knowing that they formed the foundation of that famous city which, in the words of Pericles, was the school of Hellas, and that there was neither sense nor advantage in making the foundation unsafe or unsound. Whatever the theory might be, the slaves of Attica differed little from the poorer classes of her citizens, except that they did not share in the actual rights and duties of citizenship or in the mysteries of religion.

The Helots of Lacedaemonia offered a strong contrast, showing all the characteristics of slave mentality. They were, to begin with, a conquered people—the indigenous population subdued by the invading Spartans and condemned to perpetual bondage. As such they were the slaves, not of individuals, but of the State, which bound them to the soil in what is known as predial slavery, assigning them to the localities in which they lived, and placing them, as a matter of convenience, under the immediate control of private citizens. But the rights of their so-called masters were strictly limited; they could neither free them nor sell them, nor drive them from the land. The Helots, in short, were a species of compulsory tenant, obliged to cultivate their fields and forced to hand over a fixed proportion of the produce. Apart from this duty as serfs and tillers of the soil, they were under the orders of the State which could and did employ them as galley slaves and camp-followers and even on occasion as fully armed soldiers.

The Spartans treated themselves harshly, and it is not therefore to be wondered at if they treated their slaves with no consideration. The slaves reacted as might be expected, giving no hint of loyalty nor admitting any obligation; they were concerned only with their own lot and their own hopes and fears and how they could turn to their own advantage any passing opportunity. The Helots, said Aristotle, had often risen against the Lacedaemonians, for whose misfortunes they were always lying in wait (Aristotle II, IX). The distrust was mutual. The Spartans expected no good of their slaves and took exceptional pains to keep them in subjection. According to Thucydides, most of the institutions of Lacedaemon were framed to guard against insurrections of the Helots; and each year at their election, those powerful officials, the Ephors, solemnly declared war on the slaves, in order to whitewash in advance any action they might think fit to take.

Their weapon was a secret police, a sort of early Gestapo, composed of selected young Spartans, whose task it was to spy on the Helots, and to carry out any sentences which the Ephors might pronounce against them. That they could be both cunning and ruthless is shown by the well-known story of the Ephors who, growing alarmed at the number and vigour of the Helot youth, promised liberty to those of them who claimed to have rendered the best service to the Lacedaemonians. From the most high-spirited of those who put forward claims, the Ephors selected some two thousand and led them, in ironical triumph, round the temples. Nominally they received their liberty, but within a very short time the whole two thousand had disappeared, no one knew how or where (Thuc. IV, 80). It was not becoming for Helots to be too valiant; they were 'a subject population', without root, without loyalty, without religion. Having neither personal affections nor a sense of patriotism to constrain them, they must needs be controlled, or so the Spartans thought, by a systematic terrorism. It was no wonder that they became men without hope or expectation, to whom life offered nothing but perpetual hardship diversified only by the fierce, if precarious, joys of attempted revolt.

III

Rome absorbed both Sparta and Athens, and with her coarse fibre and essential vulgarity, adopted the worst features of both, especially where slaves were concerned. In the far-off early days, when Rome had been little more than a village, she had recruited her slaves, few in number, by attacking and overthrowing neighbouring villages. The victor would drive or carry off his spoils with his own hands, a man maybe for his farm, a woman perhaps for his bed, a cow or sheep to add to his stock, and returning home would be proud of his acquisitions and anxious to preserve them. Thereafter being only a small peasant himself, he would be obliged to work by the side of his new dependants, and in the companionship of common tasks might well discover the bond of human sympathy. The slave's lot might not have been too hard in those primitive days.

But as the centuries passed and Rome went from triumph to triumph, all was changed. Rome became wealthy, the small farms expanded into large estates, and the owners grew first greedy and then luxurious. With the increase of riches the old frugal customs were discarded, the old simple virtues died out. There was a strong tendency to leave the country and crowd into the town, where money could be made without physical effort, where every form of pleasure abounded, and affluence and flaunting vice went hand in hand. Meanwhile the farm left behind—now a matter of broad acres—could be worked by slaves, and so contribute to the gains of city speculators. The result was twofold. With the precision of Gresham's law, the slave drove out the hired hand; the free labourer disappeared; and the small-holder next door, unable to compete, sold his farm to swell the possessions of an absentee landlord or a soulless syndicate. The displaced freeman passed into the town to become one of the mob, a lounger and a useless mouth, clamouring for bread and circuses, and expecting each new Emperor to dispense ever larger doles. And while the City was thus rotting in moral decay, the country was fast losing all semblance of humanity. Whatever ties may have linked the master to the man, so long as the master lived on his estate, were not merely loosened when he left for the town but were deliberately broken. The free labourer had to be paid, and being a Roman citizen was liable to be called up for military service. Such drawbacks might be patiently endured for a cherished dependant, but hardly, if there was any alternative, for a labourer who was at best a mere name in a bailiff's report. And there was an alternative in the employment of slaves, who earned no pay and were forbidden to carry arms. The free labourer must perforce yield to the slave, and did.

The change was bad in itself and worse in its consequences. Roman law gave the head of the household a power which would have been utterly intolerable if it had not been softened by love of home and family, which was one of the nobler Roman attributes. Children had no independent rights against their father. So long as he lived, he ruled with absolute sway over their persons and property. He could not only punish them, he could sell them into slavery and even condemn them to death. What the Roman could do to his children, *a fortiori* he could do to his slaves. In every sense of the word, and in the eyes of the law, a slave was the chattel of his owner. He had no rights of any sort, beyond what he could earn by his usefulness. Like any ox or ass he was fed so long as he was strong and healthy and able to work, but directly he fell ill or grew feeble, he was sold without compunction for what he would fetch. Nor had he any hope of moving his master to pity by the sight of his miseries. His master was far away in the town, and he himself was in effect the slave of a slave, the helpless instrument of an overseer whose main business was to curry favour with the distant master by making the farm pay. The terrible fate of the plantation slave is notorious—how he was branded with hot irons, how he was forced to work in heavy chains, how his back was torn and scarred with the lash, how at night he was locked into a prison, the ergastulum, often underground and always filthy. There was a proverb at Rome that a slave must either work or sleep, and in the case of the plantation slave it was more than a proverb, it was a truism.

Slavery degrades all with whom it comes in contact, master as well as man. Had the master been present, there would no doubt have been cruelty enough; but with the master's absence, conditions grew utterly bestial. Punishment turned to torture, and the unmeaning agonies too often inflicted on slaves were a measure of the inhumanity of sadistic overseers rather than of the misdeeds of the sufferers. Violence and cruelty begat their like, and in Italy, as in Sparta, the treatment meted out to slaves bore a bitter crop. Servile insurrections were persistent and bloody. Where the slaves gained a temporary success, they did as they had been done by; the masters were massacred, the women raped and the children dashed to pieces. And when at last the rising was put down, the Romans retaliated in kind—gibbets lined the roads, and thousands were crucified. It is no wonder that the Romans had yet a second and still more pregnant proverb—so many slaves, so many foes.

There was another side to Roman slavery, less physically revolting but more hideous spiritually—the position of the town slave. The Roman was a natural vulgarian, and as wealth came to him, he adopted the worst excesses of the nouveaux riches. His simplicity went. In a desire for ostentation he crowded his household with slaves—handsome and upstanding men, to form a creditable retinue when he walked abroad; practised artisans to carry out his repairs; Greek pedagogues to educate and too often to corrupt his children; and slick cockneys to overreach contractors and tradesmen. He had gentleman's gentlemen by the score, lady's-maids by the dozen, cooks, chefs and scullions, grammarians, rhetoricians, rope-dancers, painters, physicians and conjurors, any Tom, Dick or Harry who could worm his way into the rich man's good graces or play upon his superstition. There was no end to the list, for slaves were cheap and a competition in parade was the parvenu's joy. Households could number anything from a mere handful up to thousands.

All this display had a bad effect not only on the individual but on the national economy. The waste of labour was prodigious, and worse still it had the same result in the town as in the country, it drove out the native artisans and discouraged the native industries. Slaves had long performed the heavier and more uncomfortable jobs of country life, in the farms and mines, in the factories and mills; they now began to relieve their masters of the more skilled occupations of the town. Before long it was the slaves who excelled in the delicate handling of arts and crafts, who were masters of the professions, and who absorbed and became adroit in business. Work of every kind was handed over to them while the free-born Roman lazed in bed or sought the latest distraction. For him Rome had lost all the attributes of an active and self-sufficient city; and offering nothing serious to hold his attention, had become little more than a prodigious funfair, a scene of debauchery and dissipation. Of the old simple virtues nothing remained to the Roman but a debased courage—the courage to plumb the depths of vice, to explore every type of sensual pleasure, and at last, jaded and worn out, to open his veins in a hot bath. It was a life with all the satiety of luxury and all the weariness of sin.

The effect on the slave was obvious. He could, of course, and no doubt often did, take the line of least resistance, hoping to remain unnoticed among the crowd; but it was a precarious line with little attraction, for punishments were handed out with a capricious hand, and the sins of one could be visited upon all. The murder, for instance, of a master, was automatically followed by the execution of the whole household—man, woman and child, the innocent and the guilty. 'I know,' said the honest slave in the comedy, 'that a cross will be my grave.' But should the slave be ambitious, hoping to obtain manumission, and perhaps like other dexterous freedmen to amass a fortune, he needs must win the favour of master or mistress; and how more certainly than by pandering to their vices and follies? The course marked out for him was abundantly clear. In the country slaves might be physically miserable; in the town they must be spiritually perverted.

IV

With Imperial Rome, the slavery of the ancient world reached its nadir. It had lost what starveling semblance of virtue it had once possessed as the alternative to sudden death on the field or shameful sacrifice on a foreign altar. War waged between man and man has a not ignoble quality, and to serve one's conqueror is a species of homage that might not be wholly unendurable even to a proud mind. But slaves were no longer captured in fair fight; they were snared and trapped and hunted down by prowling bandits and marauding ruffians, to be sold like frightened sheep in the slave markets of Delos. Rome had long since completed her career of conquest, and the demand for slaves which the unending supply of prisoners of war had so stimulated was now met by greedy and unscrupulous merchants who sought their prey among the populations of the east. Slaves had become separate individuals who had to endure their own wretchedness. The days had passed when whole peoples were reduced to subjection and private misery could be forgotten in the general cataclysm.

Nor had the slaves now, except for a small minority, the doubtful honour of serving the state; they were not public slaves, as they had been in Greece, but the unhappy property of a single owner—often a man of less intellectual power and poorer abilities than themselves, but none the less their master to bully and torment them. Slaves, said Caius Cassius, when upholding in the Senate the law which required the execution of a household, four hundred strong, to avenge the murder of a City Prefect, slaves were the refuse and sweepings of the nations, to be kept in order only by terror. He harped on terror because in fact his world was afraid of its own slaves. Strange but true, the greater part of the Roman Empire was composed of that same refuse and sweepings of the nations; and the smaller part lived in dread of the day when its slaves would realize their power and demand their rights. The peace of the empire rested on fear; its bulwark was cruelty.

Such a state of affairs could hardly persist, and while the Roman Empire began its decline, the lot of slaves began in some tiny degree to improve. Hope for their betterment had never been entirely extinct. Lawgivers, both theoretical and practical, had always wished to impose some form of restraint, if only to benefit their own nationals. Moses forbade the Hebrews to hold their countrymen in bondage for more than a limited period; Plato frowned on the idea of Greek enslaving Greek; and Seneca even spoke of slaves as humble friends. Athens and Sparta both gave some protection, and though at the outset Rome gave none, in the decline of her empire she was less severe. There must have been many good masters, and certainly there were many grateful slaves. But the fact remains that slavery was held to be a necessary state, and to be compassionate with slaves was regarded not as a natural feeling but as a personal idiosyncracy. The slave was hardly human; he had no rights, he had no soul.

Rome was great enough to carry her slave system as well as her vicious emperors and corrupt capital. She was strong because her empire was founded on justice; her laws were sound and her administrators able. Nor was she lacking in power; her armies repelled the inroads of the barbarians, her navies kept the seas, and the Empire, feeling safe in her keeping, turned to trade and grew rich. Nor as yet were there any disruptive ideologies to disturb her tranquillity. The state-established religion was the deification of the Emperor and meant no less and no more than modern loyalty to the Crown. No patriotic Roman could reasonably object, especially as, for private purposes, he could choose any secondary religion he liked. There were sects in plenty to suit all tastes. Rome was tolerant, and rather welcomed religious festivals; indeed the more the better, since carnivals, high days and orgies gave colour to life and made for contentment. And as for philosophies, Rome smiled with equal indulgence on the Epicurean wrapped in his pleasures and the Stoic wrapped in his mantle of assumed indifference. Only slaves were debarred from the varied life of war and politics and religion. Such legislation as was passed on their behalf was mainly negative, reducing the masters' right to condemn to death, or forbidding grants of freedom if they were likely to influence local elections. The canker of slavery was only too evident, but defeated the skill of Roman legality as it had defeated the subtlety of Greek philosophy.

v

At this point the long process of emancipation began. It started in a distant province of the Empire with what must have seemed to the average Roman no more than the execution of an agitator who had been stirring up trouble in Jerusalem. But there was a strange sequel. A few obscure persons—fishermen and the like—who had been implicated in the riots and had been dispersed, suddenly reassembled, and began, with a power and conviction not to be gainsaid, to proclaim a new doctrine of resurrection from the dead, and to announce the foundation of a new kingdom apart from and over-riding the Roman Empire. More amazing still, they seemed to exercise a fascination over the mob which listened to them eagerly. It was highly disturbing, if not treasonable; and to make matters worse, the members of this new sect rejected the harmless worship of the Emperor, and looked with a jaundiced eye not only on riotous saturnalia which any strait-laced man might well dislike, but even on the good-humoured festivals of established religion. They kept themselves darkly apart from the happy-go-lucky ways of everyday life, and spoke threateningly of vengeance to come, of the world ending in fire and flame, and of a final reckoning and fierce judgment. They were dangerous people.

Such or something like it, the Christian doctrine must have appeared at its first beginning to the corrupt Roman society. But there was another aspect—the impact of Christianity on slaves—which was more immediately frightening, because it concerned not the future world, but the present; and touched on a matter which frequently troubled the Roman in his more serious moments. The slaves were a continuing and growing menace; they were necessary if life was to be worth living, but they must be kept in constant check or they would overthrow the established order of things. And the Christians appeared to be giving them ideas above their station. What the end would be, who could tell. But the Roman thought it best to keep a sharp eye on Christian doctrinaire and combustible slave alike.

From his own point of view he was right, for the effect of Christianity on the slave was immense. It did not stir him to revolt or even encourage him to self-pity; on the contrary, St. Paul's injunction was clear and precise: 'let as many slaves as are under the yoke count their own masters worthy of all honour'. But it did something which had never yet been done; it brought the slave within the pale of religion; it restored his soul to him and gave him spiritual liberty, proclaiming that in the eyes of God there was neither bond nor free. Never had he dreamt of anything like this. Hitherto the slave's share of religion had been at best no more than the duties of temple attendant and temple courtesan, to sweep the floor and pander to lust; the higher mysteries, if there were any, eluded him. And now being raised suddenly to the same level as his master, he was in danger of spiritual pride. St. Paul recognized the danger and uttered a warning: 'they that have believing masters', he wrote, 'let them not despise them because they are brethren, but rather do them service, because they are faithful and beloved'.

If St. Paul recognized the danger, how much greater did it look in the eyes of the man in the street who felt that he was face to face with a new and inexplicable phenomenon? The Christian appeared to him to be turning the world upside down, and when the slaves, who far out-numbered the rest of the population, arrived at the top, the outcome was obvious—and terrifying. Hence he was disposed to approve the persecution of Christians and especially Christian slaves. It probably added to his perplexity to find that the Christian slave seemed almost to welcome martyrdom. It was certainly amazing, yet the reason was not hard to find. The lot of the slave in this world was sad enough and precarious enough. Suffering seemed to be his destiny, and to be thrown to the lions or burnt as a human torch had this advantage over his normal fate, that it was a passport to a state of bliss which eye had not seen nor ear heard, but which the new faith offered freely even to slaves. Many no doubt shrank back when the moment of trial came, but the number prepared to endure and even to welcome a painful death was enough to stagger belief.

Slowly but surely the new faith made its way, and as it progressed, played an ever-widening part in the amelioration of the slave's lot. Throughout the Middle Ages, the Church as a whole, in spite of individual lapses, proved to be a moderating influence, encouraging the master to offer manumission and giving the slave some sort of sanctuary. Side by side with the Church's prompting, there was growing up a spirit of freedom in municipal affairs and a marked change in social conditions. All combined to soften the asperities of slavery and even to look with less tolerance on its existence, so that, over the greater part of Europe, it turned by degrees into serfdom; and its natural decease rather than its conscious abolition became a possibility. Christianity had shown its wisdom in not immediately condemning slavery as such; it could not have done so in the world as then constituted without producing chaos. There was much of the statesman's sagacity as well as the precepts of religion in St. Paul's rule, 'let every man abide in the same calling wherein he was called'. But neither could Christianity leave the position untouched; it looked forward to the healing process of a regenerate heart, and as a first step offered a new approach and a new relationship between master and man, the slave giving willing service and the master recognizing their common humanity. Out of such a relationship abolition might well spring.

But meanwhile in the outside world, the old ideas persisted; slavery continued unabated in the east and infected all lands subject to eastern influence. All round the shores of the Mediterranean there was a perennial conflict between the Moor and the European—a clash of opposing races which had been handed down from classic times, a continuation, in changing form, of the Persian invasion of Greece, and of Rome's struggle with Carthage. But since those times a fresh factor had been added, so that it was no longer simply a fight between East and West, or even between disciplined governments and Barbary pirates, but between Moslem and Christian.

The clash of these rival creeds was a fruitful source of slavery. It killed, as so often, the kindlier elements of each, breeding anger and hatred in both, and justifying so easily the selling into bondage of the prisoners on either side. The Corsair pirates from their lairs in Tunis, Algiers and Tripoli, maintained a prosperous trade out of Christian captives, whom they seized along the southern shores of Europe and sold for menial service in Moslem households. Inevitably the European nations retaliated, so that while elsewhere in Christendom slavery tended to decrease, it flourished in Sicily and Southern Italy, and especially in Spain and Portugal, both of which had long suffered under Moorish rule. Now that freedom had been won, Moors from Granada and the coasts of Africa were sold daily and in large numbers in the markets of Andalusia (Irving: *Columbus* II, 263, 295). To all the other horrors of the slave trade, there had been added the bitterness of rival religions.

II. Las Casas

I

SUCH IN outline was the position when the fifteenth century dawned. It was an age of discovery and one in which Portugal for long took the lead. Throughout the early years the Portuguese were exploring slowly and cautiously down the west coast of Africa, until at last they came to the torrid zone where they discovered a race of men entirely new to them—black men, with flat noses, thick lips and short curly hair. The sight of them horrified the sailors who, putting their appearance down to the tropical heat, were apprehensive that if they stayed too long in those regions they might themselves be similarly blighted. But in the course of repeated voyages they grew accustomed to the sight, and in 1442, more by chance than deliberation, they brought some of these black men back. It was thus exactly fifty years before Columbus set out on his voyage of discovery, that specimens of the future slaves of America were introduced into the Iberian peninsula. With unconscious symbolism they brought with them a quantity of gold dust which not they but their masters were to enjoy; for they were, of course, doomed to slavery.

By this time slavery had passed through many phases, in each of which it had picked up or shed certain characteristics. It was no longer the custom to reduce whole populations to subjection, but there had been a distinct reversion towards Aristotle's theory of natural slaves. It had come to be accepted, as the result of historical events, that certain races, principally the Moors, and certain religions, mainly the Mohammedan, were more proper for slavery than others. The negroes fitted into this pattern. Their dark skins and the popular belief that they were the descendants of Ham, steeped in wickedness, thrust them even lower than the Moors, who by contrast were comparatively white and comparatively innocent. Nor was it any longer the custom for the State to absorb all the slaves for itself, though it had not given up its interest in them entirely. It still employed them in the galleys, but had discarded the system of predial slavery, so that individual owners had in some respects rather wider powers of control. The number of slaves in private households was not so great as before, probably through lack of money and perhaps because of a better sense of proportion, while cruelty had been lessened by more humane laws and a growing sense of refinement. But, clearly, need or opportunity might at any moment revive the old excessive numbers and the old bad conditions.

The greatest change, however, was the fact that the slave was no longer cut off from religion. It was a notable advance. Yet a corrupt element had crept in even here. Christianity had once come as blessing to the slaves in a pagan world; it was now used as an excuse for creating slaves in the Christian world. The heathen savage, so ran the argument, if left to himself, would live a brutish life on earth, to be exchanged at death for an eternity of hell; but if he were enslaved he would enter the mild atmosphere of a Christian household where he might be brought to a knowledge of the true faith and given the hope of eternal bliss. The theory, which might have been good if it had not been selfish, was to have a disastrous effect. But that was in the future. For the present, slavery was accepted as a natural, and in some respects a favourable condition for certain types of humanity. Only exceptional men and women felt any doubts.

With such a belief to support them, and with the prospect of gain to entice them, the Portuguese were not slow to seize the opportunities which their explorations had disclosed. An African trade sprang up and was soon flourishing; it included innocent goods such as gums and ivory and gold, but the most profitable was the slave; and because the human crop was not entirely easy to find or to gather, the Portuguese built a series of forts, or barracoons as they came to be called, on the Guinea Coast, where wretched Africans could be rounded up and kept safe till the numbers were sufficient to justify transhipment to Spain, to slavery, to the hope of salvation—and eventually to America and the New World.

II

Columbus did not take slaves with him to America, but he took the idea. He did more than that. As a good Catholic, he took with him the Catholic doctrines of his age, and among them a firm belief that heathen nations, because of their infidelity, had neither spiritual nor civil rights: 'their souls were doomed to eternal perdition; their bodies were the property of the Christian nation who should occupy their soil' (Prescott. *Ferdinand and Isabella*, II, 419). It was not therefore surprising that when he had established a colony in Hispaniola (Haiti) and found himself at a loss how to pacify his mutinous followers, he should have introduced (1499) the system of 'repartimientos', under which the Indian lands were divided, and the Indians themselves were distributed as slaves, among the invading Spaniards (Robertson VI, 137). He even proposed to stock the farms which his followers had thus acquired by transporting natives in sufficient numbers to Spain, there to be sold as slaves and thus to provide the necessary funds for the purchase of seeds and cattle.

But the traffic in American slaves was not destined to be two-way. Columbus had owed his opportunities to the Spanish Queen Isabella and her wishes must therefore be consulted and obeyed; for it was she who had finally ended his search for a patron, imaginative enough to be fired by his paradox of reaching the east by sailing to the west, and rich enough to make his expedition possible. When all others had for years shrugged unbelieving shoulders, she had spoken with the proud voice of Castile, pledging her jewels for a chance in a great lottery which, if successful, must bring lasting renown, and might bring boundless wealth to her country. But Isabella had other characteristics besides a bold resolution and a high patriotism. She was devoutly pious and essentially pitiful. In the first aspect, she had hoped that Columbus might bring the light of the gospel to benighted Indians. In the second aspect, she was touched by reports of the gentle manners and timid docility of the natives. When, therefore, the first batch of prisoners arrived in Spain, she would not allow them to be sold as slaves until she had tried to discover the will of God by consulting a council of theologians. When, to her regret, the theologians squabbled among themselves, she gave full scope to her natural benevolence as well as her innate piety by ordering the prisoners to be returned to their homes, and by issuing positive instructions that the natives of her new possessions were to be free and all of them were to receive education in the Christian religion.

But Hispaniola was a long way off, out of range of the eye of authority and largely out of reach of its arm. The Spanish conquerors, with few exceptions, were greedy and defiant, impatient of labour and contemptuous of underlings. They were too proud to till the soil themselves, and too conceited to work in the mines; if therefore they were to live and grow as rich as their dreams, inevitably they must force the Indians to pay them tribute of corn and gold, while they themselves followed the noble profession of arms—so necessary to maintain their state. Isabella out of a weak and womanly compassion might issue what orders she liked, but there was no one to see that they were obeyed, and so far as they ran counter to the settlers' wishes they were only too certain to be ignored.

It was doubly hard on the natives, for they were not only innocent prey but by nature peace-loving and indolent, unused to heavy toil and in no sense experienced farmers or miners. Their country was extremely fertile, and having few wants and fewer ambitions, they had hitherto led a lotus-eating existence, placidly happy in their secluded Paradise. Now all had been changed. Their country had become a scene of bustling activities, a victim of progress in the modern style. Agriculture was making good the deficiencies of nature, and science helping to excavate her buried ore. Under this new dispensation the Indians found themselves forced to work in the fields as they had never yet done, not for their own advantage but for the benefit of unwelcome intruders; and they were driven into the mines to extract gold which they had hitherto regarded as of no value except for harmless adornment, but which possessed so unaccountable a fascination for their new masters. Their life which had been so happy had become toilsome and sad, and in something approaching despair they struggled to release themselves. But neither their own efforts nor Isabella's instructions had any lasting effect. They had become, and they continued to be, slaves.

The fate which befell them followed, with curious fidelity, the historic course of slavery in the old world. The Spanish adventurers were a young community, with barely enough men to provide for their own safety, and far too few to provide for their own needs. Outside labour was essential. But as the Spaniards had occupied the land without opposition, there were no prisoners of war to be set to work; nor were there any markets in the New World where slaves could be bought. In the circumstances the obvious solution, sanctioned by Church dogma and justified by custom, was to turn the Indians into a subject population, much on the lines which Aristotle had once envisaged. Hence the system of 'repartimientos', which, whatever may have been the theory, in fact reduced the natives to a condition of predial slavery. They were not the property of individuals but of the State, and, like the Helots of Lacedaemonia, were assigned by the Governor to whatever masters he thought fit. Nor as yet had they any right to any protection.

This sudden change in their fortunes made their lot grievous indeed, and with the perversity of human affairs it was made worse by Isabella's well-meant humanity. Her instructions were at first obeyed to the extent that the Indians were rewarded for their labours by a small payment—a fact which raised their status from one of slavery to one of serfdom. But these new and better conditions were short-lived. Wages were meaningless to men whose world was innocent of economics, while enforced toil was an experience that was only too real, too recent and too unhappy. The Indians gladly gave up their wages for the sake of freedom; they rejected payments and withheld their labour, relapsing with easy contentment into their old indolent ways. But in so doing they confirmed the Spaniards in their belief that the Indians were bone-lazy, and that Isabella's orders were as impracticable as they were undesirable. Compulsion followed, and with compulsion a growing restlessness on one side and an increasing ruthlessness on the other.

Everything worked against the Indians. At the outset the Spaniards had not been consciously brutal; they were too few in numbers to run risks, and Columbus had from the first, both by inclination and as a matter of policy, adopted a friendly attitude, which the Indians had readily reciprocated. But as the colony grew, and familiarity bred contempt, the harsher side of the Spanish temperament had freer play. Moreover, the character of the settlers deteriorated when Columbus, finding volunteers for the colony difficult to recruit, had looked to the

Spanish jails for fresh blood. The criminals transported to Hispaniola at his suggestion, besides providing a source of continual disaffection, carried out with them a grudge against society which they vented on the Indians. Then Isabella died unexpectedly early (1504) and with her death, her orders and regulations were either repealed or ignored. Her husband, Ferdinand, had always lacked her warm sympathy with the underdog; his interest in America was centred in the profits to be obtained from the mines, and his suspicious and coldly-calculating nature was more concerned to restrict the Governor's powers than to relieve the slaves' plight. The final hardship came when Ferdinand bethought himself of rewarding courtiers by the grant of Indian lands and slaves. It was cheap, and it enabled him to indulge his penchant for clipping the Governor's wings, by taking away from him the administration of 'repartimientos', and entrusting it to a specially appointed official, one Albuquerque. But the result was that the courtiers, having no use themselves for the land or the slaves, let the former and sold the latter. It was thus that the slave market was introduced into America and the slaves became the property of individuals.

The change boded them no good. Now that slaves cost money, their masters could no longer afford to be soft-hearted. They were not only a capital investment which was expected to pay dividends, but a wasting asset which required a sinking fund. The last ounce had to be wrung out of them. The enslaved natives had always found labour toilsome, not only because they were unaccustomed to it, but because it was beyond their physical capacity. They were in no sense 'noble savages' roaming the forests, in no sense muscular or well set up. On the contrary, like the conies, they were a feeble folk. Even under the mild rule of Columbus, the Spanish demands had overtaxed their strength, and when, with the introduction of the new system of sale and purchase, the treatment grew harsher and the demands greater, the result was startling beyond belief. The Indians died off like flies. It is said that the native population of Hispaniola fell in the first fifteen years of Spanish occupation from one million to sixty thousand inhabitants (Robertson VI, 177); and when, a few years later, Albuquerque made a fresh census, he is said to have found only fourteen thousand still existing (Robertson VI, 205). No doubt these figures are unreliable, but the fact remains that each new estimate showed a significant drop. Columbus himself told Ferdinand, shortly after Isabella's death, that, according to his information, 'since I left this Island, six parts out of seven of the natives are dead, all through ill-treatment and inhumanity;

some by the sword, others by blows and cruel usage, and others through hunger. The greater part have perished in the mountains and glens, whither they had fled, from not being able to support the labour imposed upon them' (Irving: *Columbus* III, 412).

III

Isabella's attempt to give the natives freedom had resulted in worsening their lot. The outcome of her attempts to give them religious education was to prove even more perverse. Indeed, fate dealt hardly by Isabella, twisting her very virtues awry, so that her piety, for all that it was sincere and devout, had for its fruit the monstrous Spanish Inquisition; and her brooding care for the Indians, tender and humane as it was, led to the introduction of negro slavery into America and all that negro slavery has implied.

As already related, Isabella had from the first hoped that Columbus might bring the light of the gospel to the Indians; and when the colony of Hispaniola had been founded, she determined that the natives should receive religious education. Her determination was so deeply rooted that interested persons could play upon it for their own ends. Thus, when the settlers wished to circumvent her instructions that the natives were to be free, they represented to her, in a sort of logical sorites, that without compulsion the Indians would not work; that without work, they would be cut off from intercourse with the Spaniards; that without such intercourse, the prospect of their conversion would disappear. Isabella was so impressed with the argument that she agreed to the employment of Indians, even under compulsion, provided the tasks imposed on them were not excessive and that they were paid reasonable remuneration. At the same time she gave permission for the importation of selected negro slaves—that is to say negroes who had been born in Spain and grounded and brought up in the Christian faith—under the curiously unrealistic impression that they would not only promote intercourse with the Indians but make it more spiritually profitable (Ingram, p. 41). Perhaps more wisely, she dispatched missionaries to the Island, though her choice of them was not always prudent. Yet they made for moderation, and their remonstrances moved Ferdinand, after Isabella's death, to issue orders which might have improved the Indians' lot if the settlers had not ignored them.

Among the missionaries was the celebrated Bartolomé de las Casas to whom the introduction of negro slavery into America is sometimes imputed. The charge is ill-founded; there were negro slaves in America before he arrived. Yet if he was not guilty of the first step, his influence was in the end decisive. It was in 1502 that as a young man of twenty-eight, he first went to the West Indies, and there, except for short visits to Spain, he spent the greater part of his long life, winning renown and reputation as the protector of the Indians. The moment of his arrival was one of importance in the history of Spain's colonial empire. The first flush of wonder at Columbus's discoveries had evaporated; his enemies, envious of his success, had in his absence undermined his influence at the Court of Spain, and had managed to secure the appointment of a commissioner, one Bobadilla, to investigate his conduct as Governor of Hispaniola. No doubt they hoped for damning exposures, but on reaching the colony, Bobadilla, who was plentifully endowed with the arrogance of a small mind, at once dashed their hopes, while pandering to his own conceit, by ordering Columbus back to Madrid as a prisoner, without trial and in chains. The insult and the injustice were too gross. Columbus had hardly landed in Spain before he regained his liberty and something of his old authority, but the King thought it prudent to keep him at home and to appoint a new governor in his place.

It was in the train of this new governor, Nicholas de Ovando, that Las Casas sailed. Though very different in character from Columbus, Ovando was an able administrator. Under his guidance the colony recovered quickly from Bobadilla's misrule and, so far as the Spaniards were concerned, its fortunes flourished. But Ovando was also a ruthless man; he found the Indians in a state of incipient rebellion, and instead of following Isabella's instructions or Columbus's conciliatory methods, decided to crush them once and for all. In pursuit of that end, he treated them with calculated cruelty and deliberate treachery. There is no need to paint his misdeeds or his victims' sufferings, but it is relevant to note that Las Casas was an eyewitness of what the Indians had to endure, and it was the evidence of his own eyes which ultimately impelled him to make their protection his main mission in life.

He did not act hastily. On the contrary, at the outset he followed the custom of the country, accepting his share of land and slaves under the system of repartimientos, and sending his Indians to the mines to make as large and as quick profits for him as possible. Only in his personal relations with his slaves was he in any sense exceptional—it was natural for him to treat them with unaccustomed kindness. This phase of his

life lasted for twelve years, during which time he had endless opportunities, as a priest, of studying their ways and learning their needs at
first hand. His sympathies were readily roused, but only in cases of
individual hardship which came to his notice. As yet his humanity was
neither imaginative enough, nor large enough, to understand and condemn the system as a whole.

But experience is cumulative, and at the end of twelve years his sub-
conscious horror at the cruelties and misery which he saw on every
side was touched into a live flame by the impact of some verses of
scripture and the recollection of past sermons. He underwent a species
of conversion which shocked him into action. As a first step, he went to
the governor and, after denouncing the system, gave up his own slaves.
Then in 1515 he returned to Madrid intent on wresting from the
Government itself some alleviation of the Indians' lot. Ferdinand was
then nearing his end, but was so moved by the eloquence and fervour
of Las Casas that he began to revolve in his mind schemes of amelioration which, had not death intervened (January 1516), he would certainly have put into execution. Foiled of his hopes in that direction,
Las Casas turned to Cardinal Ximenes, who, like Ferdinand, was
deeply moved by what he heard, but with a minister's natural caution
refused to act without official investigation. He appointed a commission to make inquiries, but selected Hieronymite friars for the work,
who, with the best of motives, accepted the argument which had
weighed so heavily with Isabella—that slavery was the Indians' best
hope of conversion.

Las Casas, disappointed by their conclusion, returned to Spain in
1517 with fresh petitions and a new proposal. It was now that he first
suggested the importation of negro slaves. His reason was simple;
the Indians were not merely dying off, they were dying out, because
they were being worked beyond their capacity; their constitution
could not stand the strain, nor was their heart in the work to ease their
troubles. They were not fit for the toil they were forced to undergo;
and if slave labour was essential, as the Commission appeared to
believe, it should be provided, not by weakly and effeminate Indians
but by robust and virile Africans. One negro was said to do the work
of four Indians; Africans were inured to toil and being accustomed to a
climate more trying than that of Hispaniola, would take no hurt.
Ximenes, with a foresight that was more than remarkable, rejected the
proposal—not on moral, physical or economic grounds, but because of
its potential dangers. The negroes, he argued, were a vigorous and

fertile race; in the favourable climate of Hispaniola they would breed too fast, and before long, outnumbering the Spaniards, would rise in revolt; the Island would be torn to pieces by servile wars.

Time was to confirm his prescience; but he was a dying man, and his wise counsel was rejected by the new king, Charles V, a boy of seventeen, who had been brought up in Flanders and, having only just arrived in his new kingdom, was too heedless of the old minister whom he did not know and too attentive to the Flemish courtiers whom he had brought in his train. When Las Casas suggested that each Spanish resident in Hispaniola should be allowed to import a small number of negro slaves for himself, Charles saw much virtue in the suggestion, and promptly bestowed on one of his Flemish favourites a patent to supply the four Spanish settlements of Hispaniola, Cuba, Jamaica and Porto Rico with four thousand negroes annually. This number was probably far more than Las Casas had envisaged, but the number hardly matters. The favourite sold his right to a firm of Genoese merchants for 25,000 ducats, and with the sale the hitherto fortuitous trickle of negro slaves was set on its course to become a vast torrent controlled and ordered by big business. Whether this startling result opened his eyes or whether time and experience changed his heart, Las Casas was moved to record in later years that he had acted without due thought, and that if he had known what he was doing, nothing would have induced him to make the suggestion. But make it he did, and so negro slavery was riveted on America's neck. It is a sobering thought that the untold misery of American slavery and all the problems to which it has given rise, sprang out of the unconsidered advice of a middle-aged missionary and the careless decision of a boy king.

III. Sir John Hawkins

I

LAS CASAS made his suggestion because he was a pitiful man, and living among the Indians had known and deplored their hardships, while the negroes not being within his ken had never stirred his imagination. But the fact that he could make the suggestion throws light on his times, by raising a doubt whether even so good and pitiful a man as Las Casas disapproved of slavery as such. It is true that in a debate with the Bishop of Darien, held at the King's request and in the royal presence, he declared that the Christian religion robbed no man of his freedom and violated none of his inherent rights on the ground that he was a slave by nature. But an impassioned orator does not always weigh his words with scrupulous exactness, and as, at the moment of speaking, Las Casas was prepared to accept negro though not Indian slavery, his logic at least was confused, whatever his feelings may have been. It was not till many years later that, realizing his mistake, he admitted that what applied to the Indian applied also to the negro, and that if the one must not be enslaved no more must the other. Yet even when making his recantation, he used ambiguous words, basing his objection not on the broad ground of principle, but on the fortuitous fact that the negroes 'were made slaves unjustly and tyrannically' (Ingram, p. 144); he had supposed at the time that the negroes were captives whom everyone regarded as natural slaves.

Las Casas seems to have been swayed simply by an instinctive repugnance to cruelty. If he was consciously moved by principle, he was well in advance of his age which saw nothing abnormal or undesirable in slavery. He was perhaps no less so in his reaction to cruelty; for his age—the age not only of slavery but of the Spanish Inquisition—appears to modern eyes to have been particularly heartless and inhuman. Yet if we are to pass a valid judgment on it, the influence of custom must not be ignored. Familiarity no doubt blunted perception and it is probable that his age did not realize its own ferocity. He is therefore the more to be commended for a sensitivity which transcended both habit and education. In the sixteenth century slaves were a common feature of the Spanish economy, and were not likely to become objects of pity when slave labour was said to be essential if the struggling new colonies were to be kept alive. Individual masters in the grip of necessity might be careless or cruel, but the authorities were known to be striving earnestly to keep them in order. 'The history of Spanish colonial legislation is the history of the impotent struggles of the government in behalf of the natives against the avarice and cruelty of its subjects' (Prescott. *Mexico*, p. 181).

In the matter of slavery Las Casas was consciously on the side of the angels. Perhaps he was no less so, even if more unconsciously, in the matter of the Inquisition; for the Inquisition was not wholly sadistic. Somewhere at the back of the muddled ecclesiastical mind was a conviction that the soul was of more account than the body, and that in the all-important battle for the salvation of souls, the mortification of the flesh was a potent weapon. Better by far the agony of the rack or the stake for a brief hour, better even slavery for the span of mortal life, than the pains of hell for all eternity. The sixteenth century, in spite of its slavery and its Holy Office, thought of men as a little lower than the angels. It is humbling to reflect that at Belsen and in the labour camps of Siberia the twentieth century thinks of men as no higher than the animals.

Las Casas was moved by the sufferings of Indians which he saw. He would have been equally moved could he have seen the sufferings of the negroes. How they were captured may have been a matter of doubt, but whatever the method, their misery was certain. Among the first to be brought to Europe was a batch of some two hundred captured in 1444. An eyewitness has left an account of their landing in Portugal. 'But what heart was that, how hard soever, which was not pierced with sorrow, seeing that company; for some had sunken cheeks and their faces bathed in tears, looking at each other; others were groaning very dolorously, looking at the heights of the heavens, fixing their eyes upon them, crying out loudly as if they were asking succour from the Father of nature; others struck their faces with their hands, throwing themselves on the earth; others made their lamentations in songs, according to the customs of their country, which, although we could not understand their language, we saw corresponded well to the height of their sorrow' (Azurara, *Chronicles of Guinea*. Quoted Helps. I, 24).

The first landing was no doubt memorable, but repetition bred indifference, and before long the slave trade was a flourishing business which brought wealth to the merchants and prosperity to the colonies. The Spanish Government began to take an interest in it, not as a participant—the days of nationalization were still far in the future— but partly in order to keep a restraining hand on it, and still more in order to make it a source of income. They obliged the trader to take out a licence and the purchaser to pay a duty of thirty ducats per head. As a corollary, they prohibited the trade to foreigners, who could not be compelled to take out licences and who would probably evade the duty. Obviously so lucrative a practice was to be kept within the family. But what benefited the home country was bad for the colonists. The licensed merchants could not, or at least did not, keep up the supply, and the consequent shortage, perhaps deliberately contrived, combined with the government's tax to raise the price intolerably.

Here was an opening for the merchant adventurer of the age, who was half trader, half pirate. There were fortunes to be made by bold buccaneers, and the risk was small, since the authorities were far away and the colonists eager to buy. Nor were men lacking to seize their opportunities. By the middle of the sixteenth century they were so active that a licensee, one Estebez, complained to the Emperor, Charles V, that for every hundred negroes brought openly to Hispaniola, two hundred were introduced secretly (Helps. III, 152).

II

It was at this point, according to the historians, that England entered on the scene in the person of Sir John Hawkins. They emphasize the fact, though their reason for doing so is a little obscure. Perhaps it may be traced to the American historian, Bancroft, who, not being fond of England, found it convenient to whitewash America's penchant for owning slaves by blackening England's readiness to supply them. England, it appears, thought only of filthy lucre. Alas! she 'valued Africa as returning for her manufactures abundant labourers for her colonies, and valued it for nothing more' (Bancroft. III, 404). It was bad and sad, but it had its sweet side, for America fortunately had higher aims and a higher destiny. To her 'Providence intrusted the guardianship and education of the coloured race'—mainly in her southern provinces where luckily the use of slaves was exceptionally profitable. 'All observers affirmed the marked progress of the negro American' (Bancroft. III, 408). In short, in spite of England, all was well, and continued to be well, until in 1852, eighteen years after Bancroft had written, Harriet Beecher Stowe inconsiderately published *Uncle Tom's Cabin*.

Be that as it may, Bancroft laid down that 'the odious distinction of having interested England in the slave trade belongs to Sir John Hawkins', and other historians have followed his lead. But they are not entirely right. Hawkins was not the first, nor was his example infectious. The story begins in 1554. Before that date England had long traded for gold and ivory to the Guinea Coast without giving offence, but in 1554 a certain John Lok, discovering that the negroes 'were a people of beastly living, without God, law, religion or commonwealth', carried off five of them as slaves. His depredation had a curious effect. Hitherto the negro tribes had welcomed English ships because the English, unlike the Portuguese and Spaniards, did not indulge in the practice of kidnapping. Lok's sudden aberration alarmed and frightened them; apparently the English were no better than other white men and their ships and merchants were to be eschewed as completely as the rest. The trade with England in gold and ivory came to a sudden stop and the merchants of London, properly incensed, forced Lok to return his booty, in the hope that by that means friendly relations might be re-established. The captain who took the slaves back was touched at 'the passionate joy with which the poor creatures were welcomed' (Froude. *Elizabeth* II, 183), but perhaps more important, the English regained their reputation and their innocent trade.

When Lok indulged in his escapade, John Hawkins was about twenty-five years old. His family were natives of Plymouth—prosperous merchants of the middle class, who were interested in local government but were not anxious to meddle in matters which were too high for them. The times were rough and turbulent and the Hawkinses believed that Spain, the Pope and Mary Stuart raised problems of great moment which were best left to longer heads than their own—to the Queen's Grace, God bless her!, to Cecil and Walsingham, to the Council of State and the High Court of Parliament. Nor was it fit for the respectable firm of Hawkins to indulge in privateering, for all its popularity in certain Devonshire circles. Others, if they liked, might roam the seas in search of dubious wealth; it was enough for the Hawkinses to keep to the old routes and the well-established ways of honest trade.

For a man whose name was before long to reduce Philip of Spain to angry ejaculations, Hawkins at twenty-five was deceptively mild. He stuck to business, he avoided politics, he behaved himself in foreign ports, and it was said of him that in the Canary Islands where he mostly traded he was 'growen in love and favour with the people' (Hakluyt. VII, 5). He was also growing, perhaps unknown to himself, in daring and resolution. But for the next seven or eight years he continued in his old harmless ways. In 1562, however, he began to spread his wings and, seeking for fresh outlets, asked his friends in the Canaries whether there were any openings for trade in the Spanish colonies. They assured him there were, and that he would be welcomed. They added, in the helpful way of friends, that 'Negros were very good marchandise in Hispaniola, and that stores of Negros might easily bee had upon the coast of Guinea' (ibid.). Hawkins noted the suggestion and on his return to England discussed it with his backers or, as Hakluyt prefers to call them, his 'worshipfull friendes of London'. They 'liked so well of his intention that they became liberall contributers and adventurers in the action' (ibid.). The spirit of the age was beginning to ferment in Hawkins. With the support and encouragement of his 'worshipfull friendes' he imagined he was setting out to explore the possibilities of a well-known and lucrative trade which England had hitherto unduly neglected—something with perhaps a spice of adventure in it, but a purely private enterprise with private gain as its only object. He was mistaken; he was in fact, through the curious workings of fate, placing himself in the van of that sudden upsurge of national fervour which transmuted piracy into patriotism, which wrested the mastery of the seas from Philip of Spain and which raised England from a small island to a great power and the centre of the most beneficent empire the world has yet seen.

Hawkins sailed in October 1562, and at Sierra Leone took on board three hundred negroes whom he 'got into his possession partly by the sword and partly by other means'—a mysterious statement with ominous undertones. He sold his cargo extremely well in Hispaniola 'and so with prosperous success and much gaine to himself and the aforesaide adventurers' he reached home safely eleven months after he had set out. Success encouraged him to try again, and this time he had a plethora of 'worshipfull friendes', including Elizabeth herself. But his trading was not so easy as before. Philip had heard of his previous voyage and had taken alarm; if foreigners gained an entry into the Spanish colonies, there was an end to his exclusive possession of the wealth of the Indies. They must be stopped. Philip sent out strict injunctions, which some governors felt obliged to obey, however reluctantly, but which others, with more finesse, employed as a good bargaining point for beating down Hawkins's price. When confronted with the more conscientious governors, Hawkins thought discretion the better part of valour; but with the less conscientious he was very willing to chaffer. In the last resort, he could, and did, counter the King's injunctions with a display of force; a company of armed British seadogs was a weighty argument not lightly to be confuted, and much more in evidence than his Catholic Majesty. One way or another Hawkins sold his slaves and disposed of his other merchandise, and on the 20th September, 1565, returned to Padstow 'with great profit to the venturers of the said voyage, as also to the whole realme, in bringing home both golde, silver, Pearles and other jewels great store' (Hakluyt. VII, 52).

Elizabeth was delighted with her share, and eager to tempt fortune again. She needed money to support the Protestant cause in Flanders, where Alva and the Prince of Orange were fighting the battle of religion; and no less to protect herself against the popish plots constantly hatching in her own kingdom. She was also in great need of ships and seamen to overthrow the armadas of Spain, and how could she get them more easily and cheaply than by encouraging privateers of the Hawkins type? She was more than ready to assist him, and he was more than ready to renew a traffic which was so beneficial to himself and his backers and so welcome to his customers. He set sail for his third voyage in October 1567, picked up a cargo of negroes—with plenty of violence but without too much trouble—and appeared once more in the West Indies.

By this time trading conditions had become almost impossible by reason of official bans. 'We coasted', said Hawkins, 'from place to place, making our traffike with the Spaniards as we might, somewhat hardly, because the King had straightly commanded all his governors in those parts, by no means to suffer any trade to be made with us; notwithstanding we had reasonable trade and courteous entertainment,' though at times the trade had to be 'secret', with the Spaniards making their purchases at night (Hakluyt. VII, 55). His profits were great, but on his return voyage he was overtaken by storms, and driven to seek refuge in the small harbour of Saint John de Ullua, where he was trapped by a powerful Spanish fleet specially dispatched to find and make an end of him. A desperate fight followed, in the course of which he lost all his takings but was able finally to escape himself with two of his smaller vessels and the greater part of his followers. After being buffeted in unknown seas for a fortnight, lack of provisions obliged him to land half his men on the coast of Mexico, and with the remainder he limped home. It was a sad disappointment. 'If', he wrote, 'all the miseries and troublesome affaires of this sorrowfull voyage should be perfectly and throughly written, there should neede a painefull man with his pen, and as great a time as he had that wrote the lives and deathes of the Martyrs.'

Hawkins was full of a very genuine grief, not merely nor mostly for the loss of his profits—which he chalked up as a debt to be recovered from Spain—but at the thought of his comrades left behind to the doubtful mercies of the Spaniards. He brooded over their fate. Slave-trading had no further attractions for him; his aim henceforth was to rescue the men who had sailed the seas with him and were now the helpless prey of the 'inquisition dogs and the devildoms of Spain'

His 'sorrowful voyage' had changed Hawkins from a merchant of peaceful intentions, if masterful methods, to a militant and very angry crusader. In this new character he entered inevitably into the sphere of high politics, where he showed himself cunning, persistent, resourceful and finally successful. Almost at once he became involved in the unravelling of the Ridolfi plot against the Queen's life, and handled that dangerous intrigue with the calmness and certainty of aim which he had displayed in his slave-trading transactions, though now he was not browbeating colonial governors who were half willing to be persuaded, but at one and the same time deluding the experienced Mary, Queen of Scots, outwitting the cautious and leaden-footed Philip of Spain, and foiling the Pope himself. No less important, he became treasurer of Elizabeth's navy, and dealt with it so faithfully in his official capacity, that when the moment of trial came, England's ships 'had no match in the world either for speed, safety or endurance' (Froude. *Elizabeth* V, 384). In the midst of these great matters he had no time or taste for slave-trading.

III

If Hawkins was able to beguile Philip into releasing his imprisoned comrades, Philip could at least flatter himself that he had put an end to England's commerce with his colonies, for, after Hawkins, England took no further part in the slave trade for the best part of a century. But whatever satisfaction Philip may have felt, it was personal to himself; it was not shared by the colonists. For them, England's disappearance meant merely the closing down of a new and welcome channel of supply; it did not reduce their hunger for slave labour. They still needed an unending flow of negroes, not only to work fresh plantations as they came into cultivation, but also to replace the slaves who died, especially the Indians; for slavery was then, as ever, a highly successful agent of death—physical as well as spiritual. The demand for labour was probably more urgent than Philip supposed, for Spain, not being her own purveyor, was not too well informed.

The Guinea Coast, that fruitful source of slaves, was in the area, east of the Azores, which under the papal bull of Demarkation, Alexander VI had reserved for Portugal; and the Portuguese were no more disposed to welcome interlopers into Africa than the Spaniards were into the West Indies. Spain had therefore to procure her slaves from the Portuguese, and following the precedent set by Charles V, she farmed the business out to others, choosing those others according to the political temperature of the times. The trade was thus a monopoly in foreign hands, which was very ineffectively controlled by the Spanish system of licences, and was subject to all the defects and disabilities which might be expected in such a traffic. It was cruel in its operation, and expensive in its prices. The colonists no doubt endured the cruelty with the fortitude commonly shown towards the sufferings of others, but they were ready to welcome any competition which might bring the prices down. Competition, however, except in the form of smuggling, they were not to have. The government continued the system of licences, handing them out, sometimes to courtiers, sometimes to favoured merchants, sometimes to foreigners; but the number of negroes allowed to be imported was always defined and limited, largely because of the government's lurking fear of a servile war. Frequent risings and continual unrest showed that their fear was not unjustified. By degrees as the demand grew with the progress of Spanish conquest, the system of individual licences proved unsatisfactory and the trade was vested by treaties in foreign governments, first the Dutch and later the French, with whom it remained till 1713.

IV

In the meantime England was engaged in founding her own colonies in the West Indian Islands and North America. Unlike Columbus, the colonists from England did not take with them either slaves or the idea of slavery. The condition had long disappeared from England itself and was repugnant to the English way of life. As Captain Jobson said in 1620, when offered negroes in his voyage up the Gambia, the English were a people who 'did not buy or sell one another or any that hath our own shapes' (MacMunn, p. 86). But Captain Jobson was thinking too much of his own happy England and too little of her turbulent colonies. At almost the moment of his notable remark, a Dutch ship was entering the James River in Virginia and landing twenty negroes for sale. The colonists promptly bought them and thus negro slavery was introduced into England's American colonies 'more than a century', as Bancroft reminds us, 'after the last vestiges of hereditary slavery had disappeared from English society and the English constitution, and six years after the commons of France had petitioned for the emancipation of every serf in every fief' (Bancroft. I, 176).

The slavery that had practically disappeared in the Old World, was to rise to fresh life in the New. Bancroft, ever eager to condemn England, adds that the slave traffic would have been checked in its infancy, had its profits remained with the Dutch, and offers as proof the slow growth in the number of slaves bought by Virginians before England took over the trade. But he forgot the obvious fact that the rate of growth depended on the demand. The English colonists were settlers in a land that was uncultivated and largely uninhabited; their object was to make a home for themselves, to promote agriculture and to encourage trade. Slaves were of no particular use to them in the early days and became desirable only when they had made good their occupation of the land and were turning their first painfully acquired small holdings into large plantations. It took Virginia many years to develop her tobacco and cotton. Had she been like South Carolina which, as Bancoft records, was 'from its cradle essentially a planting state', she would doubtless have done as South Carolina did, where as soon as it was recognized that the climate was more congenial to the African than to the European 'it became the great object of the emigrant to buy negro slaves without which a planter can never do great matter' (Bancroft. II, 170–1). Until moral judgments intervened and humanity had its say, the rise and fall of the slave trade was governed by the laws of economics, not by the nationality of the trader.

IV. The Assiento

I

WHOEVER was to blame, there can be no doubt that the discovery of America revived the slave trade at the precise moment when it was showing signs of extinction elsewhere. The Portuguese had taken the lead in the negro traffic because they were the first to explore the African coast, but the trade was not one in which they were much interested. Portugal, as a small country with a great reputation at sea, no doubt welcomed any new form of commercial enterprise—one forgets how few were the opportunities in those days—but she was bound to regard slave-trading as a side issue. Her main object was the same as that of Columbus—to find a sea route to India in order to tap the rich trade from the East, which Venice had hitherto monopolized.

She succeeded, as Columbus did not, by discovering in 1498 the route round the Cape of Good Hope, which at once took the eastern trade out of the hands of Venice and placed it in the hands of Portugal. In this wider world of commerce, negroes were no substitute for silks or spices; their capture was difficult and the overall profit small; nor did they offer a prospect for the future. Slavery was dying out of Europe; the market was not large and was dwindling; and in so far as it existed, Barbary offered a more popular and more easily worked source of supply.

But the discovery of the New World altered the situation. America needed slaves, at least in the opinion of its discoverers. The Spaniards, having entered the West Indies, not as settlers in the accepted sense but as conquerors eager for gold, clamoured for slaves from the first to provide them with food and to work in the mines. When their brutality had killed off the natives, they had no option but to look abroad for a new supply. The obvious source was the west coast of Africa, which was, after all, the nearest point of the Old World; and in the sixteenth century the Atlantic was too vast, and the ships too small, to encourage any but the shortest route across. Guinea became automatically the labour exchange and the slave market not of Europe but of America.

If anyone was to blame it was the Spaniards, for compared with other European nations, they had been fortunate in their first contact with the New World. Columbus had entered it through the Gulf of Mexico, at the point where North and South America join, and where alone the native civilizations had prospered. Though there were some islands in the Caribbean Sea peopled by cannibals, Hispaniola and Cuba, where the Spaniards made their landfall, had mild and friendly inhabitants, who in their pathetic ignorance welcomed to their hearts and homes a pack of ruthless oppressors, for whose benefit, all unwittingly, they had cultivated their soil, and discovered their gold mines. When, later on, the Spaniards passed from the islands to the Spanish Main, their course led them to Mexico, that great city which was 'at the time the fairest in the world, and has never since been equalled . . . the city not only of a great king, but of an industrious and thriving people' (Helps. II, 216).

It was easy for the Spaniards with their steel and their guns to overcome their lightly-armed victims; it was easy for them to live off their conquests. It would have been easy for them to avoid the importation of slaves from abroad, if they had made a more provident and more humane use of the natives at hand. Even as it was, negroes were not universal in Spanish America. They abounded only in those districts where the Indians had been wastefully destroyed because neither Government nor Church had intervened to protect them. They were at once a luxury and a writ of condemnation against their conquerors. They were never a necessity.

The other European nations, especially the English, the French and the Dutch, fared differently. Their fate took them to North America where they did not find a richly cultivated country or a race of docile men. Their first attempts at settlement mostly failed. Explaining those failures, Captain John Smith, of Virginian fame, stressed the contrast between the Spaniards and the English. 'It was the Spaniards' good hap', he wrote, 'to happen on those parts where were infinite numbers of people, who had manured the ground with that providence it afforded victuals at all times. And time had brought them to that perfection, they had the use of gold and silver, and the most of such commodities as those countries afforded; so that what the Spaniard got was chiefly the spoil and pillage of those country people, and not the labours of their own hands. . . . But we chanced in a land even as God made it, where we found only an idle, improvident, scattered people, ignorant of the knowledge of gold or silver, or any commodities, and careless of anything but from hand to mouth, except baubles of no worth; nothing to encourage us, but what accidentally we found Nature afforded. Which ere we could bring to recompense our pains, defray our charges, and satisfy our Adventurers; we were to discover the country, subdue the people, bring them to be tractable, civil and industrious, and teach them trades' (Smith. I, 172–3).

Smith was not backed by an Isabella, nor financed by a Treasury. Nor for that matter was he forbidden slaves. English colonization was a private enterprise, set on foot by 'Adventurers' and intended to produce a rich return. From that point of view the use of negroes might well have been considered, had it been the English way, for by the time that John Smith arrived in Virginia, the Spaniards had been more than a century in Spanish America, and the slave trade was in full flow. It was unlikely, however, that Smith would have taken kindly to the idea; for Smith had been a slave himself and knew from experience its physical horrors and economic shortcomings. In the course of his adventurous life, he had been captured in the Turkish wars and sold with other prisoners 'like beasts in a market-place'. He and the rest had been marched to Constantinople 'by twenty and twenty chained by the necks', and there delivered to their several masters. His final destination had been a city in the Crimea, where he had been stripped naked, his head shaved, and 'a great ring of iron, with a long stalk bowed like a sickle, riveted about his neck'. As the newest arrival he had found himself a slave of slaves, but as he said, 'among these slavish fortunes there was no great choice; for the best was so bad, a dog could hardly have lived to endure' (Smith. II, 146).

Yet Smith had endured with stoic resignation until fate and his own resourcefulness set him free. He had been given the task of thrashing in a distant farm; and there God helped him, as he piously records, 'beyond man's expectation or imagination'. His master, inspecting his possessions, wandered off rashly by himself to the barn where Smith was working, and there having nothing better to do took it into his head 'to beat, spurn and revile him', in so venomous a fashion that at last Smith, beside himself with rage and resentment, set about his tormentor and 'beat out the Tymor's brain with his threshing bat'; then 'seeing his estate could be no worse than it was, clothed himself in his clothes, hid his body under the straw, filled his knapsack with corn, shut the doors, mounted his horse', and after many adventures arrived in Russia where he was released from the iron ring about his neck and kindly entreated (Smith. II, 158). Such was the life of a slave as Smith had encountered it.

Smith was saved to become the 'Father of Virginia'; but the colony was not a dutiful child. The settlers were a thankless, improvident, quarrelsome lot; they thwarted Smith when he was present, and made difficulties for themselves when he was absent. But in Smith's philosophy, obstacles were made to be overcome, and he toiled purposefully at his ambition to emulate what he called 'the greatest honour that ever belonged to the greatest monarchs, the enlarging their dominions and erecting Common-weals'. His efforts were not without reward, but were brought to a premature end by the accidental explosion of his powder flask while he lay asleep in a boat. The explosion 'took the flesh from his body and thighs, nine or ten inches square, in a most pitiful manner', whereupon, to quote his own fascinating description, 'to quench the tormenting fire, frying him in his clothes, he leaped overboard into the deep river, where e'er they could recover him he was near drowned'. He lived to tell the tale, though the accident forced him to return to England, and it was when his guiding hand had been withdrawn that the Dutch ship arrived at Jamestown with its cargo of negro slaves. The motley collection of settlers whom he had left behind were not the sort to resist temptation; cheap labour and sweet idleness had an irresistible appeal for them, and they succumbed.

Yet it is but just to add that if Virginia was the first American colony to admit slaves, she had been anticipated not only by the Spaniards but also by the West Indies. Negro slaves had been employed in Bermuda since at least 1617, or three years before the Jamestown episode occurred (Lucas, p. 13).

II

With the introduction of negro slavery into America, the interest passes for the moment from the victims to the trade. The shop window was the Guinea Coast; the first purveyor was Portugal; and originally the only customer was Spain. As Spain felt a delicacy about intruding into that part of the newly-discovered world which the Pope had assigned to Portugal, she acted through agents, who bought the slaves at the Portuguese 'factories' and made arrangements for their transport to America. Other nations did not feel the same delicacy, and when, after colonizing some West Indian island, they found the need, or at least the advantage, of negro labour, they tended to set up their own 'factories' on the Guinea Coast and to become their own purveyors, as well as carriers for the others, whenever the chance arose.

The Dutch were among the first. In the great days that followed their fight for freedom, they made a bold bid for the carrying trade of the world, and were eminently successful. But the carrying trade was not in those days remarkable for its size or variety. Wharves might appear to be busy and warehouses full, but the scale was minute by modern standards. There were no widespreading factories and consequently no vast range of commodities; no machinery or machine tools, nor any of that immense output dependent on motors and electricity, on conveyor belts and mass production. Populations were mainly static and for the most part self-sufficient, so that international trade was largely restricted to natural products of a non-perishable kind such as corn, and the more fundamental types of manufacture such as woollens and textiles. With the scope so limited, the demand for slaves offered a new and expanding trade, and their transport became an object of desire. The Dutch quickly made it their own; the ship at Jamestown was not merely evidence of Dutch commercial supremacy, but an enterprising attempt to break into a new market.

The Dutch could not expect to go unchallenged, and by the middle of the seventeenth century, the English were becoming their rivals. England was just such another small seafaring nation, with even less prospect of expansion by land; and when, like Holland, she had broken free from the menace of Spain, it was natural for her to look to the sea as the source of wealth and prosperity. The sea was open to all who had the courage and skill to explore its paths; it was owned by none; and though outwardly barren and cruel, was certainly the gateway to high adventure, and possibly the road to affluence. It appealed to every part of the English spirit. Inevitably, as England rose in the scale of power and influence, she became more and more determined 'to foster commerce, and the necessary condition of commerce, maritime power' (Gardiner. *History of the Commonwealth* II, 151). The determination found a potent aid in the Navigation Act of 1651, by which Cromwell threw down the gauntlet to Holland. He was not contemplating war— his challenge was commercial—but the Dutch wars followed, as the night the day, and in the end gave England the prize for which she was contending. She had wrested the carrying trade from the Dutch, and with it the transport of slaves.

It is a curious and sad fact that her first venture in the slave-carrying trade was not concerned with the transport of negroes but of her own sons, and was not directed to foreign settlements but to her own colonies. In the course of his ruthless advance to power, Cromwell took prisoners in Scotland, England and Ireland, and was hard put to it to know how to dispose of them. He must have had some bowels of compassion, for 'I pray you' he wrote in 1650, the year before the Navigation Act, 'let humanity be exercised towards them; I am persuaded it will be comely' (Gardiner. I, 295). But he offered no solution himself, leaving the decision to Parliament; and as civil war never was, and never will be, comely, Parliament showed no slightest trace of any weakness or any tenderness. Its first thought was to sell the prisoners to foreign powers for military service; and when no foreign powers appeared as buyers, it offered them, for a consideration, to the merchants trading to Guinea, for employment as slaves in the African gold mines. When there also it had no success, it bethought itself of the colonies, and such of the prisoners as still survived were sent to Bristol for shipment to New England. There they were sold to the settlers, not in perpetuity, but for a term of years, after which they were to recover their freedom. The precedent was followed by other parties and sects as the wheel of power revolved. Royalists, Parliamentarians, Jacobites, Catholics and Dissenters were all, at one time or another, shipped from Bristol to become slaves. Some of these unhappy prisoners were lucky in their fate, rising after their release to fortune in their new country and one may hope to happiness as well; but the lot of others was more hard; their right to eventual freedom made them of less value than negroes in the eyes of their masters; their welfare was no one's concern; and they were worked to excess in order to extract the utmost value from them before the opportunity was lost.

III

But to return to the main story. Whilst each nation, as it acquired settlements in the New World, tended to follow the Portuguese example and set up its own slave 'factories', there was one nation—Spain—which did not follow the usual practice, but continued to rely on others. The Spanish contract was therefore a matter of interest to all the competing countries, and not the less so because the Spanish demand was, for long years, by far the greatest; the right to supply it was eagerly sought by all the European nations. As already related, originally the monopoly had been granted to the Genoese; they were succeeded for a time by Dutch, German and Swedish companies, and then by the French.

The English were comparatively late-comers, taking no part in the trade for the best part of a hundred years after Hawkins's isolated enterprises. Being busy elsewhere England largely ignored Africa. She had still to evolve the most convenient method of trading with distant countries and during the first half of the seventeenth century developed a fancy for a system of great corporations, established by charter and backed by the City of London, corporations such as the East India Company, founded in 1600, and the Virginia Company founded six years later. In each case the company was buoyed up by the hope of a widespread traffic emanating from one or more trading settlements overseas. It was intended in due course to adopt the same system for Africa, but there it proved less successful. The trade envisaged by the first African companies was simply the trade in gums, gold and ivory, but the volume was small and the prospect of settlements remote. The slave trade might have made a difference, but the companies had little interest in slaves, since in those early days the demand from the English colonies was either non-existent or at best very small, and without the Spanish contract did not warrant the cost of a 'factory'.

As the century progressed, however, the increasing prosperity of the sugar plantations in Barbados and other islands, created a growing demand for slave labour, which the company as a matter of commercial development wished to satisfy, and the Government for the sake of its colonies wished to encourage. According in 1662, and again in 1672, fresh African companies—the third and fourth of that name—were incorporated, the King himself being among the subscribers, and were given the express duty of importing three thousand negroes annually into the British West Indian Islands (Lucas, p. 64). It is improbable that anyone thought of the plight of the slaves, or the moral objection to what, after all, was an old-established custom. What mattered was the welfare of the colony, and the fact that the traffic was profitable for traders and settlers alike.

But the element of profit—and it was great—had its disadvantages; it encouraged 'interlopers', those bugbears of all chartered companies, to break into the trade, snatch what business they could, and skim off the cream, without contributing a farthing towards the cost of the company's overheads or the upkeep of 'factories'. The quarrel between the monopolist company and the interlopers was perennial, and finally attracted the attention of Parliament. The problem was very real. On the one hand the company was obliged to carry out the terms of its charter, obliged to build and maintain its 'factories' and forts; on the other hand it was exposed to the competition of 'interlopers' who could undercut it precisely because they had no obligations and no charter. As the interlopers were trespassing into an area from which they had been expressly debarred, the company felt that they had a right to look to Parliament for redress. On the other hand, the interlopers argued, not altogether without force, that monopolies were bad and expensive, and if the company were not controlled by competition, the price of slave labour would become prohibitive, and the plantations would be ruined. No doubt they exaggerated, but it is hardly necessary to add that colonial opinion supported their contention wholeheartedly (Trevelyan. *The Peace and the Protestant Succession*, p. 148).

In an effort to effect a compromise, Parliament, in 1698, decided to give the interlopers a legal footing by throwing the African trade open to all comers; and at the same time to impose a tax of ten per cent on all goods, out of which the African company could be reimbursed the cost of its forts and armaments. The compromise suffered the fate which so often overtakes Parliamentary incursions into commercial affairs; the duty was hard to levy and seldom paid; what was collected proved insufficient; the company remained dissatisfied and was finally ruined;

the interlopers could not meet all the demands; and the colonists lost the benefit of cheap labour. Some change seemed to be inevitable if the trade was not to cease altogether.

The opportunity came at the end of Queen Anne's wars, when the Government determined to solve the problem by the terms of peace to be imposed upon France and Spain. England's victories deserved some reward, and what better reward could there be than a new and flourishing trade with Central and South America, based on the Assiento, or contract to supply negro slaves to the Spanish colonies? France was in immediate enjoyment of that contract, but, as a defeated country she must surrender it, while Spain, as another defeated country, must award it to England. A new corporation, to be known as the South Sea Company, would be set up to carry it into execution, and should receive, with the Assiento, certain other trading rights, including the privilege of sending annually 'at the time of the fair' a ship of 500 tons burden to trade with the colonies (Jenkinson. I, 398). The prospects were much too dazzling to allow room for scruples of a moral kind, which had never been raised before and would certainly have appeared superfluous. The Tory statesman, Harley, in whose brain the idea was conceived, saw nothing in this new company but a rival to the Whiggish Bank of England, a means of reducing the National Debt, a benefit to English commerce and a fillip to the policy of expansion overseas (Churchill. *Marlborough* IV, 402).

The company did not fulfil all that was expected of it; but by the Treaty of Utrecht (1713) Spain gave it a firm contract to supply the Spanish colonies in America with a total of a hundred and forty-four thousand negro slaves over a period of thirty years, with an added right to supply further slaves as and when they might be desired. The treaty did more than that. Hitherto there had been restrictions on the number of ports at which slaves could be landed. Those restrictions were now removed, on the ground that 'the provinces which had not had them [slaves] endured great hardships for want of having their lands and estates cultivated, from whence arose the necessity of using all imaginable ways of getting them, even though it were fraudulently' (Jenkinson. I, 378)—an admission which throws an interesting light not only on the urgency of Spanish needs, but also on the extent of interloping activities. A demand so clamant that it had resulted in wholesale smuggling would have overborne the scruples of most traders in most ages, certainly in an age when slaves were a commonplace and no feeling of moral revulsion had as yet been awakened.

V. The Trade

ENGLAND had now acquired the first place in the coveted traffic in slaves, a position which she held for over ninety years. No doubt it was because of this long pre-eminence that she has not only been held up to obloquy ever since, both at home and abroad, but has managed to obliterate the memory of whatever reproach others had incurred. It is curious with what self-abasement English historians insist that as the Crown shared in the profits, not only those directly concerned, but the whole nation must be held responsible for maintaining a trade which was 'shameful in itself, politically hurtful, and economically, in spite of appearances, unsound' (Woodward, p. 173). England was wicked; England was stupid; and the historians have nothing to say on her behalf. More curious, because even less justified, is the tendency to make Hawkins the villain of the piece. The belief is so widespread and so ingrained that in any book dealing with negroes or their activities one may come across such a statement as 'Sir John Hawkins himself could hardly have foreseen the extremes of barbarity to which the victims of the movement *which he founded* were subjected' (Rex Harris. *Jazz*, p. 22. The Italics are mine).

Slavery nowadays carries its own condemnation to all right-minded men, and the duty of the historian is surely not to emphasize that truism, still less to propagate falsities, but to understand and explain the attitude of men in other times and with different outlooks. At no point in the world's history, either past or present, has slavery been non-existent, and over by far the greater period it has been accepted as right, or reasonable, or at least desirable. That England at the beginning of the eighteenth century should have been no wiser and no better than other nations is not a matter for surprise. It is much more significant that, owing to certain elements in the English character, the transfer of the trade into English hands was to prove the first effective step towards its abolition. It must of course be admitted that at the outset England took up the trade with vigour, and having done so, ran it with greater efficiency and more ruthlessness than her predecessors; she made an outstanding financial success of it; and to this day there are probably many families who owe their wealth and position to the skill of forefathers who trafficked in slaves.

But the traders were not the whole of England. There was another part, which may indeed have included the trader in his more serious moments. In that other part there burned bright the most fundamental of English characteristics, the love of liberty—a characteristic which must always sooner or later be fatal to the concept and practice of slavery. The average Englishman may not have been very conscious of his own convictions, but, for all that, he was as firmly convinced in the eighteenth century as Captain Jobson had been in the seventeenth, that the English were a people who 'did not buy or sell one another or any that hath our own shapes'. That belief, however emphatically contradicted by the existence of the slave trade, was ingrained, and sprang from an outlook on men and matters which, if it was not entirely new, at least had rarely been voiced before and never acted upon in other parts of the world. The nearest approach to an absolute condemnation of slavery had come from Leo X who had told the Dominicans from Hispaniola that not only religion but nature herself cried out against slavery (Roscoe's *Leo X*. II, 258). He did not, however, follow up his words with deeds, and apart from him no one in earlier ages seems to have denounced slavery as such, but only acts of cruelty. It was left to England to challenge the principle as opposed to the accidents of slavery, and probably she might never have done so, if her eyes had not been opened by her experience of the trade. The terms therefore of the Treaty of Utrecht should be regarded with a measure of forbearance, for until England meddled with the Assiento, slavery had never been regarded as a sin, but only as a fact of life—a fact no doubt peculiarly subject to abuse but still no more than one of the natural phenomena of a far-from-perfect world.

The old traders were doubtless too callous in their actions, but modern historians are sometimes too impassioned in their judgments. In retrospect slavery must always appear a grievous thing—'infamous' as Gardiner says—but the English historian, intent on blaming his country, tends to make it more grievous than it was, and in doing so, comes near to missing the essential point. 'Torn from the most distant parts of Africa,' says Lecky, 'speaking no common language, connected by no tie except that of common misfortune, severed from every old association and from all they loved, and exchanging in many cases a life of unbounded freedom for a hopeless, abject and crushing servitude, the wretched captives were carried across the waste of waters in ships so crowded and so unhealthy that, even under favourable circumstances, about twelve in every thousand usually died from the horrors of the passage. They had no knowledge, no rights, no protection against the caprices of irresponsible power. The immense disproportion of the sexes consigned them to the most brutal vice. Difference of colour and difference of religion led their masters to look upon them simply as beasts of burden, and the supply of slaves was too abundant to allow the motive of self-interest to be any considerable security for their good treatment. Often, indeed, it seemed the interest of the master rather to work them rapidly to death and then to replenish his stock. All Africa was convulsed by civil wars and infested with bands of native slave-dealers hunting down victims for the English trader, whose blasting influence, like some malignant providence, extended over mighty regions where the face of a white man was never seen' (Lecky. II, 14).

Within limits, this is no doubt a true description, yet it tends to lose the essence in a crowd of biased incidentals. What difference could it make from which part of Africa the slave was torn? What great hardship was lack of a common language to those who would never meet again when the voyage was over? How could it matter whether or not the face of a white man had been seen in the regions where slaves were hunted, and why is it only the English trader for whom the hunting was done? Why, too, but to blacken the picture, is the Atlantic turned into a waste of waters, and why is mention made only of the caprices of irresponsible power and the erroneous views of masters? To have mentioned palliating factors would not have weakened the case. On the contrary, it would have emphasized its inherent badness, for it is clear that had the slave been taken from the nearest part of Africa, had he spoken the same language as all the rest, had the passage been smooth and comfortable and the master kindly and sympathetic, it would still have been infamous and a crime to deprive the slave of his liberty, turning him not so much into a beast of burden as into a piece of property. Slavery is not made bad by cruel masters, nor good by tolerant masters; it is an insufferable wrong in itself, and betrays its true nature by its fruits—the perpetually recurrent unhappiness of the slave, the inevitable brutalization of the master. It is not the trappings of slavery, but slavery itself which is wrong. In every case, not only in the many cases of which Lecky writes, the slave exchanges a state of freedom for one of abject, hopeless and crushing servitude, for that is the nature of slavery; it debases the sufferer from a man in the image

of God to a chattel in the possession of a fellow-creature. Until that
basic fact was recognized, there was no visible end to slavery, nor even
the least hope for the slave except in the character of his master.

II

At the time of the Assiento, England had not yet appreciated the true
nature of slavery. In her eyes it was still simply a form of commerce, 'a
trade', as John Cary wrote in 1695, 'of the most advantage to this
kingdom of any we drive and as it were all profit, the first cost being
little more than small matters of our own manufactures for which we
have in return gold, teeth [ivory], wax and negroes, the last whereof is
much better than the first, being indeed the best traffic that the kingdom hath as it doth occasion and give so vast an employment to our
people both by sea and land. These are the hands whereby our plantations are improved, and 'tis by their labours such great quantities of
sugar, tobacco, cotton, ginger and indigo are raised which being
bulky commodities employ great numbers of our ships for transporting hither, and the greater number of handicraft trades at home'
(Quoted. MacInnes, p. 28). The negroes, in short, might without
much exaggeration be described as the promoters of full employment
and a rising standard of life. Cary's picture was not without its attractions for an Englishman; he was a good patriot, and cannot altogether
be blamed if he had not learned, with Nurse Cavell, that patriotism is
not enough.

Cary's outlook was typical of the merchant at home. The slave trade
was, on the whole, considerate in its organization, and for the most
part not consciously cruel in its operations. If the merchant in his
office ever had a sneaking suspicion that all was not as it should be, his
doubts were easily allayed not only by the prospect of large profits but
even more by a belief that the negroes were hardly human. Nor were
they. Lok, as already recorded, had found them 'a people of beastly
living, without God, law, religion or commonwealth', and he had not
been far out.

A hundred years later, another trader, one Owen, lived some years
on the Sherborow River. Though not a literate man, he was in his own
quaint way of an inquiring turn of mind, and his researches led him to
the conclusion that 'the inhabitants are hardly above beasts, ignorant
of all arts and siances, without the comforts of religion or the benefits
that an engenous mind or person could show them, without industry

of cultavateing or manageing thier land to its perfection, destatute of all
wholsom laws and past perswasion to enter into the civel society with
the rest of mankind' (Owen, p. 61). They were, according to him, lazy
and improvident, with the result that their food was poor and scanty.
Possibly for that reason they had 'an inhuman custum in this river of
eateing yong children. . . . I have seen some instances of this inhuman
practice' (ibid., p. 32).

The various tribes differed in their characteristics, some being more
ferocious, some more tractable, but most of them indulged in human
sacrifices; many were cannibals, and all alike were superstitious, savage,
barbarous and dirty. It was not difficult for a merchant, if he ever gave
the matter a thought, to believe that by putting them to honest work in
a country where they might taste the benefits of civilization, he was
raising them to an infinitely higher level. It was the newest form of the
old Spanish excuse that the slaves were being put into the way of
salvation. Any awkward doubts could always be stifled by such
arguments but probably doubts were few and far between. 'Some
people', said Owen, 'may think a scruple of congience in the above
trade, but its very seldom minded by our European merchts' (ibid.,
p. 45).

If it was seldom minded by those on the spot, it was still less minded
by those in charge of the trade at Bristol, London or Liverpool. The
merchants at home did not regard themselves as in any sense missionaries or trustees for backward nations. They were traders; and their
proper business was to grapple with the problems of organization consequent on the nature of their trade. It was enough for them if the
instructions which they drew up for their captains paid attention to the
health and happiness of the slaves as well as the profits of the company.
The two after all were intertwined, for ill-treatment would benefit no
one; it would smack of inhumanity and, more important, damage
the negroes and so reduce their value. The captains accordingly were
ordered to buy only the best specimens, rejecting any that were
'maimed or decrepit'; and to see to it that these best specimens 'have
their provisions regularly and be no ways molested but treated with all
the lenity that security will permit of' (Instructions to Captain
Duncombe, 1759. Quoted. MacInnes, p. 47–8). The merchants were
not unkindly men, merely unimaginative, and not at all inclined to
quarrel with their bread and butter.

III

The captains and crews who actually did the work had a different and more realistic outlook. In the eighteenth century life at sea was always hard, not only in the slave trade but in the best of services. The ships were small, the accommodation cramped, and the ventilation mainly to seek, so that the stench below decks was often overpoweringly disgusting. The food, never luxurious, became in the case of long voyages nearly uneatable. Scurvy was rampant and the medical services rough and incompetent.

Discipline tended to be brutal. Punishments were always harsh and often excessive; men were thrown into irons, or tied to the masts and flogged unmercifully for what must often have seemed to them venial offences. There were, of course, many good officers who displayed a sense of responsibility towards the men under their command, but there were plenty of others cast in a coarser mould; and for those seamen who incurred the displeasure of a martinet, or, still worse, the malice of an evilly disposed captain, life in the confined space of a ship must have been unendurable indeed.

Nor were the men who formed the crews at all likely to improve matters. Too frequently they were the offscourings of the gaols, the flotsam and jetsam of seaboard towns, swept up by impatient press-gangs or rascally crimps. What was true of the best of services was even more true of the slave trade, which had its own especial drawbacks to discourage the better type of sailor. At the outset there was the risk of trouble in collecting the slaves. 'Upon our setting ourselves on shoar,' Owen records of one expedition, 'we ware secur'd by the natives, put into irons, and hove down upon the ground in a barborous manner, striping us of all our cloaths, and in short made a prize of us' (Owen, p. 37). It was all in the day's work and Owen relates it in a matter-of-fact style, passing on in the same business-like way to record that 'in this adventure we lost four years' pay all in gold'. Nor was this first risk the only hazard. When a cargo of slaves had been secured, it was noisome in itself and the conditions under which it was carried were only too likely to breed disease. Sailors were well aware that the resultant mortality could not be confined to the negroes, and for that very reason shunned the slavers. Lastly, there was ever present the chance that the slaves might make a desperate bid for freedom. 'Lately,' says Owen, 'we have the malloncoly news of Captain Potter's being cut of by the slaves at Mano and the ship drove ashoar; the captain, second mate and doctor are all killed in a barbarous manner by the slaves' (ibid., p. 106). Little wonder that, after weighing the pros and cons, Owen preferred his life as a resident trader in Africa, poor as it was, to his life as a sailor. 'Some people', he remarks, 'may condem this kind of life, and perferr that of a venturious sailor or valliant soldier, but I can tell them to try both first and then to take thier choice. One of these lives I have tried 8 or 9 years both in pace and war, and found nothing to intice a man of a good disposition to a continuance in an imployment wherein vice and ignorance bare the garland from virtue and honour' (ibid., p. 85). It was unlikely that crews who suffered so much themselves and were generally of so low a class would see any need to be tender towards the slaves who formed their cargo.

IV

There was a third component in this traffic, of which a word should be said—the agent or broker at the receiving end. The arrangements for disposing of slaves under the Assiento were elaborate, but the Assiento was important only for the impetus which it gave to England's participation in the trade; it was never of the expected value; it opened the door to interminable disputes; and in due course was brought to an end to the mutual satisfaction of all parties.

The trade to America and the West Indies was quite different; it soon became well organized; it was highly profitable and it persisted. It took the form of a round trip, divided into three parts—first, the voyage to Africa where 'the small matters of our own manufactures' were so gainfully bartered; secondly, the voyage across the Atlantic, usually known as the middle passage, to the port of debarkation where the slaves were handed over to the broker; and thirdly, the return voyage to England with a fresh cargo, picked up in America. There were thus three separate profits to be obtained, and, in fact, the net earnings of a successful round were often well over one hundred per cent of the original outlay. The amount of the profit depended to a large extent on the ability of the brokers. Their task was not confined to selling the slaves; they had also to arrange for the return cargoes, and to pass on to the captains any news or instructions received from England. In a word they were agents doing their best for the company which employed them, and for the most part faithfully representing its views. Normally they were sound business men, respectable citizens with a reputation to lose in their home towns. Their enemies represented them as monsters of cruelty, but in fact they had no time or inclination to treat the slaves harshly; it was neither their desire nor their duty to be brutal; they looked upon the negroes as merchandise, entitled to the same care and regard as any other item of commerce—no more and no less—and they dealt in them with the same detachment that a farmer might show in selling a herd of cattle. Their arrangements were a great advance on the crude methods in force before the trade was properly organized, and were improved from time to time as the agents gained in experience.

It is thus apparent that, apart from the general odium which must attach to the trade, the main charge should be levelled not against the merchants in England, nor against their agents in America, but against the methods of capture adopted in Africa, the conditions obtaining in the middle passage, and the treatment which the slaves received at the hands of their masters across the Atlantic. These matters concern the slave rather than the trade.

VI. The Raw Material

I

In the early days of discovery and for centuries thereafter, Africa was a mystery which no one was disposed to investigate. It was enough for the Portuguese to coast round the outside; they had no desire to penetrate into the interior. Others followed their example, so that it was not till the nineteenth century that exploration began on a scientific basis. This lack of interest in the country was matched by the lack of sympathy with its inhabitants. Indeed the attitude of the Europeans towards the Dark Continent in all its aspects is a phenomenon well worthy of study from a psychological point of view. The natural curiosity which might have been expected to arise, as it did in the case of other continents, seems to have been damped from the first by a species of racial antipathy which showed itself in a reluctance, as determined as it was unreasonable, to admit negroes into the circle of the human family.

To the European the negro was an enigma who bred doubt upon

doubt. Was he a man or an animal? Was he capable of civilization? Had he a soul? Did he share in the hopes and fears of mankind or was he a devil in semi-human form? The suspicions were real; the matter was hotly debated, and settled only by degrees. 'Methinks', argued Godwin in 1680, 'the consideration of the shape and figure of our negro's bodies, their limbs and members, their voice and countenance in all things according to other men's; together with their risibility and discourse (man's peculiar faculties) should be a sufficient conviction' (Godwin. Negro's and Indian's Advocate. Quoted Klingberg, p. 115). Yet clearly his own conviction required bolstering. Even a hundred and fifty years later all doubts had not been completely resolved. 'The opinion', wrote Eliot in 1832, 'that the negro is not only inferior in endowments to the European, but that he belongs to a species altogether distinct, has been frequently advanced by the advocates of the African slave trade' (*Christianity and Slavery*, p. 195).

The lack of interest in the negroes' home was due to the fact that the slaves were supplied by native agents on the coast. The European trader, therefore, had no need to penetrate inland, and no ambition to inquire into the agents' methods. If questioned, he allowed his imagination full play. Africa, so he assumed, held in its interior a number of primitive tribes, living in dirt and poverty and dominated by savage superstitions. Slaves abounded, and the most powerful influence was witchcraft—the dread Obeah which disposed of human lives in secret session. No doubt the tribes made war on one another, as such tribes will, and no doubt tribal conflicts resulted in numerous captives. War and witchcraft and the surplus of home-bred slaves were sufficient sources for the merchandise which the trader bought.

To some extent the trader was right, but his assumptions fell woefully short of the truth. The life of a savage offers few occupations, other than that of a concubine, to which a slave could well be put, and it may be doubted therefore if slaves as such were particularly abundant. Chieftains, whether so-called kings or so-called nobles, all had their followers who were required to do their bidding, but rather out of loyalty as members of the clan than consciously as slaves. As for prisoners of war, the tribes do not appear to have been particularly bellicose. Such prisoners as were taken seem, as a rule, to have been butchered on the spot, or else reserved as offerings for the tribal god, or as victims for a witch-doctor's unholy but exciting rites. No one pitied them. Nor was any stomach turned at the so-called 'customs' which meant the murder of whole hecatombs, whether of slaves or clansmen, to accompany the august dead into the next world. Life was cheap and death could be horribly cruel. The African's methods were not pleasant. In 1817 one, Bowditch, saw and described 'a most inhuman spectacle' at Kumassi, the capital of Ashanti. 'It was a man whom they were tormenting previous to sacrifice. His hands were pinioned behind him, a knife was passed through his cheeks, to which his lips were noosed like the figure of 8; one ear was cut off and carried before him; the other hung to his head by a small bit of skin; there were several gashes in his back, and a knife was thrust under each shoulder-blade; he was led with a cord passed through his nose by men disfigured with immense caps of shaggy black skins, and drums beat before him' (Buxton, p. 233). The Africans' loathsome deeds gave the upholders of slavery their strongest, indeed their only valid argument, which was that 'if the present European exportation of slaves should be discontinued, the whole number of slaves usually so obtained, which is said to be about seventy thousand per annum, will be annually murdered' (Francklyn, p. 157).

Be that as it may—and obviously it was grossly exaggerated—the slaves were conjured out of the interior, no one knew how. There were only theories to explain the mystery. What can be said with some degree of certainty is that while the trade was still in its small beginnings, the merchants persuaded African chiefs that it was more lucrative to sell their criminals than to execute them. The chiefs were apt pupils, and finding the resultant trade profitable and much to their liking, quickly learnt to multiply the number of crimes for which sale into slavery was the appropriate punishment; and probably before long did not balk at selling men who had not even had the satisfaction of first committing their crime. In short, a plethora of ne'er-do-weels became an open sesame by which the happy chief gained entrance to an Aladdin's cave of coloured beads and tinkling bells and gaudy clothes, or, more deadly, of cheap muskets and kegs of rum.

But the slave trade was a lusty and gargantuan child; it soon outgrew the supply of criminals, real or feigned; and when that source failed, it was only natural for chiefs, whose yearning for finery could never be sated, to turn their minds to so-called prisoners of war. Before long, at the instigation of the merchants, or spurred on by the wickedness of the human heart, Africans began to prey upon one another in order to obtain the black currency which bought the traders' trumpery. They became ruthless where before they had been peaceable; they became predatory where before they had been mild. Two centuries earlier Purchas had discovered at Benin 'a gentle, loving people', who would not 'do injury to any, especially to strangers' (Purchas. *Africa*. Quoted Buxton, p. 232); and so they might have continued, had not greed and temptation combined to pervert their natures; for even after two centuries of slave-hunting, Buxton maintained 'on the authority of public documents, parliamentary evidence, and the works of African travellers' that 'the principal and almost the only cause of war in the interior of Africa, is the desire to procure slaves for traffic' (Buxton, p. 74).

The methods of the slave-hunters were at once crude and wasteful, no doubt because they were robbers and not warriors. Their practice was to surround some village which they had marked down for their prey, silently and at night. It was a collection of primitive mud huts thatched with bamboos and palm leaves, all highly inflammable, which they set alight without compunction, generally at early dawn. As the inhabitants woke to the crackling of flames and struggled into the open, they were rounded up and made prisoners. Any who resisted were cut down; the slave-hunters had no mercy for them. Nor had they any use for the old or infirm or for babes, all of whom they killed out of hand. Only men and women in their prime and adolescent boys and girls were spared, to be carried off into slavery, leaving behind them dead bodies and dying ashes where once there had been happy homes and a living settlement. The waste was out of all proportion to the prize. But waste, wanton waste, was the hall-mark of negro slavery, from its first moment to its last. Wherever it reared its head, death, disease and destruction were its invariable concomitants.

II

The victims of these raids had to be driven down to the barracoons on the coast, like cattle to market. If their village had been near a river, they might almost be called lucky, for then they would have a ride down the stream, free and for nothing. It would, of course, be their fate to lie naked, under a few coarse mats, at the bottom of a canoe, trussed up like fowls and shivering in the bilge water, but at least they had no further effort to make; their vessel carried them on all too swiftly to their doom, with much beating of drums and fluttering of flags.

Those captured far inland were less fortunate, for they had to march to the coast on their own feet—a dreary pilgrimage over many miles of thick forest and rough desert ways. They too were naked, with no protection against sharp thorns or jagged stones. To prevent escape, they had heavy forked poles, about three feet long, fastened round their necks; their hands, if they were troublesome, might be secured through holes in a rough wooden board, and they were fettered with chains on their ankles. Linked together by ropes, the long files known as coffles trudged miserably on towards a terrifying fate; for all Africa knew that the white men fed on the negroes bought from the barra-coons. Their captors drove them relentlessly forward, ignoring wounds and lacerations, and physicking weariness by plentiful flicks of the whip. If any succumbed, they were thrown on one side; if any became too ill, they were left to die, or more mercifully knocked on the head. The hunters were hardened and callous—they could hardly be anything else—but probably not for the most part intentionally cruel. They were too occupied with their own affairs, and their urgency had a reason. A slave coffle, like an army, moved on its stomach, and its com-missariat was greatly to seek. There were no depots, no storehouses, no shops; the coffles had to carry their own food on their heads and not infrequently their drink as well, and if the march lasted too long, they must all inevitably die of starvation. It was a choice between swollen feet and empty stomachs, between excoriated backs and starved bodies. The hunters wanted their money; the slaves may still have wanted their lives. Both had to hurry; it was part of the trade, one of its least disadvantages. So they came to the barracoons and the middle passage.

III

The middle passage! At the outset of his campaign, Wilberforce and his friends decided, for reasons to be mentioned hereafter, that their best course would be to attack, not slavery itself, but the slave trade. Their decision, whether right or wrong, had the effect of cramping their style. To damn the trade they should have exposed all its horrors from beginning to end, but they found that there were practical limita-tions. They knew little or nothing about the capture of slaves—no one did, or at least no one admitted knowing—and they hesitated to say too much about the treatment of slaves at the hands of the planters for fear of antagonizing the colonies. They were forced, therefore, to concen-trate mainly on that fleeting experience in the slave's life known as the 'middle passage'. It was only with considerable difficulty that they were able to collect any facts about it, and naturally they made the most of those which were most lurid. They exaggerated, not in details, but in cumulative effect by seizing on the bad and dwelling on the worst, ignoring whatever might explain or excuse. 'Never,' wrote Wilberforce, with a faint foreshadowing of a more famous dictum, 'never can so much misery be found condensed into so small a space as in a slave ship during the middle passage' (Wilberforce. *A Letter on the Abolition of the Slave Trade addressed to the Freeholders and other inhabitants of Yorkshire*, 1807). It is a tribute to his skill that ever since it has been customary to speak with bated breath of 'the horrors of the middle passage'. But the horrors must be approached with a more critical eye than Wilberforce was disposed to use.

There were horrors enough in all conscience, but they were peculiar to the slave trade only in part; they lasted a mere matter of weeks; and had they proved to be the sum total of a slave's distresses, his life would not have been too unendurable. Like all horrors, too, they tended as time went on to diminish. In essence, they can be listed under two heads—physical and psychological, the former being more spectacular and perhaps more fatal to life, the latter more pregnant of misery and perhaps more fatal to reason.

The negro driven down from the interior had never seen the sea, nor yet ships which he called moving or flying houses. Even when free he was apt to be terrified of both. Livingstone tells the pitiful story of Sekwebu, a native who had accompanied him on his travels through Africa and wanted to return with him to England. But the sea greatly daunted him, and he kept murmuring 'What a strange country is this— all water together'; and was so bewildered by all he saw and suffered on board that the strain was too much for him. In the course of the voyage, he became insane and threw himself over the side (Livingstone. *Missionary Travels and Researches in South Africa*, p. 683).

If a free negro 'a favourite with both men and officers', travelling with a trusted protector and looking forward to the wonders of civilization, could be so affected by the strangeness of his environment, it is not surprising that the wretched slaves on the middle passage, with no protector and no prospects, going they knew not where and expecting they knew not what, should usually have seemed dejected and not infrequently have gone out of their minds. Nor was it surprising that many, like Sekwebu, threw themselves overboard if the chance came their way. They hardly needed the goad of added cruelty, though in fact they received no encouragement from their surroundings. The slave ships made no pretence at comfort. They were often intolerably overcrowded, and the reason is not far to seek. Captains were paid a commission on slaves sold, and being for the most part simple and rather stupid men, 'made', as one of them said in evidence, 'the most of the room and wedged them in' (An Abstract of Evidence, p. 35) The slaves had barely space to lie side by side. If illness supervened and they died like flies, it was in the captain's view, just too bad, not the result of his own foolish greed. Deaths were frequent and in Wilberforce's eyes were 'evidence which is absolutely infallible . . . a sure ground of proof' of the terrible conditions (Speech, 12th May, 1789. Quoted Coupland, p. 123). It seemed so unanswerable that inevitably the reformers tended to exaggerate the numbers and overlook the various causes. Undoubtedly the losses were large, but it is not without significance that when in 1787, the reformers, with Government assistance and the best of intentions, dispatched from England a party of four hundred and sixty negroes to settle in Sierra Leone (see p. 123), no fewer than eighty-four, or over eighteen per cent, died on the voyage. Perhaps, after all, death was not such conclusive evidence as Wilberforce thought!

IV

Granted fine weather and a reasonable captain, the middle passage was soon over—a matter of six weeks or so, and with luck was not too utterly uncomfortable. The men were allowed on deck during the hours of light; their food, though coarse, was sufficient; their drink— half a pint of water per meal—about the same as was allowed to naval ratings. They were encouraged to sing, however lugubriously, and also to exercise themselves by skipping or jumping, which was usually described as dancing and was sometimes enforced with whips on very reluctant and no doubt sea-sick merrymakers! The worst part of their lot was at night when they were crowded below decks, and one might almost say fitted into bunks, generally known as platforms, which were never more than two or three feet high, and destitute of bedding. In these bunks they were shackled together in twos, the right hand and ankle of the one to the left hand and ankle of the next, a condition which was hardly conducive to sleep and could give rise to trouble if one of the two, wanting to answer nature's call, could not persuade a sleepy or sullen or sea-sick partner to accompany him to the buckets which formed the sanitary system. The reformers laid great emphasis

on the lack of height between the platforms, and indeed it was deplor-
ably small; but the fact remains that the conditions of the slaves did not
differ appreciably from the conditions which Smollett, when he acted
as a naval surgeon, found in the hospital ships of the Royal Navy.
Describing the expedition against Carthagena in 1740, he recorded
that the wounded 'languished in want of every necessary comfort and
accommodation . . . they were pent up between decks in small vessels
where they had not room to sit upright; they wallowed in filth;
myriads of maggots were hatched in the putrefaction of their sores'
(Smollett. *Expedition to Carthagena*). The slaves would not have
envied them, or perhaps have noticed any particular difference, for the
slaves' plight stands out more terribly against the background of
modern conditions than in the setting of their own age. It was a rough
and brutal age for all except the favoured few.

Yet, if the horrors of the middle passage could be matched elsewhere, they were none the less real; they were not a mere invention of
soft-hearted reformers; they existed and became glaringly evident in
rough weather, when the slaves were perforce kept below deck by day
as well as by night, and the portholes had to be shut. Negroes were
more seriously affected by sea-sickness than Europeans, and in stormy
weather may well have been too ill to think about the buckets provided
for their use; but in any event the buckets were almost inaccessible in
that mass of human wretchedness, where it was hardly possible to walk
without treading on others, and those trodden upon were apt to retali-
ate by biting the intruding foot. Sooner or later the slaves were
obliged to wallow in their own vomiting and filth, and the stench in
the confined area became overpoweringly foul. Nor was it made better
by the stifling heat and the lack of air. Many a fight and many a death
took place when men less prostrate than others struggled and bit and
fought to get near the gratings, through which alone came some
semblance of fresh air. In such an atmosphere, epidemics were only too
likely, and dysentery could run through the ship, carrying off numbers
not only of the slaves but also of the crew. The misery was intense; it
explained and more than justified the efforts at insurrection which were
often made and were sometimes successful. Where the insurrection
failed, the vengeance taken was fearful in its barbarity; captain and
crew driven on by fear, vied with each other in devising tortures. When
it succeeded, captain and crew paid the penalty; they were massacred
wholesale.

Bad weather had other effects. It prolonged the crossing, and by so doing added to the sum total of suffering. If it were too prolonged, it might lead to shortage of food, when the rations of the slaves would naturally be the first to be cut. If the shortage became too threatening, the slaves could be, and sometimes were, thrown overboard to reduce the numbers. The crew did not usually trouble to kill them first; they simply left them to drown.

The lot of the women slaves was slightly better; they were nearly as crowded below decks but they were not shackled and were allowed to wander where they would. They paid for this freedom by becoming the natural prey of the crew. Sometimes, though not often, they were able to revenge themselves by assisting their husbands and brothers to get weapons and start a revolt; but for the most part their fate was just to be raped.

But in fair weather or foul, in spite of diseases and deaths, and for all the insurrections and suicides, every year the ships brought thousands of slaves to America and the West Indies. The number rose to its maximum in 1768 when one hundred and four thousand were landed, and probably in the leanest of times the total never fell much below half that figure. They came in ships of many nations—French, Dutch, Portuguese and Danish—but rather more than half were brought in English ships that had sailed from Bristol, London or Liverpool. Year in, year out, they were set ashore, diseased or whole, resigned or despairing, and were lost for ever to the land of their birth.

v

To what did they come? First, to a brief period of relief, whilst they were being polished up for the shop window. It was not to be expected that they would land in fine fettle, and the captain, anxious for his employer's profits and especially his own commission, took such steps as he could to cure, or at least to cover up, cuts and sores and abrasions, and all signs of illness and disease. Wilberforce looked on these efforts with a suspicious eye; he believed that 'the astringent washes which are used to hide their wounds, and the mischievous tricks employed to make them up for sale' were a cause of mortality. Possibly they were, for it is unlikely that rough sea-captains should be exceptionally skilful or particularly cautious in medical affairs, or indeed that they should care for anything but immediate and superficial results. But the slave welcomed the attention; it was not for him to grumble at better food and some relaxation nor to reject a salve which he supposed would heal his wounds. At the least it should improve his chance of being sold to someone on dry land, and surely anything was better than a return voyage over the dreadful ocean.

When the grooming was complete the sale began. Originally it had taken place on the ship, generally by what was known as 'the scramble'. The men were placed on the main deck, the women on the quarter-deck, and the would-be purchasers collected on the quay. When all preparations were complete, a gun was fired, on which the buyers 'rushed through the barricado with the ferocity of brutes' and proceeded to label the slaves they fancied. Sometimes, however, a middleman would buy the lot, and hawk them around from plantation to plantation; it was significant of his methods that he was known familiarly as a 'soul driver'. But as the trade became better organized, and the merchants appointed agents at the ports, the system became more orderly, though not more seemly. The slaves were sold at auctions, being brought in stark naked, men and women alike, and mounted on a chair, where the bidders handled and prodded them and felt their muscles and examined their teeth and made them jump and flex their arms, to satisfy themselves that they were not bidding for a diseased or disabled lot. As the slaves were bought singly, it followed that often husband and wife, children and parents went to different owners; and the loss of kith and kin and all that the slave held dear was added to the loss of liberty. So the slave left the auction room, bereaved of everything, to begin a new life of 'abject, hopeless and crushing servitude'.

VII. The Slave at Work

I

THE USES of servitude, like its abuses, never change; they are the same all the world over and from one age to another. In America and the West Indies, as in ancient Rome, or in Greece, or in the dim beginnings of history, slavery was divided into two broad types—domestic slavery and the slavery of the works or plantations.

The former tended to be less oppressive, because the duties were lighter and more varied, and especially because they were performed

in and about the owner's house. It would never have occurred to him
to live as he required his plantation slaves to live, and the domestic
slave, therefore, had a cleaner, a richer and a more attractive environment. Except for this matter of physical comfort, the lot of the domestic slave was determined by the character of his owner. Inevitably the
master became accustomed to his personal attendants but how he
treated them depended not on law, or custom, or contract, but on
his temperament; he might grow fond of them as one grows fond of
animals; and even, in forgetful moments, think of them as human
beings; equally, he might be testy and intolerant and allow familiarity
to breed its usual quota of contempt. Some masters were naturally
good and their families kind, and then the lot of the slave was comparatively happy. Thomas Mann Randolph, we are told by a slave of
twenty-six years' standing, was 'one of the finest masters in Virginia;
his wife a mighty peaceable woman; never holler for servant; make
no fuss nor racket; pity she ever died' (*Memoirs of a Monticello Slave*'
p. 38).

Others were different and their actions could be deeds of darkness.
Lewis Hayden, a fugitive slave from Kentucky, told this tragic story
of his mother. She was a 'very handsome woman', and the sight of
her roused the desires of a man in Lexington who sought her favours,
and when she would not respond bought her from her owner. Finding
her still reluctant, his appetite turned to hatred, and growing vengeful,
he sent her to be flogged, and punished her in so many and various
ways that at last she lost her reason. She tried to commit suicide, and
even attacked her children in order to save them from a slave's fate
(*A Key to Uncle Tom's Cabin*, p. 378). The majority of owners no
doubt came between these two extremes, and may perhaps be represented by the rumbustious Colonel Cary, a friend of Thomas Jefferson,
who, we are told by one of Jefferson's slaves, would in the course of
a visit 'whip anybody' if the whim so seized him and no doubt
thought he had made amends when, on leaving, he tipped the servants
'sometimes five or six dollars among 'em' (*Memoirs of a Monticello
Slave*, p. 36). The qualities he betrayed were those one might expect
to find in a master of slaves—an inability to put himself in a slave's
shoes and a good conceit of himself.

Slaves were cheap and the owners liked to be luxurious. Hence, in
America and the West Indies, as in Rome, the number of domestic
slaves tended to multiply in the houses of the rich. They performed
all the ordinary household duties; they were the butlers, gardeners,

grooms, postilions and handymen; the cooks, parlourmaids, nurses, washerwomen and sempstresses; they were also the valets and lady's-maids, the secretaries, major-domos and chatelaines. They belonged to the house in more senses than one and if they married, their children were equally slaves of the house, and were brought up as part of the estate. They had to pay their way, and the boys, if there was no obvious job for them, were apprenticed to some trade, such as tinkering or carpentry, which would be useful to their owner; and the girls could be put to help in the kitchen or laundry, or, if they were good-looking, could be hired out as prostitutes. It was common practice for a host to offer his guests the use of a slave girl at night (Mathieson. *British Slavery 1823–38*, p. 59). So much for the domestic slaves; they were furniture about the house and implements on the estate, and as such commanded a certain degree of consideration.

II

The lot of the plantation slave was harder. The job assigned to him was, from his point of view, skilled; he was to cultivate a crop hitherto unknown to him—for the most part sugar in the West Indies, cotton or tobacco in America—and, in that his work was novel, he endured a heavier burden than his counterpart in Greece or Rome or among the serfs of Europe. They had been set tasks which at least were familiar to them, but a savage fresh from the wilds of Africa was not accustomed to sugar or tobacco, still less to the process of extracting and refining the one or curing the other. Nor was he naturally a good farmer or even inured by practice to heavy agricultural labour, coming as he did from a country where the soil was bountiful, and the wants of the inhabitants simple and easily satisfied. All was new and strange to him; he had, therefore, to be broken in; he had to be taught his new duties; he had to be seasoned, as the saying was.

'Seasoning' was a euphemism for a harsh discipline, which was reckoned by the opponents of slavery to carry off not less than twenty per cent of those who underwent it. Maybe that was over the mark, but it must none the less be admitted that large numbers died. The discipline was painful, and there was little to ameliorate and much to embitter its severity. That the older slaves, into whose charge the pupils were committed, were skilled instructors or patient teachers, is not to be supposed. They were poor, ignorant creatures themselves, not much advanced, if at all, in the ways of civilization, and no doubt they often took that delight in tormenting those in their power which is character-istic of the half-fledged and the barbarous when they are drest in a little brief authority. Often, too, the instructors did not speak the same dialect as their pupils, so that some means of communication had to be devised, and language had to be taught as well as the rudiments of agriculture. If the old slaves were impatient or cruel, the new slaves, one may believe, were not submissive. On the contrary, they were probably resentful; they were certainly sad; and in many cases may still have been suffering from the effects of the voyage.

The reformers were given to comparing the deadliness of the various stages in the slave's progress from Africa to the plantations; but when each stage added to the suffering, their cumulative effect makes it difficult to draw distinctions between them; they all merge in together. This was particularly true of the 'seasoning', for beyond doubt a large proportion of those who died under its discipline would have died in any event from the effects of the middle passage. Experience showed that the greater number of those who were weak or emaciated on arrival, died soon afterwards whatever they did. The medical author-ities put this down to 'the long confinement in slave-houses previous to embarkation, want of cleanliness and ventilation while on board the slave-ships, alterations in dress, food and habits, and, not the least, change of climate' (Buxton, p. 188). But they agreed that there was something more—a psychological or spiritual malaise, which they described, perhaps a little portentously, as 'the sad recollection of perpetual expatriation, the lacerated feelings of kindred and friendship, the rude violation of all the sacred and social endearments of country and relationship, and the degrading anticipation of endless unmitigated bondage'. This when added to the physical hardships too often dis-solved the will to live, and the slave seized the first chance to do away with himself, or more simply, pined away and died.

But, here again, for all the suicides and deaths, thousands passed through the discipline alive and in due course took their place in the plantations. Except that life is sweet, one might suppose them to have been less fortunate than those who fell by the way, for too often the plantations had little to offer beyond toil and sweat and blood and tears.

The toil varied with the crop, being heaviest on the sugar, and lightest on the coffee, plantations. 'The discipline of the sugar planta-tion', said Ramsay, who spoke with the knowledge gained by nineteen years in St. Kitt's, 'is as exact as that of a regiment; at four o'clock in the morning the plantation bell rings to call the slaves into the field.

Their work is to manure, dig, hoe and plough the ground, to plant, weed and cut the cane, to bring it to the mill, to have the juice expressed and boiled into sugar' (Ramsay. *Essay on the Treatment and Conversion of African Slaves in the British Sugar Colonies*, p. 69). The work went on till about seven in the evening, though it was interrupted twice in the day when the slaves were dispatched 'to pick up about the fences, in the mountains, and fallow or waste grounds, natural grass and weeds for the horses and cattle' (ibid.). This aimless search for fodder was, said Ramsay, 'a most cruel and oppressive business' (Letter to Tobin, p. 32 and Ramsay's Reply, p. 87), for the supplies were scanty and scattered, and the slave in order to obtain his quota too often trespassed, of necessity or by mistake, on to private property when, if he was found, he was deprived of his gleanings, and in their place received a flogging, which his own master repeated when he appeared empty-handed.

The work in the field continued roughly from July to December. From January to June the canes were harvested and treated in the mills to produce sugar and rum. During this period the slaves were worked not only from morning till evening, but every other night as well, feeding the mills and skimming the copper cauldrons in the boiler houses. At such times they were apt to become drowsy, and being half asleep, not infrequently lost a finger, a hand or even an arm in the machinery. Yet on the whole, in spite of accidents, in spite of the extra work, the slaves were happier in the time of harvest; for, being allowed to eat the cane tops, they were able to some extent to assuage their almost universal hunger, and had also a chance of stealing some rum while it was being distilled.

What they did with their leisure, with their brief public holidays, their Sundays and such off times as they might be granted, does not much matter. Probably, in large part, they were occupied on the allotments which they were usually given and on which they grew vegetables or kept pigs and poultry, partly for their own use, partly for sale. They delighted in crude colours, as they or their fathers had done in Africa, and were fond of dressing themselves up, when they could afford it, with gaudy handkerchiefs and flashy jewellery. They amused themselves in their own way, mostly and of necessity a limited way, indulging in dancing, singing and sexual excesses, as often as not continuing throughout the night and until the day broke. A composite picture of a system which lasted for several centuries and was spread over many lands is bound to be full of contradictions; so much would depend on the time and the place and the master's character. Stories of kindness would contrast with stories of cruelty, stories of happiness with tales of woe. What might be true of one country or one century might be far from true of others. Nor would the variations in detail matter; none of them would affect the core and essence of slavery.

There is, however, one connecting link which from the days of Pharaoh to the present time has run without deviation through every type of slavery. From one century to another, from one plantation to the next, the symbol and sign of slavery has always been the whip. If a slave was late, he was whipped; if he was lazy, he was whipped; if he was stupid and forgetful, he was whipped; and if by chance he was happy and worked well and was successful, his reward was, simply, not to be whipped. For minor lapses he was flicked by the 'driver' who presided over the gang with a short-handled whip of 'plaited cowskin'; for more serious offences he was held on the ground for a sound thrashing; for major sins he was handed over to a professional flogger. This professional went by the title of Jumper. In the normal course he waited for his clients; but if business was slack, he would tout for orders from door to door, like any pedlar or commercial traveller. His presence and functions were taken for granted—except by visitors to whom he could appear as a distressing phenomenon. One such visitor has left an account of the scene when a Jumper knocked at the door. The master of the house had no occasion for his services, but the mistress decided that two of the maids waiting at table would be all the brisker for a good beating. The visitor, horrified, protested; but in vain. There and then, we are told, the Jumper 'ordered one of the women to turn her back and to take up her clothes entirely, and he gave her a dozen on the breech. Every stroke brought flesh from her. She behaved with astonishing fortitude. After the punishment, she, according to custom, curtsied and thanked him; the other had the same punishment and behaved in the same way' (MacInnes, p. 119). The whip took the heart out of a slave as well as the flesh off his back. Fear may be an incentive, but only so long as it remains a threat; with the fall of the lash fear becomes pain and incentive dies. So it was with the slaves.

III

A point generally overlooked in any description of slavery is that the ties which bound the slave to the master, also bound the master to the slave. The effects were reciprocal, and though different in kind were perhaps equal in degree. No one would willingly have become a slave; but equally no one who prayed that he might not be led into temptation should willingly have become an owner, for slave-owning was a never-ending temptation which resulted too often in spiritual decay and not infrequently in material disaster. The point is worth a moment's consideration. It is notorious that power corrupts. Power over a slave was almost absolute and it was natural therefore that it should have fertilized and nourished in the masters whatever tendency they had to cruelty, avarice, insolence and pride; their path to heaven was more full of snares than that of other men.

Nor were they helped by law or custom. Acts and regulations, coming from the mother country and based on second-hand information, were spasmodic and followed no regular plan; sometimes they aimed at curbing the physical brutality of the master; sometimes at promoting the moral welfare of the slaves. But whatever their object, they could be, and largely were, ignored in the colonies. The local assemblies and the local courts were controlled by the settlers, who inevitably partook of the local prejudices, however anxious they might be to do right and to administer the law justly—desires, incidentally, that did not obtrude themselves unduly. Nor were their best efforts aided by the universal custom of refusing to allow negro evidence except against another negro. How then could the masters ever be brought to justice? Morally, the whole weight of slavery was on the devil's side, so far as the masters were concerned.

Nor was the position better in the scales of human happiness or practical politics. In the British colonial system countless English men and women have consciously toiled for the good of backward nations, and in so doing have found happiness and a reasonable livelihood. But slavery was the reverse of this system; the slave was the stepping-stone by which the master hoped to rise, at another's expense, to a richer, if not a better, life. It was the epitome of selfishness which could not benefit the slave and did not benefit the master.

IV

The masters were, to begin with, emigrants from Europe, and as such not only had their individual, but also their national characteristics, conforming in a greater or less degree to the outlook and laws of their mother countries. There were consequently at least five types of owner and five forms of negro slavery—Spanish, French, Dutch, Danish and British—without counting American, which at the outset was British.

Apart from these national distinctions, there was one difference which produced its own peculiar effects, dividing the colonies into two broad categories—those which granted the slave the right to religious instruction, and those which withheld it. The point arose at an early date. The first settlers were the Spaniards, and owing to Isabella's wistful hopes, and the character and calling of Las Casas, they were placed squarely in the first category by being enjoined to see that all slaves were educated in the Catholic faith. The settlers themselves showed no enthusiasm, but the Government saw to it that the injunction was obeyed by sending out priests and missionaries. The spiritual benefit to the slaves no doubt varied with the individual, but all of them profited physically by the rest to which they were entitled on the feast days and festivals of the Roman calendar. Moreover, their status was raised, and they received a greater degree of attention from the law. The masters' powers were curbed; they could no longer, at least in law, ill-treat their slaves with impunity; there were limits beyond which they could go only at their own peril.

At the same time, on what may be called the social side, they were obliged to recognize the marriages of slaves which had been blessed by the Church, and they were forbidden by law to separate husband and wife, or to break up families in sales for debt. Elaborate and comparatively liberal arrangements came into force for enabling the slave to buy his freedom, and the Church encouraged manumissions as a pious duty, so that the number of freedmen in Spanish colonies attained considerable proportions. In short there began to be a link, however slight, between white and black; and the attendance of both together at Mass gave the slave some semblance of honourable standing and the master an opportunity of recognizing his moral obligations.

The full effect appeared when in due course the nature of the Spanish settlements changed. Originally the conquistadors had thought only of gold. They had crossed the ocean to make their fortune, and in order to mine the precious metal of their Eldorado, they had sacrificed, without compunction, the whole race of native Indians, and were ready to do the same by the imported negroes. But their avarice overreached itself. No one from outside was to share in their new-found wealth, and to ensure this, trade with other nations was strictly forbidden; foreign ships, if Spain could help it, should never approach her American possessions. The gold mines, however, were not aş copious as had been hoped and in due course were exhausted, but not before the conquistadors had contracted the lazy habits which naturally attend on a slave-borne opulence. Thereafter without either mines or trade or the large plantations which trade might have encouraged, they had no means of increasing or even maintaining their wealth except by smuggling or corruption, and no good reason to struggle against their natural indolence. The primary splendour faded; the colonies took on a seedy aspect; and the conquistadors sank from notable grandees to petty proprietors and small-holders. In this humbler, though possibly happier, state, the Spaniards, like the primitive Romans, worked or lazed side by side with their slaves, grew familiar with them, and began to intermarry. The laws and regulations tended more and more 'to promote the moral and social welfare of the slave' and less and less to protect him from an ill-treatment which was less and less in evidence (Mathieson I, 40). Spanish slavery which had once been more ruthless and brutal than any other, now became the least onerous.

But only until the Spaniards awoke to the short-sightedness of their trade policy, as at last they did. By a series of edicts extending from 1765 to 1809 they gradually withdrew the restrictions which prevented intercourse with other nations; and in order to build up an export trade, began to develop large plantations, with growing quotas of slaves. They had the advantage of a rich and as yet unexhausted soil, but they had also the disadvantage of their natural greed and inborn brutality, both of which revived with the hope of better times. The treatment of slaves ceased to be kindly, and from being the least onerous became once more the most ferocious. 'So terrible were the atrocities,' said one spectator, 'so murderous the system of slavery, so transcendent the evils I witnessed over all I had ever seen or heard of the rigour of slavery elsewhere, that at first I could hardly believe the evidence of my senses' (Madden. *Cuba*, pp. 25, 39). The results were the same in the Spanish colonies as elsewhere; the white population began to diminish; the slave population to grow; fear and suspicion flourished and cultivation declined. Slavery was trailing its universal slime!

The French had followed hard on the heels of the Spaniards across the Atlantic, but had concentrated on the northern mainland rather than the West Indies. In Canada they had become famous not only for their work of exploration, but for the selfless devotion with which the Jesuits had toiled and suffered to convert the Red Indians. When, therefore, in the middle of the seventeenth century, Colbert acquired for France a number of islands in the Antilles, complete with slaves, it was natural for Louis XIV to insist on the baptism of the negroes and their education in the Catholic faith. The French islands thus fell into the first category, and at one time seemed to be shaping the lot of their slaves on the lines of the milder of the two Spanish forms. The process might have continued, if the Code Noir, which Louis XIV drew up for the governance of slaves, had included any executive principle. But it included none, and the character of French slavery therefore came to be moulded by the character of the French settler, whose one object was to grow rich as quickly as he could and return to France. Those who succeeded, did return; those who failed, with true Gallic fervour, exhausted themselves and died (Mathieson. I, 51). In such an atmosphere of bustle and grab, the Code Noir, which was little beyond exhortation, was bound to be ignored; the religious instruction was entirely neglected; and the slaves were mercilessly overworked. From all of which it might be thought that the French islands should not be placed in the first category; yet they must be included, because the original impulse given by religion did ensure the slaves a certain protection against the extremes of cruelty, and certain rights in the matter of food and clothing, which could not be denied them without a deliberate flouting of the law.

There was a third nation whose colonies fell into the first category— Denmark. Her overseas possessions were few and not important, but her planters had the distinction—and it was an enviable one—of behaving towards their slaves with a higher degree of humanity than any other nation. From the first they promoted happy relations and favoured religious instruction. By way of reward, they had at the end of the eighteenth century entirely freed themselves from the fear of insurrection, and found no difficulty or objection to taking a leading part in the movements towards abolition which arose about that time.

The two remaining nations, Holland and Great Britain, fell into the second category. Neither of them gave, or sought to impose, religious instruction; on the contrary, their tendency was to deny religion to the slaves, for fear that it would make them restless and more liable to revolt; ignorance was to be the key to submission. The Dutch had, besides, a natural antipathy to black races; their reputation in the West Indies and Guiana was of the worst; 'their system of slavery had no redeeming features, and the unfortunate negroes were driven by merciless masters, unrestrained alike by the dictates of conscience or the law of the land' (MacInnes, p. 104). The characteristics which they betrayed in America, they betrayed also in their colonies at the Cape, proving hard masters to the Hottentots. Indeed they do not seem to this day to have lost the reputation which they then earned of never being tender in their dealings with native peoples (Woodward, p. 282).

Great Britain's attitude, though not unlike that of the Dutch, had certain features of its own, which had best be dealt with in a separate chapter.

VIII. The Slave in the English Colonies

I

SLAVERY WAS not an English institution, nor, as Captain Jobson had pointed out, did it comport with the English character. None the less over a period of something like two hundred years slavery was not only planted but sprang up and flourished in the North American and West Indian colonies of Great Britain, displaying itself there in peculiarly revolting colours. It may be some explanation, though not an excuse, that the early colonists were sorely tempted and were not of the type to resist temptation. In his history of the founding of Virginia, John Smith wrote, with feeling recollection, that 'everything of worth is found full of difficulties, but nothing so difficult as to establish a commonwealth so farre remote from men and meanes' (Smith. I, 93). The task was indeed stupendous and was made no easier by the character of his companions. They were incompetent, quarrelsome, resentful of authority and lacking in foresight. Nor were they remarkable for high-mindedness or virtue. Smith described them as 'this lewd company wherein were many unruly Gallants, packed thither by their friends to escape ill destinies' (ibid. I, 189). Nothing in their surroundings or their disposition was likely to deter them, when the opportunity arose, from adopting a system which was already in existence in the New World, and which they fondly supposed would relieve them of all toil and trouble.

When the fatal Dutch ship arrived at Jamestown, it found receptive soil in which to sow its tares. Everything conspired to start slavery and to start it on the wrong lines—the character of the settlers, the disadvantanges of the climate, the type of work to be done, the absence of established law and order, and the very novelty of the institution. Being uncontrolled and in the hands of rascally men, British slavery developed the worst possible traits, outstripping in brutality practically all the others. Writing in 1785, Ramsay felt bound to record that when buying slaves from the English, 'foreigners, except perhaps the unfeeling Dutch and Americans, may boast that they take these wretches out of the hands of severe task-masters' (Ramsay. *A Reply to the Personal Invectives*, etc., p. 59).

Slavery had no sooner been adopted than it began to grow with luxuriant haste, and when the colonies, especially the islands, shortly afterwards turned to the cultivation of sugar, the pace increased and with it the number of slaves. By the same token the white population declined. Nor was this surprising. Sugar plantations to be economical must be large; they tended, therefore, to expand, and the small proprietors who had struggled to win a living, poor at best, by the cultivation of cotton, ginger or indigo, were soon bought out and disappeared. Meanwhile the opulent owners of large estates fell more and more into the habit of leaving the work of superintendence to overseers and managers—attorneys, as they were generally called— while they themselves preferred to return whenever possible to England and live upon the profits. The attrition of the white population thus proceeded from both ends, while the demands for labour multiplied on all sides. In short, the invariable outcome of a combination of sugar and slavery was a rapid increase in the number of negroes and an equally rapid decrease in the number of whites, changing the proportions and disturbing the balance of the population.

The statistics of negro slavery and colonial immigration, especially in the early years, are mainly conjectural, but such figures as are known to be accurate afford a tolerably clear picture. There is no need for more than a single example, and that of Barbados will do as well as any other, Barbados being the second oldest of the islands acquired by Great Britain in the West Indies, and for long the best known and most important. Though claimed for England in 1605 it was not occupied until a few settlers were landed about the end of 1624. A year later the population—all white and engaged in growing cotton, ginger or indigo—amounted to about 1,400. As conditions proved favourable, immigrants flocked in, their numbers reaching a maximum of some 37,000 by 1648. It is not known when negroes were first introduced but certainly at an early date, for in 1636 slavery was formally legalized by a local Act. Probably to begin with the slaves were few in number, and were employed mainly on domestic duties. Five years later, however, in 1641, sugar planting began, and was so successful and spread so rapidly to the neighbouring islands that Barbados came to be known as the mother of the sugar colonies. From that moment the real influx of negroes started and though for a while the prospect of making a speedy fortune continued to attract European immigrants, the Gresham-like law which governed sugar and slavery soon began to exert its irresistible pressure; the white population was steadily overhauled by the black, and before long began to decline. Thirty-five years after the first plantation there were no more than 21,000 whites; and in another thirty-five years only 12,000. In the meantime the negroes had risen to about 40,000, outnumbering the whites by more than three to one.

The other islands and the colonies on the mainland all showed the same tendency, differing merely in the actual figures. The grand total of slaves owned by British masters will never be known; but some idea can be gathered from the writings of those who supported the trade, and who consequently were unlikely to exaggerate. Francklyn, one such writer, spoke in 1789 of an annual export of 70,000 from Africa, of whom it may be supposed, from other evidence, that half went to English colonies in America or on the islands. Wilberforce in 1823 gave the number in the islands alone as 800,000, and one of his opponents, Sir Henry Martin, valued them at above thirty-five million pounds (Martin, *Counter-Appeal*, p. 44). Whatever the right figure, the numbers were staggering.

II

By the eighteenth century, British slavery had acquired a bad reputation. It would be easy to explain that reputation by recording instances of shocking cruelty, but not very profitable. It is better to concentrate on the causes which gave rise to the cruelties and the reputation alike. There were two main causes—the type of slave preferred by the British planters, and the official indifference of both Church and State.

As to the first point: Among the tribes of Africa, the Koromantis from the Gold Coast stood in a special category. Unlike the majority of their compatriots they were notoriously savage and intractable, and when any of them were rounded up and offered for sale, the planters of other nations fought shy of them. But not so the British, who, on the contrary, showed a pronounced preference for them, admiring their thews and sinews, and reckoning that, if they were fierce, they were also strong and would make excellent workers when once they had been bent to their masters' will. So the British bid for those black panthers—powerful brutes, snarling, restless and strong—and having acquired them, got down to their 'seasoning' with resolution and energy. To break their spirit, to crush all prospect of revolt and to turn them into so many blind Samsons at their 'task of servile toil', was a harsh and dangerous job that almost demanded cruelty. At all events cruelty abounded, and the result was that the slaves, as Wilberforce declared, 'were systematically depressed below the level of human beings' (Wilberforce. *An Appeal*, etc., p. 10). Such treatment inevitably reacted on the masters. The more the Koromantis were lashed and starved and bullied into submission, and the more they crouched like Caliban, sullen and smouldering in their wretched huts, the more the planters came to look on them as beasts and dangerous beasts, and the more surely they treated them as such. The slaves were unmercifully degraded, and by their very degradation vitiated the masters' judgment of what was needful for their bodies and souls.

The world in general had by now resolved the doubts which had assailed Godwin in the seventeenth century; but the lingering impress of those doubts still existed in the planter's mind. He must, of course, have admitted, had he been asked, that the negro was a human being; but he would have done so with reluctance, stubbornly cherishing an ingrained belief that, in spite of a common humanity, the slave stood on a lower plane than the European, not only mentally and morally, but in nature's scale. Nor can he be altogether blamed when it is recalled that the same belief has been hinted at even in this present century (See Sir H. Johnston's *The Negro in the New World*, p. v). In the heyday of slavery any planter could readily have subscribed, without mental discomfort though one may hope also without conviction, to Long's disquieting suggestion that it would be no dishonour to a Hottentot woman if she were to take an ourang-outang for her husband (Long. *History of Jamaica*). Wilberforce thought that the slaves' degradation in 'the intellectual and moral scale and in the estimation of his white oppressors' was the most intolerable of his sufferings (*An Appeal*, etc., p. 9). But Wilberforce was a highly refined product of civilization with the sensitiveness appropriate to that state; and one may well doubt if he would have won the assent of the witch-obsessed and obscene-minded negro.

The slave realized only too acutely his physical smarts—they were thrust on his attention with impressive iteration—and in the aches and pains of the flesh had no inducement and little time to brood over spiritual disabilities of which he was not aware. It was his master's shame rather than his own fault that he knew nothing of intellectual interests, of the consolations of religion, of the pleasures of art and the fascinations of science. He had been stripped of everything but bare life and a mean subsistence, so that it is no wonder if, sinking into a trough of sexual vice, he became too often riddled with venereal disease, and with corrupt flesh and foul environment, found his span of existence to be 'nasty, brutish and short'. That it was nasty and brutish affected the slave alone; that it was short affected the master as well, ensuring that slavery should be expensive as well as incompetent. So was the slave avenged.

III

All slavery is brutal in greater or lesser degree, and the British form was particularly ferocious. Had England followed the example of Spain, and given scope to law and religion as ameliorative factors, the ferocity might have been qualified. But England did nothing of the sort. Her State and Church both showed themselves indifferent, the former deliberately, the latter possibly through ignorance. 'The Slave Trade', said Newton when he had given up his connection with it, 'was always unjustifiable, but inattention and interest prevented, for a time, the evil from being perceived' (Newton. *Thoughts upon the African Slave Trade*, p. 7). Whatever the reason, State and Church stood aloof, an attitude which seems deplorable to modern eyes, and which yet, in the inscrutable workings of fate, proved in the end to be the salvation of the slaves. But that is anticipating.

The State's indifference had nothing to do with the type of negro preferred; it arose out of an idea of slavery, very prevalent in the planter's mind, which had been adopted at an early date by the legal profession. To the planter the slave appeared not as a man, but as a chattel, a piece of property, a possession which he had acquired by purchase or inheritance, in the same way as possessions are acquired by other men. That view was always present to his mind, but was formulated with its greatest precision when compulsory emancipation seemed to be imminent. 'I must solemnly implore our legislators,' ran one typical appeal, 'individually and collectively, before they are called upon to vote away the property of their fellow subjects, the Planters, to consider deeply ere they adopt the dangerous principle of *setting might against right*; for the British legislature can with no more justice emancipate the Negroes against the consent of the Planters (without giving them the most ample compensation) than they can seize their property in the public funds, or their estates in England. It cannot do either without committing a most flagrant breach of national honour and destroying that fundamental principle of the British constitution, *which secures to every man his property*' (Martin. *A Counter-Appeal*, etc., p. 48). The law accepted this view from the very beginning; as early as 1668 Barbados declared by an act of her legislature that her negro slaves were real estate; Mansfield did not dissent when judging the Zong case; and at the very end Parliament itself subscribed to the doctrine, at least implicitly, when, in freeing the slaves, it decided that the planters were entitled to compensation.

The adoption of this view led to certain conclusions which, if possibly embarrassing in practice, were yet unassailable in logic. For all practical purposes it cut the slave out of the law's jurisdiction, enabling his master to commit against him, with complete impunity, acts which must appear to the better class of citizen as dreadful wrongs and the worst of crimes. Yet they were not illegal, and there seemed no way of preventing them. The law had never intervened between a man and his possessions; he could do what he liked with his own; he could destroy his property wantonly; he could waste his substance in riotous living; he could whip his dog; he could kill his livestock; no one could say him nay, and provided he left others alone, nobody much cared what he did in an age when life was violent and cheap, and public opinion had not yet crystallized into societies for the prevention of cruelty. How the planter dealt with his slave was his own affair, and he acted according to his character, supported or at least unhampered by the law.

Yet Englishmen are not happy with a logic which is liable to end in cruelty; they are even less happy with a logic which condones the mutilation and murder of men and women who, even if they are regarded as merely pieces of property, are none the less sentient beings. As evidence accumulated of injuries crying to heaven for redress, the law became uneasy. Reluctantly and by degrees the local legislatures were compelled to pass Acts restraining the powers of the masters.

But they moved at a snail's pace. Writing in 1784, Ramsay lamented that 'the English have not paid the least attention to enforce by a law, either humanity or justice, as these may respect their slaves. Many are the restrictions, and severe are the punishments, to which slaves are subjected. But if you except [three trifling laws] I recollect not a single clause in all our colony acts (and I perused the several codes with a view of remarking such) enacted to secure to them the least humane treatment, or to save them from the capricious cruelty of an ignorant, unprincipled master, or a morose, unfeeling overseer' (Ramsay. *An Essay on the Treatment and Conversion of African Slaves*, pp. 62–63). After he had written, the pace was a little quicker, and the results a little more effective; but not much, because of the masters' tendency to ignore Acts that did not please them.

None the less Acts were passed—the outward expression of a changing climate of opinion. Antigua led the way, in 1787, by granting slaves the right to trial by jury in the case of serious offences. Two years later Bermuda dropped an ancient enactment which decreed that a white man who had killed a slave, could not be punished by forfeiture of either life or estate. The Bahamas in 1796 and the Leeward Islands in 1798 regulated by Acts such matters as the food and clothing of slaves, their right to marry and the amount of punishment which could be inflicted on them at any one time. But, in some ways, the most interesting of these new Acts was the Consolidated Slave Act of Jamaica (1792), which laid down *inter alia* that any person, whether master or not, who should 'mutilate or dismember any slave' should be liable to a fine not exceeding £100, and imprisonment not exceeding twelve months. The punishment was mild enough, but sufficient to mark the growing revulsion against the wanton cruelty practised on the slaves— a revulsion springing not out of hearsay but first-hand knowledge. At the same time it offered proof, not the less convincing because it was local, that the accusations of the reformers had substance behind them, and that the pretty pictures of negro felicity drawn by the planters' advocates were not the whole truth, even if they had a modest foundation in fact.

IV

The legal aspect influenced the attitude of the Church—more perhaps than it should have done. The planter exercising his powers, either forbade or at least made it difficult for his slave to attend the church or to be visited by the parson, partly out of fear that the Christian doctrine would create unrest in his mind, and partly out of a widespread, though erroneous, belief that baptism would confer freedom on him. 'We know', said the Dean of Middleham in 1787, 'how invincibly unwilling the white people are to admit the slaves to the privileges of Christianity' (Nickolls. *A letter*, etc., p. 9). For precisely the same reason, the planter opposed any effort to educate the negro; knowledge would make him discontented and dangerous; he must be kept in perpetual mental darkness, if only for his own peace of mind!

But the darkness merely served to emphasize another anomaly of his position—the undoubted fact that his status as a chattel destroyed the whole basis of morals. He was entirely dependent on his master, without responsibility, and without freedom of action. How then could he be either virtuous or vicious? The problem became strikingly evident in the matter of marriage. As a chattel he had neither the capacity nor the right to marry; yet as a man he could not be denied a partner, however much under the rose. He did inevitably cohabit with a fellow-slave as a wife, and often enough, as and when he was sold to another master, found himself taking a fresh wife in fresh surroundings. Even if fortune and inclination allowed him to remain true to his original partner, there was nothing legal or binding or sacramental about the position, and consequently from the point of view of the Church his sexual life was one long act of fornication—a thought which distressed the more earnest parsons, such as Eliot, who implored 'every owner of slave property'—note the phrase—'in the West Indies to exert his influence in checking, and if possible altogether suppressing the shameful concubinage which prevails on his plantations' (Eliot. *Christianity and Slavery*, p. 117).

Because of his negative standing in the world, the slave's religion, if he could be given one, must of necessity be faith without works, which according to St James is dead. Whether it was because of legal fictions, or spiritual difficulties, or the attitude of the planters, or a bad choice of incumbents, the fact remains that the Church had little influence over the negro population, or indeed connection with it. The majority of the clergy confined their ministrations to the whites, and those who took an interest in the blacks were either thwarted in their endeavours by the ill-will of the planters or were unworthy members of the Church who succumbed to the colonial atmosphere and, having slaves of their own, ill-treated them in the prevailing fashion. 'Christianity', said Buxton, 'has made but feeble inroads on this kingdom of darkness, nor can she hope to gain an entrance where the traffic in man pre-occupies the ground' (Buxton. *The Slave Trade and the Remedy*, p. 10–11). The planters hedged the slaves about from all contact with religion, and the clergy were not very vigorous in attempting to break their way in.

IX. Thistlewood

I

No SINGLE picture of negro slavery, even in the limited sphere of English possessions in the eighteenth century, can be wholly complete; there was too great a diversity of experience. When the reformer and the planter came face to face, each took his stand on facts that were true but conflicting, the one supporting his point of principle by tales of cruelty, the other relying on stories of negro devotion to bolster his claim to possession. Both were speaking the truth, though not the whole truth—a fact which embittered their fight—but there can be little doubt on which side the weight of evidence lies, or what sort of verdict follows. The thumbs turn down. As a check, let us take the unvarnished story set out in the journals of Thomas Thistlewood.

Thistlewood went to Jamaica as a young man of twenty-seven, determined to make his way in the world. He soon gained the confidence of a certain Mr. Cope who appointed him overseer of one of his plantations. Thistlewood remained in Jamaica, with hardly a break, for the rest of his life, and from 1748 to 1786 made brief notes of each day's happenings in journals which are still preserved at Lincoln, the home town of his family. No one can pretend that the journals make attractive reading either in style or substance; the notes are generally terse and to the point, no more, as a rule, than a line or two for each day; but their continuity over the years and their occasional longer entries supply the place of literary skill, and by degrees an extremely clear picture emerges, not only of life on the plantation but also of Thistlewood himself.

What sort of a man was he, and how far can his evidence be accepted? Undoubtedly he was an excellent type for a colonial life—hard-working, hard-living, hard-bitten. Beginning in the smallest way, he succeeded in making a comfortable if modest fortune for himself, and ended as a Justice of the Peace and a man of weight and distinction. He was honest and outspoken, if not particularly upright; conscientious towards his employer but unscrupulous towards the tax-collector; courageous but not merciful; affectionate but not constant. In his youth he was insensitive and callous, as young men often are, but underneath there was a kindly streak which, without ever overcoming his hardness, broadened and mellowed with the passing of years into a species of grudging compassion. No one could call him a moral man, though he possessed a queer sensibility, or perhaps a feeling of shame, which induced him to record his sexual adventures in a kind of dog Latin. He never married; but his escapades were plentiful, and their venues quickly transcended his Latin vocabulary. *'Cum Phibbah in illa domo'* was not much more than a flash in the Roman pan; he did not know, and could not invent the Latin for such places as the boiler house, the curing shed, or the edge of the plantation. English supervened; but the 'cum' was retained to the end—perhaps as a veil for modesty. Yet here again for all the multiplicity of his *affaires*, there was an underlying element of faithfulness.

From first to last, for nearly forty years, the queen of the harem was Phibbah—a strange name, but possibly the negro or Thistlewood version of Phoebe—and the references to her, short and abrupt as they are, provide the material for an odd sort of idyll. Thistlewood had a genuine affection for her and she for him; and though he strayed too often from the narrow path, their mutual affection lasted to the end. The notes of lovers' quarrels, of Phibbah's 'sauciness', of 'words' with Phibbah; the simple record of Phibbah's jealous fits and Thistlewood's urgent desire to coax her back again; the quaint catalogue of little presents from him to her, from her to him—a few beads, a black ribbon, a coloured handkerchief, a negro purse—and the satisfaction of restored harmony, are not the less revealing for their brevity; nor the reference to the still-born babe, and the frequent visits to Phibbah in hospital; nor, indeed, the gift, in old age, of a pair of spectacles as Phibbah's eyes 'begin to be so bad she cannot sew without them, except very coarse indeed'. Phibbah represents, on a somewhat high plane, an aspect of slave life that was universal. She was lucky. The lot of her less fortunate sisters is not hard to imagine, nor did Thistlewood seek to cover it up; but his treatment of Phibbah puts him comparatively high in the list of white masters, and adds weight to his evidence.

Such then in brief was the man—a mixture of good and bad, with a few virtues and some vices—not clever enough to distort the truth, nor sensitive enough to hide it. The entries in his journals are plain records of fact, unemotional and usually of no more than ephemeral interest; but clearly veracious, as, for instance, 'I am very unwell today, owing to drinking more than enough yesterday.' He inspires confidence by his very lack of imagination, but his journals must be read in the light of his limitations. There is no introspection and little philosophy to be found in them, and it is all unconsciously that they bring to light two striking facts, first that he himself was dominated by the slaves, and secondly that the slaves were dominated by hunger.

The first fact seems startling in view of his obvious self-reliance and the firmness of his control. It is easy however to explain, and serves as evidence of the blighting effect of slavery on master as well as man. Thistlewood could not escape the influence of his environment and the environment in which he lived was predominantly black. True, he had white neighbours, but they were few in number and widely scattered. Sometimes he realized their absence with a tinge of regret: 'Have seen no white man since Mr. Plaister went, now above a fortnight'; or again: 'today [8th Jan] first saw a white person since Dec. 19th that I was at Black River.' Not that he missed much from the social, or intellectual, or moral point of view. Colonial society in his neighbourhood was rough and uncouth, and his records of it hardly attractive. 'Today old Mr. Jackson dined with us. He is accounted a very honest man and worth 8 or 10 thousand pounds; yet goes without stockings or shoes, check shirt, coarse jacket, Oznaburgh trousers, sorry hat, wears his own hair.' Mr. Collgrove, not unlike old Mr. Jackson, was 'remarkably slovenly, even to nastiness', and in addition was given to 'raising scandals' on his acquaintance. Mr. Allen may, or may not, have been smarter in appearance, but was clearly a testy individual. 'Mr. Allen told me this forenoon that if I shot any of his negroes, he would have me lay wait for to be shot, and would as soon shoot me himself as he would a mad dog.' An unsavoury, quarrelsome lot, it seems, by no means patient masters for unruly slaves, or shining lights for dark, untutored minds. Their main virtue, if it may so be called, was the herd loyalty of the white man against the black, a loyalty that had no regard to truth or justice, and was founded, whether they knew it or not, mainly in fear.

Thistlewood's lack of neighbours was not counterbalanced by the presence of white men on the estate. As a rule there were none but himself; but in 1764 there was a temporary change, not perhaps much for the better. His nephew, John, came to stay for a couple of years, in order to learn the business. Like his uncle, he kept a journal, and from it we learn that in 1764–5 a creole was with them for half the year, and there were visits from a Scotsman who left in a month, a cooper who was present on business for six weeks, and lastly an Irishman who for eight months was a sluggard by day and an irritation by night, uproarious in his cups and a terror to the women; his going was unlamented. The list is hardly inspiring, but the fact it represents is important. In judging Thistlewood and his dealings with slaves, it must never be forgotten that for the greater part of his time he lived, a single young Englishman, alone among fifty or more unhappy, degraded, resentful negroes, with no neighbours or police or troops to whom he could look for help in the event of trouble. His living, in more senses than one, depended on his ability to control the slaves and, if necessary, to face and subdue them. Had they been contented and willing, the task might have been easy; but they were neither, and so presented Thistlewood with a danger that was always latent and at times active. Consciously or unconsciously, his knowledge of that danger settled his attitude towards the slaves, who in their turn were inevitably affected by the treatment he meted out to them. There was here the makings of a vicious circle. What was true of Thistlewood was true of his neighbours. Their lives were dominated by the slaves, and the perils which the slaves presented—moral, physical and intellectual.

II

The danger began in Africa the moment a negro's liberty was stolen. He had been and was a savage, but in his own land he had been free, and he left it a slave, with a burning sense of injustice and a wild longing to be free again. However carefully he was 'seasoned', the longing remained and was voiced from time to time sadly, fiercely, regretfully according to his nature and temperament. 'Wanicher says in the ship she was brought over in, it was agreed to rise, but they were discovered first. The piccaninnies brought the men who were confined knives, muskets and other weapons.' The attempt had come to nothing, but it gave Wanicher a melancholy satisfaction to recall dead hopes and recount them to Thistlewood.

Wanicher was a woman, and there was little the women could do to sublimate their sense of frustration; their only outlet was to steal and lie and indulge a perverted pride among their fellows by becoming the mothers of mulattoes. It was different with the men. They had clasp-knives for their work, and when the madness fell on them, would draw those knives against their oppressors. 'About 10 a.m. one of George Gooding's negroes came at me with an open knife and an outstretched arm, in the morass, down from Bimba Back. He was landed at my usual fishing place and came resolutely towards me, although I offered to defend myself with the harpoon. Coffee stood by me with my fishing rod in his hand. Yet he would not desist till I called for my gun, though God knows I had no one nigh me, but it frightened him so that he ran away.' That was Thomas Thistlewood, the uncle. His nephew, John, had a similar story to tell ten years later. There was trouble in the Salt Savannah, where a band of marauding negroes were robbing Thistlewood's men of their fish. John went down to put matters right; but when he arrived on the scene 'one of them drew a large clasp knife and swore that he would strike me with this. I was a little frighted and thought myself in a good deal of danger as they were much in superior numbers to us. Therefore it made me begin to think of some expressions to save our lives as we were but seven and they near thirty in number. Therefore I swore that if any of them offered to stir, I would take out my pistols and blow his brains out. With mentioning the word pistols, it made the fellow that had the knife in his hand run immediately into the Bush, and the rest became quite calm, so that I took six of them and brought them to the house, and each of them had a good whipping and dismissed about their business; so that mentioning the name of pistols did me as much service as if I really had had them with me' (15th April, 1764).

The fright to which John confessed was universal, and because of it the colonists made the drawing of a knife on a white man a capital offence. Any such incident could drive them into a display of almost hysterical savagery. 'Saw a negro fellow named English, belonging to Fullerswood, tried, cast and hanged upon the first tree immediately for drawing his knife upon a white man, his hand cut off, his body left unburied' (1st Oct. 1750). Probably the same fear was the reason for the bitterness felt against runaway slaves. The loss of a valuable 'property' was annoying enough in itself, but was greatly enhanced by the fear of what a negro, at large and armed with a knife, might do when overtaken by hunger or cold or the memory of past wrongs. The bitterness could even result in the pursuit of vengeance beyond the grave, that unhallowed toil, as Shakespeare calls it. 'Yesterday, a runaway negro being dead and buried while we were away, Mr. Dorril caused him to be took up, his head stuck on a pole and his body burnt' (18th May, 1750). This mixture of fear and savagery was not peculiar to the islands or to the eighteenth century. Nearly one hundred years later, Harriet Beecher Stowe made a collection of advertisements from American papers, in which rewards were offered for the apprehension of runaway slaves dead or alive—50 dollars for the head of a runaway slave; 25 dollars for a runaway negro dead or alive; 100 dollars for satisfactory evidence of a runaway having been killed; and so on (*Key to Uncle Tom's Cabin*, p. 40—41). The fear and anger must have been great when men were ready to pay for useless corpses.

III

The second fact which emerges from Thistlewood's journals—that the slaves were dominated by hunger—is the key to much that might otherwise be obscure.

The masters had four weapons in their armoury for keeping the slaves in submission—the death penalty, ignorance, hunger and the whip. The first was a weapon of despair, and though used lightly enough when occasion arose, could never become common. The second was in effect a weapon of precaution; the slaves must never learn the depth of their degradation or the means by which they might rise. It was negative in itself and only dimly realized here and there by the victims. 'My poor mother', wrote Thomas Johnson in his auto-biography, 'taught me what she knew. The whole of her education consisted in a knowledge of the alphabet, and how to count a hundred. She first taught me the Lord's Prayer. And as soon as I was old enough, she explained to me the difference between the condition of the coloured and white people, and told me that if I would learn how to read and write, some day I might be able to get my freedom; but all that would have to be kept a secret . . . for the law was very strict with regard to slaves in this matter—they were forbidden education' (*Twenty-eight Years a Slave*, p. 3).

Hunger and the whip went hand in hand; they were far from nega-tive; but while the use of the latter was intermittent, the use of the former was never-ending. The slaves were deliberately kept on short commons, both to tame their spirit and as a measure of economy. It was foolish, as all such parsimony must be; their work was hard physical toil in the open air, 'holing' sugar-canes, making roads, mending fences, burning scrub, gathering in the harvest and feeding the boilers. The slaves worked none the better for being half starved; their thoughts were centred on their bellies, not their job. But there was another, and more distressing, result; their pangs drove them to steal food; the thefts led to floggings; the floggings, or fear of them, persuaded the slaves to run away; and running away had its own peculiar horrors.

Thistlewood sympathized with the sufferers, but not to the extent of turning a blind eye on their thefts. 'They complain', he noted, 'very much of hunger, and not without reason, I believe,' and he contrived from time to time to add some trifling morsel to the herring apiece which, under his instructions, he distributed to them at noon. He would give them 'half a dozen heads of corn' if they happened to be available, or a plantain, when the stock was 'like to rot and be lost', 'or a bit of bad salt beef' that had been left in the bottom of the barrel. He indulged the slaves with such meagre titbits because they were hungry. He was not hungry himself, but he could on occasion suffer from ennui, and when he did, found consolation in food. The plantation, he recorded on one occasion, 'now seems very dull. However I had a bottle of good ale at my supper, which I mixed with sugar and water and grated some nutmeg over it; roast beef, roast turkey, cold tongue, cheese etc to my supper'. No doubt he was cheered, and slept well. It was otherwise with the slaves. When they suffered from depression on top of their hunger, the cure was different: 'today Nero would not work, but threatened to cut his own throat. Had him stripped, whipped, gagged, and his hands tied behind him, that the mosquitoes and sandflies might torment him to some purpose.' Nero was less lucky than his fellow-slave, Tom, who also suffered from depression, and when he was found dead was 'judged to have poisoned himself'.

But depression, at least in so marked a form, was not the usual cause of either death or punishment. Hunger and the thefts it occasioned were much more potent. There was no disguising a theft or the reason for it, however hard one tried. Take the case of the fine young kid which disappeared from the flock. Old Sambo, the goatherd, had to account for it, and bringing in the bones, declared that he had found them in a rock hole. No one supposed that he was telling the truth, and Thistlewood merely records that 'as there was no certain proof to me what was become of the flesh, had him given one hundred lashes to make him more careful for the future'. When, again, Cyrus, the fisherman, came back at night without any fish, no one imagined that he was a luckless angler or that fish were scarce. He was simply 'secured in the bilboes' and flogged the next morning. When Derby was discovered stealing corn out of Long Pond Cane Piece, and made a show of resistance, he 'received many great wounds with a mascheat in the head etc. particularly his right ear, cheek and jaw almost cut off'. No one was surprised; it served him right.

But perhaps the most spirited and persistent of these old-style 'hunger-strikers' was the Boy George. Like Odysseus he was much-enduring. His story begins, as all the others, suddenly and without preface: 'the Boy George this morning when going to work ran away with Tony and Wanicher's breakfast which he was carrying in a basket and has not been seen since.' The next night, being still at large and presumably hungry, he robbed one of the watchmen; and the next day threatened one of the maids with a knife. But without food or money, and with every man's hand against him, escape was hopeless. He was caught after a few days and Thistlewood—so runs the record—'gave George an hundred lashes, loosed him and took him to work this afternoon. Had Accabah and Will (one of Mr. Barton's negroes) all whipped for letting loose the Boy George on Wednesday night'. But the Boy George was not yet conquered. Twelve days later he ran away again, 'and in the forenoon when everybody was at work, he came and broke into Tony's house, took out cassava, plantains and some pork'. He was recaptured that same afternoon by Dick who, no doubt much to his indignation, 'made him bring back all he had left of what he had stolen'. A fortnight later he made his third dash for freedom, which alas! was cut short that same evening. Thereafter he watched and waited for eighteen days, and then on the 22nd November, broke away for the fourth and last time, once more taking 'two of the negroes' breakfasts with him'. His story ends as abruptly as it began; there are no further records, but one must needs hope—however faint the hope may be—that on that day in late November his perseverance and pluck received a fitting reward and he escaped for good and all. Though the Boy George was more persistent than most, he was only following the fashion. Running away was all too common, and all too unsuccessful. It was a fruitful source of punishment.

The tales of thefts and floggings or attempts at escape become monotonous; but one story remains to be told, if a full picture is to be given—a story of cold-blooded murder. In October 1764, as Humphrey, one of Thistlewood's slaves was fishing, the occupants of a passing canoe (three coloured men and one white) tried to steal his fish from him. When he resisted they shot him in the back and neck with double duckshot, wounding him so severely that in spite of the doctor's efforts he died that evening. Thistlewood sent his nephew John into the nearest town to see if he could collect evidence. John was successful; he found a mulatto who knew the whole story and was ready to tell it, but when John took him before a Justice of the Peace to make an affidavit, he was told that as a white man was involved, a mulatto's affidavit would 'not be good for anything'. None the less Thistlewood demanded an inquest, and insisted that the culprits should be brought up at the next assizes on a charge of the wilful murder of a negro. The herd loyalty of the white men promptly came into action. The body had to be buried and exhumed more than once before a sufficient number of reluctant white men could be collected to form a jury, and when the inquest was at last held, the white defendant, James Salter, promptly offered to turn King's evidence against the other three, and was accepted as such. It was an easy way out.

Injustice and cruelty were not peculiar to Jamaica; far from it. They were universal, but they lose their force by repetition, and one further example must stand for a multitude. Some thirty-five years after Humphrey's murder, Josiah Henson, whose autobiography inspired the writing of *Uncle Tom's Cabin*, was born, a slave, in Maryland. His first memory was of his father staggering into the room with a bloody head and a lacerated back. The story he had to tell was one of villainy and bad faith. The overseer where he worked had assaulted his wife, Josiah's mother, and he had rushed to her protection. Having mastered the overseer he was about to kill him, when Josiah's mother entreated him to stop, and the overseer promised that, if he were spared, nothing more should be said of the matter. Josiah's father let him up, and the promise was promptly forgotten. For assaulting a white man he was condemned to receive one hundred lashes on his bare back and to have his right ear nailed to the whipping-post and then severed from the body. 'That,' said the awed spectators, 'that is what he got for striking a white man.'

The evidence is clear and overwhelming; slavery was infamous. Yet it had its bright points, like stars in a black night, though even the bright points are often veiled in tears. The planters called them in aid against the reformers; they were true and here is one from Thistlewood. When Mr. Cope died, 'a negro man about 24 years of age, so soon as he heard his old Master was dead, stole to the negro house privately and shot himself to accompany him into the other world and there wait upon him. His name was Roger'. His old Master was not so old—only fifty-six—and a shadowy figure in Thistlewood's journals. Maybe he was no more deserving than the Mr. Collgroves and the Mr. Allens of the colony, but surely there must have been some good in him since, as St. Paul says, 'scarcely for a righteous man will one die; yet peradventure for a good man some would even dare to die'. Roger dared for Mr. Cope.

PART TWO

◆◆◆◆◆◆◆◆◆◆◆◆◆◆◆◆◆◆◆◆◆◆◆◆◆◆◆◆◆◆◆◆◆◆◆◆

EMANCIPATION

PART II : EMANCIPATION

X. 'The People called Quakers'

I

It is a notable fact that, riddled as negro slavery was with every form of wrong and oppression, no one ever proposed its abolition until the trade had fallen into British hands. It is the more notable, because the Indian slavery, which went before it and out of which it sprang, had aroused misgivings in many persons who could, had they wished, have crushed it in its first beginnings—in Isabella, who had felt a womanly compunction; in Ferdinand, whose conscience had been troubled; in Charles V, who did indeed impose a few regulations, though they were generally ignored; and in Leo X who made a profound but ineffective *pronunciamento*. Yet, as soon as negroes had replaced the Indians, authority, both civil and ecclesiastical, dropped the subject and with it their hesitations, displaying thereafter a surprising degree of indifference. Almost overnight, negro slavery became, like the slavery of the pre-Christian world, an accepted fact—a mere matter of trade, which was of no interest to polite society or powerful hierarchies, or even philosophical academies. Civil authority, it seemed, had adopted the popular view that the negro was less than human; and ecclesiastical authority the equally popular view, that he was under the curse which Noah had pronounced against Canaan: 'cursed be Canaan; a servant of servants shall he be unto his brethren' (Genesis 9. 25). For rather more than one hundred and fifty years this state of indifference continued; and then, as England entered into the trade and the facts of slavery began to seep through, the English conscience was stirred; and with that stirring, hope for the slave, was born. In less than a century, England had abolished the trade, and in less than a century and a quarter had freed all slaves on British soil. She had brought about a revolution in public morals, giving, in the words of a one-time slave, 'the death-blow to slavery throughout the world' (Johnson. *Twenty-eight Years a Slave*, p. 25).

II

That fruitful stirring of the conscience was not the outcome of simple pity or a mere revolt against cruelty; there was too little pity and too much cruelty in the world to be effective in such a cause. It was essentially a religious movement, springing out of a conviction that slavery was a sin in the eyes of God, and therefore not only wrong in itself but bound to be a constant source of misery, ruin and degradation. Because it was a sin, there was nothing to be gained by applying a surface salve, or tinkering with symptoms; the cure must reach down to the root of the evil. Humanity and slavery could not exist together; the one must destroy the other; and it was the duty of all good Christians to see that victory inclined to the side of righteousness.

As the movement was religious, the type of religion professed by the country which was to be the protagonist, was clearly of importance. It so happened that, in the matter of religion, England had certain advantages denied to the other slave-trading countries—to Spain, France and Portugal. They were Catholic countries, and in a Catholic country religion belongs to the Church; the priest celebrates Mass at the altar on behalf of the people; the monks and nuns pray for the world in the seclusion of their cells; the parish priests and curés come and go at the bidding of authority, and being vested with a mystic and awful power to bind and to loose, are representatives and ambassadors of the Holy Father. Though often saintly and devoted men, eager to do good to those in their charge, their main duty is to enlarge or at least maintain the bounds of the Church and enhance her power and prestige. All that is left to the laity is to watch the elevation of the host from afar, and kneeling in the confessional to receive absolution and blessing from a superior order of beings. The laity are in the Church but not of it; they accept, they do not originate, the dictates and objects of religion. In Catholic countries therefore, any impetus towards the abolition of slavery, in so far as it was a religious movement, must have come from the Pope; and he showed no disposition to move. Without his judgment the laity were ignorant whether or not slavery was a sin; without his lead, they gave no thought to the matter.

In England, on the other hand, religion belongs to the people; the priest is a minister; the sacrifices of God are contrite hearts, and prayers are the spiritual aspirations of the whole congregation. Religion thus holds a precarious, but pregnant, position, being strong or languishing according to the progress of individual pilgrims. When it is weak, it falls below the Catholic Church in vigour, for the Catholic Church is little affected by the attitude of the laity; but when it is strong, it attains by its dedication of a whole people a far greater momentum and a far more powerful urge to victory than can be achieved by any close institution or privileged priesthood. It has one further advantage—the beauty of variety; that variety which is at once the evidence and the spice of life, the mainspring of endeavour and the vehicle of inspired strength. It enables religion from time to time and in unexpected quarters, to burgeon into those deeds of love and charity without which faith must die. It was so in the case of slavery. The first impetus came, not from the Established Church, but from a much derided and even despised body, the Quakers.

III

It was towards the middle of the seventeenth century that England began to take a lively interest in the slave trade, and the third quarter of that century had not been completed before the first suggestion of a doubt made its appearance. It came from George Fox, the founder of the Quaker sect, a man in whom much that was trivial, ignorant and even absurd, was shot through and made splendid by a great spiritual insight and a profound yearning for human perfection. In 1671 he visited Barbados in the course of an evangelizing mission, and there, seeing the condition of the slaves with his own eyes, was moved to exhort the owners not only to 'deal mildly and gently' with their negroes, not only to 'bring them to the knowledge of the Lord' but also to set them free after certain years of servitude. No doubt in this he was founding himself on the precepts of the old Mosaic law, but his exhortation contained the first germ of future emancipation. Two years later his gentle admonition received a brusque reinforcement from a celebrated Nonconformist divine, Richard Baxter, who declared without mincing his words that slave-hunters should be regarded as the common enemies of mankind, and the slave-owners who ill-treated their slaves as devils rather than Christians (*Baxter's Christian Directory, 1673*). Other isolated voices began to be heard here and there, in established churches, in dissenting chapels, in pious homes, voices apparently crying in a wilderness of ignorance and indifference, but invisibly moulding that public opinion, which by its silent but irresistible pressure was to force a bewildered Parliament and a hesitating

Government to advance by one reluctant step after another towards the goal of complete emancipation.

But if many religious bodies took part in the onward sweep of reform, the main impetus came from the Quakers. Their motives and their methods afford a striking contrast to the efforts at amelioration in Catholic countries. Isabella, Ferdinand, Charles V and Las Casas had all felt concern at the fate of the slave; they had attempted to lighten his burdens and to shield him from cruelty; and above all they had striven to ensure that he was taught the Catholic faith. The impulse they gave towards reform, perhaps because it lacked the Pope's imprimatur, soon slackened and died, but in any event it could never have led to emancipation. The Catholic authorities were concerned solely with the physical comfort and spiritual health of the slave, not with the contractual relations between him and his master. Taking slavery for granted, they turned the beams of religion on to the negro in order to lighten his darkness and make him a member of the Church.

The Quakers were equally ready to lighten his darkness, but they used the beams of religion first as a searchlight to illumine their own hearts and consciences asking, not whether the slaves' condition could be improved but whether slavery could be justified in the eyes of God. It was a fundamental difference of approach, and in that difference lay the possibility, and indeed the certainty of ultimate emancipation; for no one of Quaker principle could escape the conviction that slavery was a sin, and in that conviction could never accept the dictum of Lord North that the slave trade 'was in a commercial view become necessary to almost every nation of Europe'. There is no unbreakable tie between sin and necessity.

The progress of Quaker thought was slow but sure, and their example a standing reproach to the world. Unlike the generality of slave-owners they had little need for Fox's exhortations; they already treated their slaves with Christian consideration, and did their best to 'bring them to the knowledge of the Lord' by allowing them to attend their meetings. Indeed, their proselytizing zeal worried and disturbed their fellow-colonists, in whose eyes religion was a combustible very unfit for slaves. They demanded that the Quakers should give over their dangerous practices; and failing to turn the Quakers from their ways, were disposed to turn them out of the islands. In 1661 Nevis passed an Act forbidding Quakers to land. Antigua and the Bermudas followed suit, while Barbados prohibited all Quaker meetings, whether attended by slaves or not. But these were temporary set-backs. The Quaker scruples blossomed both in America and England; and first in America where the presence of slaves brought the matter more sharply to their notice. In 1688 the German Quakers of Pennsylvania voiced a doubt whether there was any valid distinction to be drawn between those who stole men in Africa and those who purchased them in America; and in 1696 the Yearly Meeting of the Friends advised their members to be 'careful not to encourage the bringing in of more negroes'. It was a cautious beginning which failed for some time to develop. Slaves, after all, were a familiar sight, and familiarity can breed forgetfulness as well as contempt. As they were commonplace, it was natural to overlook them; as they were useful, it was tempting to retain their services. For the present it was enough to hold sin at bay by avoiding further importations.

In England, where slaves were not in evidence, the movement was more tardy, and the emphasis was on the trade rather than on the slave. Conscience, without the goad of sight, moved with a slow and measured step, but it moved; and in 1727 the Yearly Meeting in London put on record its conviction that the traffic in negroes was neither a commendable nor an allowed practice for Friends. Though the lead given in London was thus firmer and more unmistakable than the lead given in America, it, too, failed to develop; and reform, if it does not advance, is apt to regress. In spite of resolutions at the Yearly Meetings on both sides of the Atlantic, in spite of the earnest efforts of individuals such as Benjamin Lay and John Woolman, in spite of an increasing flow of pamphlets, the number of slaves owned by Quakers, and the number of Quakers connected in one way or another with the trade, tended to mount, and the collective conscience to be correspondingly uneasy.

The uneasiness came to a head in America, in 1754, when the Yearly Meeting issued a more solemn and heart-searching exhortation. The Friends were entreated in a letter of earnest eloquence, addressed to each one personally, to bear in mind 'the royal law of doing to others as we would be done by' and urged 'never to think of bereaving their fellow creatures of that valuable possession—liberty, nor endure to grow rich by their bondage'. They were told that 'to live in ease and plenty by the toil of those, whom violence and cruelty have put in our power, is neither consistent with Christianity nor common justice; and we have good reason to believe, draws down the displeasure of Heaven'. Four years later the English Meeting passed a resolution on similar lines, warning their members to 'avoid being any way concerned in reaping the unrighteous profits arising from the iniquitous practice of dealing in negro or other slaves', and telling them that to have any part in such practice was 'in direct violation of the Gospel rule', and would be 'to the unspeakable prejudice of religion and virtue, and the exclusion of that holy spirit of universal love, meekness and charity, which is the unchangeable nature and the glory of true Christianity'.

From that moment the Quakers in England moved steadily forward. Three years later they thought the time for warning had passed and decided to exclude from their membership anyone who should be 'concerned in the unchristian traffic in negroes'. In another two years they went further, extending the ban to anyone who should aid or abet or in any shape give encouragement to the trade. So by 1763 they had washed themselves free from all taint, and now felt enabled and indeed constrained to appeal to others who were not of their own communion. In 1783 they presented a petition to Parliament for an end to be put to England's participation in the slave trade—the first such petition ever to be laid before Parliament—and the next year extended it to the whole country by printing and distributing a pamphlet entitled *The case of our Fellow-Creatures, the oppressed Africans, respectfully recommended to the serious consideration of the Legislature of Great Britain, by the People called Quakers*. But more important as an earnest of their determination, a number of them collected together as a working group and at their first meeting on the 7th July, 1783, set themselves 'to consider what steps they should take for the relief and liberation of the Negro slaves in the West Indies, and for the discouragement of the Slave-trade on the coast of Africa'. So the first Anti-Slavery Society came into being, and the machinery for the slaves' deliverance was set in motion.

XI. Granville Sharp and the Law

I

WHILE THE Quakers were treading the path to reform, the slaveowners were treading a path of their own, widely divergent, and yet, as it proved, leading to the same goal. Unlike the emigrants from other countries, the English planters had as a rule no desire to settle permanently in the West Indies. Their ambition was to make their fortune quickly and to return to England in order to enjoy the proceeds. If they could retire for good, so much the better; but even if they could not, it was pleasant and profitable to revisit the old country from time to time, perhaps to consult the City merchants on the raising of fresh capital or perhaps simply to enjoy a holiday. In either case, as the return journey was likely to be tedious and uncomfortable, they tended to prolong their stay. There was much to be seen and done in England —the newest fashions to be studied at London and Bath, the reigning toast to be ogled at the theatre, portraits to be commissioned from famous artists, the latest gossip and the wittiest lampoons to be picked up in the coffee houses—in short, all the elegance and wit and *ton* to be found only in the metropolis, and all the satisfaction of appearing in the great world and moving at the centre or at least on the outskirts of high society.

But if they had much to see and do, they hoped they had also something to offer. They had left England poor; they were returning rich, and they liked to parade their wealth. Hence, partly to impress their friends and partly for their own convenience, they were in the habit of bringing a few of their domestic slaves with them, and flaunting them as gentleman's gentlemen of an unusual and striking type. They brought them in such numbers that by the third quarter of the eighteenth century there were said to be fifteen thousand of them resident in England. In bringing them over, the planters had been thinking only of themselves—their comfort and personal standing; they would have been prudent if they had thought also of the slaves and the impact which they would make on the ordinary Englishman; for the effect was not what the planters had imagined.

'Slaves', wrote Cowper about this time, 'cannot breathe in England'—but Cowper was writing as a poet. They could and did breathe, and the air of England went to their heads like wine, rapturous and intoxicating. To the negro 'Britons never shall be slaves' meant vastly more than to the ordinary Englishman, being for him something quite beyond a patriotic boast—a new outlook on life, a squint-hole into Paradise. He noted with envious eyes that the work of a white servant was the same as his own, but how different the reward! At the same time he noted with sanguine eyes the opportunities for escape offered by a crowded city. In the colonies, where the dice were ineluctably loaded against him, he had run away time and again, though he had run always without hope. How could he fail to run away now, with his hopes as high as his heart, in the favourable conditions of an English town. But to his confusion, the conditions were not so favourable as they seemed. In the West Indies, a runaway slave was not immediately recognizable amid a crowd of blacks, and yet he was generally recaptured. What chance then had he in England where he was only too conspicuous amid a crowd of whites? The masters pursued their fugitives; they found them too easily and haled them back too violently.

The masters were acting as they were accustomed to do at home, where no eyebrows would have been raised, whatever the treatment of a slave; but the sight of a negro buffeted and beaten and dragged violently away, was a new and disturbing sight for the Englishman, and one, moreover, which he did not like. He began to take an interest in the slave, and before long was asking himself whether he ought not to intervene. The conclusion to which he came was typical—a compromise which had no logic about it, but which satisfied both his feeling of pity for the slave and his somewhat indignant recognition of the master's rights. He persuaded himself that a negro, if still a heathen, was justifiable prey; but if baptized, must be regarded as free on English soil. It was a compromise without a shadow of sense, but was almost universally adopted; and the slaves, quickly getting wind of this new idea, were not slow to take advantage of it. They looked round for parsons willing to perform the ceremony and warm-hearted citizens willing to stand as godfathers—and usually they had not far to look!

The practice became so common and the good-natured godfathers so troublesome that the masters grew seriously alarmed, especially as they had other grounds for uncertainty. In the reign of William and Mary, Lord Chief Justice Holt had declared that 'as soon as a negro comes into England, he becomes free'. The declaration had not been a decision given in court but an expression of opinion, and not being legally binding had since been ignored and largely forgotten. But it now began to be remembered, and joined to the new popular doctrine of the efficacy of baptism, added greatly to the masters' worries. They felt it wise to get the matter resolved once and for all, and with that object approached the two Law Officers of the Crown, Yorke the Attorney-General and Talbot the Solicitor-General, who on the 14th January, 1729, gave it as their opinion, categorically and in writing, that a slave did not become free by coming to England, nor did baptism bestow freedom on him or make any alteration in his temporal condition. They added that the master might legally compel the slave to return to the plantation.

Twenty years later Yorke, now the Earl of Hardwicke and Lord Chancellor, reaffirmed his opinion. It was reluctantly accepted by the people at large, and was hailed by the masters as their Bill of Rights. In the revulsion of their feelings they became insolent and overbearing and flouting the popular sense of their conduct, began to treat their slaves in England as they treated them in the West Indies. Not only did they drag their fugitives back with whatever violence seemed to them good, but they advertised for them openly in the papers, offering rewards for their apprehension and return; not only did they buy and sell slaves by private treaty, but they put them up brazenly to public auction. That seemed shocking enough to the ordinary good-natured Englishman, but worse still in his eyes was the nefarious trade which, under cover of the right to ship slaves for return to the colonies, the more unscrupulous shipowners were rapidly building up—the trade of smuggling kidnapped innocents on board for transportation and sale. The traffic was too open; the scandal too notorious; it shocked the public conscience, and prepared the way for reform as nothing else.

II

The reform when it came was one of the most remarkable that the world has ever seen. It was neither spectacular nor sudden; it was not initiated by the Government or by any powerful interest; it was not promoted by Ministers in Parliament or by leaders of society outside. It was the work of England's conscience, interpreted and made manifest by a band of devoted reformers, unknown to the great world then and, with the exception of their mouthpiece in Parliament, still unknown to the great world, though not to the hapless negroes for whom they toiled. They were driven on by the goad of a deep religious conviction, and were carried to victory by the silent but massive support of the man-in-the-street. They needed all the help they could get, for they were opposed by the law and by Parliment, by the cities of London, Bristol and Liverpool with their large West Indian communities, by shipping, commerce and vested interests of all sorts, which used every artifice to hold them back and every endeavour to delay their progress and destroy their work. Yet after years of patient and unremitting effort they succeeded not only in bending Parliament to their will but in laying the foundation of a movement which was to affect first England and her colonies and then the whole world.

At the outset, their main, and indeed their only, asset was a favourable atmosphere, to which several sources contributed. Easily first came the Quakers who had set an example of what should be done by washing their hands of the trade and emancipating their own slaves, and had shown by an increased prosperity that the wages of virtue can sometimes be wealth. But the Quakers were a people apart; their methods were mysterious; they offered an ideal too difficult for the average man, in whose eyes it was more to be respected than followed, more to be admired than practised. Just for that reason their influence, though good, was restricted. On a different plane there stood the philosophers and poets and men of letters—authors such as John Locke and Montesquieu, Alexander Pope and William Cowper, Daniel Defoe and Dr. Johnson. They had all denounced slavery in their several ways —with philosophic detachment, or poetic fervour, or robust common sense. But philosophers and poets and even men of letters appeal only to a limited class; their influence is evanescent, at least until after their death. Yet they too in their degree helped to mould public opinion. Most potent of all, however, was the indignation felt at the planters' doings, and the latent hostility which it produced in the minds of the common people. England's village Hampdens, her little men, had always disapproved of slavery in the abstract and now were shocked by its manifestations in the flesh. They felt a growing malaise, an uneasy consciousness that evil was present and must be destroyed. But the man-in-the-street is tongue-tied and helpless in the face of great problems. He can create the conditions for reform; he can lay the train; but in himself he cannot provide the spark to set it alight. There was urgent need of a protagonist. Whence was he to come?

III

Granville Sharp, who was to fill the role, was born in 1735. He came of a clerical family well known in the North, but did not himself follow the family tradition. As a youth he was apprenticed to a linen-draper in London, and after following that occupation for seven years, obtained a post as clerk in the Ordnance Office. There he remained without distinction for eighteen years, and then resigned as a protest against the war with the American colonies. Thereafter, so far as worldly affairs were concerned, he lived on a small income derived from his brothers. Such, in brief, was his official career; it held no interest for him, or for us. Far more important was his character; far more effective his researches into obscure and erudite subjects; far more pregnant of results the chance encounter which put him in the way of immortality.

Coming from a clerical family, it was not surprising that he was of a religious turn of mind. What prevented him from taking holy orders is not known, but probably his own peculiar brand of diffidence. He could not face an assembly, and to his dying day was reluctant even to take the chair at a meeting. Preaching was clearly not his forte; but if he could not exhort a congregation, he was ready to argue with anyone. During his career as a linen-draper, the shop in which he was employed was owned, in turn, by a Quaker, a Presbyterian, a Roman Catholic, a Socinian and a Jew. Sharp found a keen delight in arguing points of religion with them all, and in order to hold his own, taught himself Greek and Hebrew in his spare time. His propensity to argue might almost have put him into the category of sea-lawyer, if it had not been for his principles and his lack of personal ambition. He did not argue for his own benefit, or for the fun of defeating an opponent, but out of an abstract love of the truth and a desire to do good. There was in his make-up a high degree of that selfless devotion which was, or should have been, the hall-mark of knight-errantry, a burning desire to redress wrong and destroy evil. His early activities were varied, curious and not without interest, but do not concern us except as they emphasize his altruism, his tenacity in the face of difficulties, and his patience in research.

The turning-point of his life came in 1765, when he was thirty years of age. Going one day to visit his brother, William, a surgeon in Mincing Lane, he met a negro whose condition was so deplorable that it demanded notice. The negro gave his name as Jonathan Strong, and said he was the slave of David Lisle, a planter from Barbados. Lisle, who was visiting England and had lodgings at Wapping, had lost his temper with Strong and, for whatever reason, had so belaboured him that Strong was hardly able to walk and had nearly lost his sight; then, under the impression that he was no longer capable of service, Lisle had turned him out to fend for himself or failing that to die in the streets. Such a procedure was common enough in Barbados. Jonathan in his pain and misery was making his way to William Sharp, having heard of his reputation for kindness to the poor in the east end of London.

William did not belie his reputation; he took Jonathan in, gave him first aid and then procured him admittance to St. Bartholomew's Hospital. Granville had been as touched as his brother at the man's plight and when a few months later Strong was discharged as cured, found him employment as a messenger in an apothecary's shop. For two years Strong prospered, growing hale and hearty and happy. But London in those days was a small place, and in 1767 Lisle caught sight of his reconstituted slave. Deciding that obviously he had made a mistake in throwing away so likely a piece of property, he made up his mind to recover him, and suborned a couple of scoundrels to lure him into a public house in Fenchurch Street and there kidnap him. The plot succeeded, and Lisle, once more in possession, sold his prey for £30 to John Kerr, a planter from Jamaica.

Pending shipment to the West Indies, Strong was confined in the Poultry Compter but managed to get a message through to Granville Sharp, appealing for help. Sharp took immediate action, hastening to the Lord Mayor, Sir Robert Kite, and persuading him to intervene. Strong was brought into court, and after his case had been heard, was discharged on the ground that he had been arrested without a warrant. Though now at liberty, he was not necessarily safe. Indeed as he was leaving the court, the captain of the ship which was to have taken him to Jamaica, attempted to seize him as a runaway slave, and only desisted when Sharp threatened him with an action for assault. It was evident to Sharp that though Strong had been rescued for the time being, his position was far from satisfactory and his future precarious. His release had been procured on a technical point, not on a point of principle, still less on one which touched the heart of the matter. There was nothing to prevent Lisle or Kerr from making a further attempt on his freedom, with greater precautions and very possibly with greater success. Strong was still a slave, and still without security. Was there no method of giving him real protection? His case cried aloud for investigation and Sharp, very conscious of the fact, determined to take in hand the whole question of the status of slaves in England. It was work which appealed to him from many angles, offering as it did full scope for both his chivalrous spirit and his capacity for research, besides giving present help to a man in trouble.

The danger clearly lay in the Law Officers' ruling of 1729. Was it impossible to overthrow that ruling and reinstate Holt's opinion? Sharp thought it could be done, and applied to a number of lawyers, including the eminent Dr. Blackstone, for confirmation of his views.

When they all failed him, Sharp, with characteristic determination, resolved that as he had once taught himself Greek and Hebrew to support his theological convictions, so now he would teach himself law to support his legal convictions. He set to work with a will, and as a result of two years' hard study was able to write a treatise—*A Representation of the Injustice and dangerous Tendency of tolerating Slavery in England*—in which he maintained his views with a wealth of learned argumentation. Having written it, he distributed copies among the legal fraternity. It was not without its effect. Sharp was now embarked on his crusade in good earnest.

IV

To have secured Strong's release was good; to have shaken the legal pundits, in however small a degree, was better; but best of all would be a favourable decision in the courts, settling once and for all the status of slaves in England. Sharp could not be content until he had obtained it, but there were two difficulties. First he had to find a suitable case to take to the courts, and then he had to find a willing judge. Neither was easy. The owners were not anxious to put their rights to the hazard; they were growing chary; they became less blatant in their actions, hurrying their slaves on board without fuss or ostentation. The judges, in their turn, had no desire to challenge Hardwicke's authority; he had been a famous Chancellor and a ruling given by him was not lightly to be set aside. The doubts which Sharp was voicing might some day have to be resolved, but why seek trouble before it was necessary? Even if the existing state of things did run counter to an amorphous public opinion—and it was not clear that it did—any alteration could hardly fail to result in much legal confusion and certainly also in real financial hardship. Better to let sleeping dogs lie. So it came about that though Sharp was able from time to time to secure the release of individual slaves, snatched, as a rule, just as they were on the point of transportation, in each case the judges burked what seemed to Sharp the main issue; they invariably gave as the grounds of release the lack of a proper warrant, or disputed ownership, or some other such technical matter, but never the indubitable rights of the slave given him by law.

At last, after three years, Sharp found the case for which he had been waiting. James Somerset, a negro from Virginia, had been brought to England by his master, Charles Stewart, had escaped, been recaptured, and on his master's instructions taken on board the *Anne and Mary* to be shipped to Jamaica for sale. His case was ideal. There was no question of warrants or disputed ownership to confuse the issue. There was no doubt about the facts. The only question was how far Stewart was justified in seizing and selling Somerset. If by coming to England Somerset had automatically obtained his freedom, then clearly Stewart had no justification. If, on the other hand, he had not obtained his freedom, it had still to be settled to what extent Stewart had rights over him and how those rights could be enforced. In January 1772 the matter came before Lord Chief Justice Mansfield. He found it a heavy burden, for though he was an able judge, he was a timid man, shunning responsibility and frightened of popular disfavour. He could not deny the validity of Sharp's contention, but, being acutely aware of the probable results, was very unwilling to admit it. To avoid the necessity of a legal decision, he did his best to persuade Stewart to manumit Somerset and so put an end to litigation. But by now the owners had taken alarm, and thinking it best to face their opponents and fight for what they claimed to be their rights, had rallied to Stewart's support, subscribing the funds to enable him to brief the best counsel procurable. Battle had been joined and neither side was willing to withdraw—certainly not Sharp now that at last he had succeeded in getting a test case and forcing the judicature. Mansfield held back as long as he could, trusting in vain to the chapter of accidents; but, after dragging the case on through three separate sessions, was at last obliged to give judgment. He did so on the 22nd June, 1772—a memorable day! His decision was all that Sharp could desire—final, conclusive, incontrovertible. He held that the seizure and sale of a man was so high an act of dominion, and the state of slavery was so odious in itself that nothing could justify the one or the other but positive law. There was no such positive law in England, and Somerset must therefore be discharged. Mansfield had pronounced judgment, and to still the quakings of his heart, had muttered '*fiat justitia ruat coelum*'. But the heavens did not fall. Instead, Mansfield had atoned for many earlier sins. From that day forward, no man in England could be a slave, and no slave could set foot on English soil without becoming free.

The verdict given with so much misgiving chimed in well with a decision given three years earlier by John Jervis, afterwards the Earl of St. Vincent. In 1768 that formidable sailor had been in command of the *Alarm*, frigate, in the Mediterranean, when two Turkish slaves had jumped into the *Alarm's* boat and wrapped themselves in the British flag. Their owners had tried to take them back to captivity, but were warned off by Jervis who told them bluntly that any slave who touched the British colours could claim freedom as a right. Both Jervis and Mansfield had given voice to the profoundest of British convictions— a passionate belief in personal freedom.

Yet for all Mansfield's verdict, the traffic in slaves was not yet dead— not even in England, though the first blow had been struck. The sale and transportation of slaves which had once been carried on openly and unabashedly in the streets of London had now become the hole-and-corner affair of racketeers and smugglers.

XII. Clarkson writes an Essay

I

THAT AN unknown and somewhat eccentric clerk in a minor government office should have bothered his head about the status of slaves might well be considered unusual. That in the short space of five years the same unknown clerk should have secured the freedom of the fifteen thousand slaves then resident in England and of all who might thereafter land on English soil, must be regarded as little short of a miracle. After such an achievement Granville Sharp had every right to rest on his oars, but he preferred to move forward in his own unexpected style. One of his first actions was to write to the Prime Minister, urging him to abolish the slave trade and to free all slaves throughout the British dominions at the earliest possible moment. He could hardly have chosen a worse time or, for that matter, a less sympathetic auditor. The Prime Minister in question was Lord North who was slithering into war with the American colonies, and could hardly be expected to endanger an already explosive position by flinging such a bombshell into the existing mass of colonial grievances. He took no action.

But Granville Sharp, nothing discouraged, approached the problem from the other end, and helped to keep alive the flickering lamp of abolition which the Quakers had lighted in America, by entering into correspondence with Anthony Benezet, an American Quaker whose pen and money were both employed in the cause of negro freedom, to

his ultimate honour but not to his immediate popularity. Bancroft
called him disparagingly 'the amiable enthusiast'—(Bancroft III, 408).
The prospects in America looked bright, but the appearance was
greater than the reality. In 1772 the colonists were at loggerheads with
the mother country. They believed that the only method of forcing
England to redress their grievances was by touching her pocket. A
boycott on her trade would work wonders, and how could America
inflict a greater or more immediate damage on England's commercial
prosperity than by putting an end to the slave trade, her highly
profitable monopoly? Hence there came across the Atlantic a series of
resolutions, culminating in one passed by the Congress of 1774 which
banned the importation of slaves altogether. But it was only part of
what today might be called a cold war. The resolutions, except in so
far as they originated among the Quakers, were mere political gestures.
It was England's trade, not America's addiction to slavery at which
they were aimed: 'the question of tolerating the slave trade and the
question of abolishing slavery', as Bancroft was careful to point out,
'rested on different grounds' (*History of the United States* III, 410).
He did not explain the difference, but in short the one would hurt
England, the other the colonists.

The resolutions seemed at first to have some effect, for the War of
Independence which followed soon after, automatically reduced the
volume of trade; but not the desire for slaves, as the Americans proved
clearly enough when the war was over, by showing themselves as
eager to renew the purchase of slaves as the traders were to provide
them. The outlook in America therefore was less hopeful than Sharp
thought, but his correspondence with Benezet helped to unite into one
body the reformers on both sides of the Atlantic. Meanwhile Sharp kept
eyes and ears open for other steps which might be taken. There was
more work for him to do.

II

Somerset's case had received great publicity and roused widespread
interest. Mansfield's judgment had dealt only with slaves in England; it
did not apply to any other country, not even to Scotland, which had to
await a similar decision of its own in the Joseph Knight case some five
years later. But inevitably his pronouncement drew attention to the
whole question of slavery. People began to ponder over it more
deeply; to study its foundations in history; to weigh up its effect on

economics; to examine its justification in religion; and to moralize on its desirability or otherwise in the conduct of human affairs. It had its defenders in plenty among the vested interests at home and the solid phalanx of planters in the colonies, but it had also its opponents—for the most part a silently disapproving company, but not without a vocal element. Indeed attacks on the system came with increasing frequency and mounting intensity from a number of quarters. Adam Smith argued that it was financially unsound; Dr. Robertson, the popular historian, denounced it as repugnant to humanity; and Wesley, going even further, dubbed it 'that execrable villainy, which is the scandal of religion, of England and of human nature'. Yet in spite of considered criticisms from philosophers and economists, in spite of condemnation by the leaders of religious thought, the trade, carried on in English ships, continued to flourish and slavery to increase rather than decrease in the colonies. It was a deep-rooted and ancient evil, which was entrenching itself more firmly every day.

The revival of the trade at the end of the war, the welcome it received in the colonies, and the wealth it produced, encouraged a recklessness of behaviour which soon brought its own retribution. In 1783 England was shocked at what became known as the *Zong* case. The owners of the *Zong*, a slave-ship trading from Liverpool, claimed, under their insurance, the full value of a hundred and thirty-two slaves lost in a voyage from St. Thomas to Jamaica. There was no dispute about the main facts; the slaves had been thrown overboard and deliberately drowned. Neither the captain nor the owners made any secret of the fact, nor did the insurance company regard it as a reason in itself for refusing payment. The only point at issue was the captain's motive. According to the owners the crossing had been prolonged, the water supply was running short, and the slaves had been thrown overboard to save the lives of the rest. The insurers, on the other hand, maintained, and the evidence proved, that the captain's motive had been altogether different and that the claim was fraudulent. There had been no shortage of water, nor any peril from that cause to either crew or slaves. The true fact was that in the course of an unusually long and stormy voyage dysentery had broken out; a number of slaves had died and many more were in a sickly condition and likely to die. It seemed inevitable that the voyage would be a financial loss, part of which would fall on the captain. He had therefore proposed to the mate that the slaves should be jettisoned, on the ground that if they remained in the ship and died of dysentery the loss would fall on the owners, whereas if they were thrown overboard to meet a case of necessity, the insurers would become responsible.

At the trial, neither side paid any attention to the loss of life, except by way of emphasizing that it was, in the words of the Solicitor-General, acting for the owners, merely 'a throwing overboard of goods and of part to save the residue', merely 'a case of goods and chattels'. It is true that counsel for the insurance company made some play with the argument that the slaves were as much entitled to their share of the water as anyone else, but even he did not stress the enormity of the captain's action. Mansfield contented himself with describing the case as a 'very uncommon one', and directed the jury that the only matter for them to decide was simply 'whether it was from necessity', declaring that 'they had no doubt (though it shocks one very much) that the case of slaves was the same as if horses had been thrown overboard'. It was, he repeated uneasily, 'a very shocking case'.

So the rest of England thought. Sharp, at his own expense, employed a shorthand writer to take a full note of the proceedings, which he sent to the Admiralty and the Duke of Portland, the then First Lord of the Treasury, demanding that the men who had thrown the negroes overboard should be brought to trial for murder. The Government took no action, but the country was profoundly stirred. A trade which could perpetrate such wholesale murder with impunity was not a trade which should be, or could be, tolerated.

III

The first reaction came from the Quakers who in the month following the *Zong* trial sent their petition to Parliament (see p. 102), conceiving themselves, as the preamble stated, 'engaged, in religious duty, to lay the suffering situation of that unhappy people before you, as a subject loudly calling for the humane interposition of the legislature'. It was the first such petition, and for two years it stood in honourable isolation, until in 1785 it was joined by one from the inhabitants of Bridgwater, expressing their ardent hope 'to see a British parliament, by the extinction of that sanguinary traffic, extend the blessings of liberty to millions beyond this realm, hold up to an enlightened world a glorious and merciful example, and stand foremost in the defence of the violated rights of human nature'. They had many years to wait, but in the end they were to see their hopes fulfilled. Meanwhile the Quakers had followed up their petition by the appointment of a standing committee, their Meeting for Sufferings as they called it, which was to blazon abroad the enormities of the trade, and wherever possible to bring relief to 'our fellow-creatures, the oppressed Africans'. Nothing can deprive the Quakers of the honour of having offered the first practical example of what the nation should do, by renouncing slavery for themselves, nor of having presented the first petition to Parliament, nor of having set up the first society for the abolition of slavery. They were in a true sense the conscience of the nation.

In 1784 they received a powerful ally in the person of James Ramsay, who for nineteen years had been one of the five Anglican ministers in the island of St. Kitts, and in 1783 or thereabouts had returned to England to become the vicar of Teston, a village in Kent. Distressed by what he had seen at first hand of the evils of slavery, he was anxious to promote reforms, and with that end in view published, on his return home, *An Essay on the Treatment and Conversion of African Slaves in the British Sugar Colonies*—a book which he had planned and largely written while still in the island. Coming, as it did, from the pen of a man who had been so long resident in the West Indies, it was bound to carry weight. The authoritative picture which it painted of the use and abuse of slaves was at once convincing to the layman and intensely irritating to the planters. But the facts which he gave were not, in the long run, so important as the attitude which he adopted. It was a constructive attitude but also restrained, for he had been taught caution by the comparative failure of his own relations with his own slaves. He had treated them with Christian forbearance and they had not responded in the way he had expected; so that, as he sadly admitted, 'he possessed not a single slave on whom he could place dependence'.

In his book, therefore, he approached the problem in a somewhat cautious fashion. It was no use merely harping on natural rights, or on the villainies of slave-traders or on the cruelties of owners. They might be, and indeed must be, described; for they were the foundation on which his book rested. But other facts also had to be faced; and it was a fact glaringly evident that in the ignorant, helpless condition in which most of the slaves stood, 'full liberty would be no blessing to them' (p. 118). On the contrary 'to make a slave free, who cannot earn an honest living would be inhuman and impolitic' (p. 283), for it would merely encourage him in his bad habits of robbery, stealing and getting into drunken brawls (p. 186). What then could be done? Could any steps be taken, not to abolish slavery overnight by a violent revolution, but to turn it from a curse into a blessing?

The first essential was to appreciate the existing state of things. Slavery, at all events in the colonies, was 'an unnatural state of oppression on the one side, and of suffering on the other'; the slaves were treated with 'unconcern and unfeeling neglect', and as a consequence became treacherous and cunning. What more could be expected of men and women 'who were moved only by present feeling, who had no reputation to support, no lasting interest to care for'. Hunger, mistrust, oppression and ignorance were bound to breed worthlessness and crime. The position would seem utterly hopeless if it were not for the existence here and there of slaves cast in a finer mould and of masters endowed with a kinder nature. Broadly speaking, slaves suffered most, and reacted worst, when they were 'the property of an ignorant, low-minded, narrow-hearted wretch, or of one indigent and involved, or of a man who made a figure beyond his income in England, or when they were submitted to some raw lad, or untaught unfeeling manager or overseer'. And such men, Ramsay added, were to be found in too great numbers.

Yet when all was said and done, in spite of their deplorable conditions and depraved natures, the prosperity of the sugar colonies rested on the slaves. They were the foundation and source of the wealth which poured into England from the West Indies—some six to eight million pounds every year. Even in their degraded state they were a highly valuable commodity, and there could be no doubt that their value could be largely increased by a sane, sensible, humane treatment; if, in short, they could be raised in the social scale and given a proper wage. As free men, secure in the possession of their families and their own property, they would work far more effectively for their masters, and in addition would provide an immense and as yet untapped market for English goods and manufactures. Financial interest, therefore, joined with humanity and religion in proclaiming the need to adopt a new and more liberal attitude towards the slaves.

Ramsay supported his general argument with facts and figures that were clear and not unconvincing. His suggestions for raising the status of the slaves were equally clear and given in some detail. He recognized that lifting the slaves up to a point where they could safely be emancipated, must be a long and slow process; they would have to be educated to a new conception of life and the responsibilities it entailed. During this interval of preparation the ideal would be for the Government, the Church and the owners to combine in speeding the work, but that could hardly be expected. There were bound to be some owners who would show themselves unwilling, unable, or recalcitrant. The Government, therefore, would be obliged to place some restraint upon them as a body, while the Church through her ministers should busy herself as never before with the welfare of the slaves. The minister must have free access to them, and must pose as their instructor and benefactor, acting as a mediator between them and their master, so that 'their esteem for his person, and gratitude for his kindness, may stand them in the place of law, may produce in them a love for his doctrines and be a pledge of their good behaviour'.

The proposals were not really practicable. The owners could hardly be expected to surrender the control of their slaves in so great a degree to outsiders, even if those outsiders were ministers of the Gospel. Nor for that matter was it at all certain that a sufficient number of ministers with the necessary qualifications would be forthcoming. It was very improbable that the owners would welcome Ramsay's proposals, and in fact they reacted violently. Ramsay found himself involved in a furious and highly personal controversy, which continued until his death in July 1789, and indeed is said to have hastened it. One of his opponents, Molyneux by name, wrote exultantly: 'Ramsay is dead—I have killed him.' Perhaps he had; but perhaps he flattered himself, for even the highly sensitive rarely die of controversy. But whether killed by slander or by something more normal, Ramsay had made a serious contribution to the cause of reform by exploding the tendency in some quarters to sentimentalize over the negro, by explaining the practical difficulties of emancipation, and by offering a reasoned prospect of financial gain as an inducement for a forward move.

IV

The Quakers had given the country a lead; Granville Sharp had obtained a definite interpretation of the law; and Ramsay had lighted the fires of controversy. They had all three been working towards their particular ends in isolation. It still remained for them to combine before the actual work of reform could start. The motive force was to come from yet another man, also working in isolation. In 1785 the Vice-Chancellor of Cambridge was Dr. Peckard, the Master of Magdalene College. It was part of the Vice-Chancellor's duties to choose the subjects for the Prize Latin Essays, and as Dr. Peckard was a convinced opponent of slavery, it was not surprising, especially in view of the publication of Ramsay's book, that he should have set the senior B.A.'s to answer, in the best Latin they could muster, the question 'Is it right to make men slaves against their will?' As a subject for a Latin essay it was new and it was topical.

Among the senior B.A.s was Thomas Clarkson, who had won the junior prize the year before and hoped to repeat his success on the higher level. He did; again he was first. His *Essay on the Slavery and Commerce of the Human Species, particularly the African,* which he published the next year (1786) in an English dress, gained for him considerable and indeed excessive notoriety, for it had the defects usually to be found in the work of an academic young man of twenty-five. It gave much relevant information and many striking facts, but they were embedded in long dissertations on the origins of society; on the rise, nature and design of governments; on the laws of nature and of God, and on other such vast topics of which Clarkson had little knowledge and less experience. The *Essay* was dogmatic, it tended to exaggerate, and generally speaking was heavy and dull. There was plenty of scope for replies, which were not slow in coming.

Perhaps the best was from the pen of one Francklyn, a widely read man with an easy style, who had no difficulty in tripping Clarkson up on the more irrelevant portions of the *Essay,* and in casting doubts very artfully on his conclusions by emphasizing his exaggerations, and pointing out that his facts rested for the most part on 'the simple declaration of an obscure student in an English university' who had failed to name his authorities or to give any corroborative evidence. But Francklyn himself was forced to admit the potency of an *Essay* which, in his own words, had 'persuaded so many people to consider the commerce itself as infamous, and the purchasers of slaves in the colonies as so many savages devoid of every principle of humanity' (Francklyn, p. 21). Certainly the *Essay* had its effect on the world at large, but for us it is of interest mainly for the light which it throws on Clarkson's character. The first point to be noted is not the tone nor the contents of the *Essay,* but the steps which he took to obtain his material. The time allowed for the composition was short—a few weeks—and the subject, so far as Clarkson was concerned, entirely new. He needed powder and shot, and took considerable pains to find them. College and university libraries were not enough; he went up to London to buy books which were otherwise unobtainable, and, more important, he searched round for information from other than printed sources, seeking, as the result of a hint, to get access to the manuscript papers of a deceased trader, and questioning any of his acquaintances who had ever been to the West Indies. The experience which this gave him of collecting information was to stand him in good stead later on; and attacks made by such men as Francklyn taught him the need to sift evidence and the value of corroboration.

The second point of interest and the most outstanding is the effect which the writing had on Clarkson himself. Clarkson, like Granville Sharp, came of a clerical family. He was by nature and upbringing a deeply religious man, and his ambition at the moment was to enter the Church. He had many qualifications, being of a serious, and indeed solemn, turn of mind, and blessed with sufficient verbosity to make sermon-writing easy. He was not afraid of hard work or comparative poverty, and was capable of devoting himself whole-heartedly to any cause which he had adopted. It was less satisfactory that he lacked the sense of humour without which it is hard to deal successfully with mankind, but to make up for this deficiency, he was highly charged with emotion, surprisingly so in view of his heavy physical build and slow mental reaction. The *Essay* in its preparation and composition played upon his emotions to an extraordinary degree. He had entered for the prize from a proper sense of ambition, but the *Essay* had from the first taken complete control of him. It had opened the door on to a new and horrifying world, the existence of which he had never imagined and which stirred his over-sensitive nature to its foundations. He could neither forget nor disregard the harrowing scenes disclosed by his researches and magnified by his emotions. His mind was full of them, waking and sleeping; they disturbed his rest, they preyed on his thoughts.

When he had won the prize he was summoned to Cambridge in the usual way to read his production before the Senate. This awe-inspiring ceremony increased the perturbation of his mind, and while riding back to London, he was so overcome that as he was approaching Wades Mill in Hertfordshire he dismounted from his horse and, in his own words, 'sat down disconsolate on the turf by the roadside'. There it was borne in upon him that if the horrors which he had described were true, it was more than time that someone should put an end to them and the heavy load of misery they entailed. At the moment he did not consciously assign the role to himself; but it was a mere matter of time before he did. Whilst he was slowly reaching his inevitable conclusion, he decided to ease his feelings and test the ground by translating and publishing his *Essay* so that it might reach a wider public and perhaps give an indication of the direction in which his duty lay. It was while making the necessary arrangements that he came into touch first with the Quakers and then with Granville Sharp and Ramsay. With that the stage had been set, and soon afterwards Clarkson while walking by himself in the woods around Teston made his final choice—to renounce ambition, to sacrifice what he believed to be bright and indeed brilliant prospects, and to devote himself body and soul to 'the cause of the oppressed Africans'.

XIII. Slave Trade or Slavery?

I

HAVING MADE his choice, Clarkson returned to London, intent on breaking the news to his friends. He took himself with youthful and engaging seriousness, discussing endlessly how he was to fulfil his object, and what his dedication of himself entailed. It was not easy to decide, for Clarkson, though earnest and persevering, was not a born leader with the born leader's knack of pre-eminence; his talents lay elsewhere. Nature had given him, with his strong emotions, a retiring disposition, so that while his emotions made him declare war against slavery, his disposition marked him out for a role which, however important, was essentially behind the scenes. The function which fate had ordained for him was to become the ordnance factory of the movement, producing ammunition for others to use.

The first essential was for him to recognize that function, and here his friends were a help. They pointed out that the only sure road to success was by way of parliamentary action, based on sound knowledge and bulwarked by public support. He should therefore get in touch with members of Parliament, giving them copies of his *Essay* and if possible enlisting their active sympathy. As the advice chimed in with his inclination, he was easily convinced. He turned the matter of procedure over in his mind with his usual meticulous care, coming finally to the conclusion that the best method of winning politicians to the cause would be to visit them personally; and as they might ask questions and even raise objections, it was highly desirable that he should enlarge his own knowledge. He set to work at once, enlarging his knowledge by haunting the docks, in order to board vessels from Africa and enter into conversation with the seamen; while at the same time he obtained introductions wherever he could to Members of Parliament.

Among those on whom he called was Wilberforce, who appeared to be more truly interested than any of the others. Clarkson cultivated his acquaintance, which proved immediately useful in an unexpected quarter. For some time, half aware of his own limitations and realizing acutely the need for funds and assistance, Clarkson had been anxious to join forces with the Quaker Committee, believing that they would provide the ballast which he needed. He had approached them and found them not altogether unwilling but undoubtedly cautious—more ready to listen and encourage than to make common cause. When, however, he told them that he was in touch with Wilberforce, they became more interested, agreeing to unite with him 'as soon as ever Mr. Wilberforce would give his word that he would take up the question in Parliament' (Clarkson I, 251). Clarkson hurried away to ask for the required promise, but when he came face to face with Wilberforce displayed the essential flaw in his character by allowing his emotions to overcome him. They affected him to such an extent that the question stuck in his throat; he was quite incapable of asking it either then or thereafter. Deeply chagrined, he had to bespeak the help of a friend, who a few days later, at a dinner-party, specially arranged for the purpose, made the necessary inquiry on his behalf. Wilberforce, with becoming modesty, replied that he would have no objection to bringing forward a motion in Parliament when he was better prepared and provided no more suitable person could be found. On the strength of this offer, the Quakers joined forces with Clarkson, and on the 22nd May, 1787, their original committee was reformed to include, amongst others, the two non-Quakers, Clarkson and Granville Sharp.

II

The union came about at a critical moment. It was now fifteen years since Mansfield had given his memorable judgment, and there had been ample time for the fears which had haunted his imagination to materialize. In fact they had done so, and if they had not taken quite the shape he had expected, none the less they had proved sufficiently real. Mansfield had been concerned mainly with the financial loss to the owners. Slaves were property, and fifteen thousand of them trained for domestic service must be worth, in real money, not far short of a million pounds, and perhaps a good deal more. To think that a few words from him would deprive the planters, in a flash and without notice, of property worth so large a sum, was enough to daunt any man with a sense of responsibility. Certainly it oppressed Mansfield, and no doubt he awaited the outcome with deep anxiety.

To some extent his fears proved well founded, but nothing like to the extent he had anticipated. Actually the financial results might be described as moderate. A large proportion of the liberated slaves had stopped with their old masters; the only change, so far as they were concerned, was that they now received a small wage, which their masters could well afford, while those more valuable elements of their erstwhile condition, their service and in many cases their devotion, continued unchanged. The attitude of the ex-slaves went far to justify the planters' claim that they were happy, and to support such a verdict as that of Lady Nugent, who after ten months' residence in Jamaica as the Governor's wife, was rash enough to declare that 'generally speaking, I believe the slaves are extremely well used' (*Lady Nugent's Journal*, p. 117). But of course in both cases the slaves to whom they were referring came from the domestic, not the plantation class. Of the liberated slaves who had not remained with their old masters, many had obtained work on their own account and settled down happily. But there had been a residue, a few hundred strong, who in the first moments of freedom had broken away from their old life, and either because they were lazy or drunken or worthless, had failed to obtain new, or indeed any, jobs. They had sunk rapidly to the ranks of vagabonds and beggars, and for the most part had drifted to London where they were a burden to themselves and a nuisance to the authorities. Perhaps even worse, they tended to become 'Poor Blacks' in the eyes of the more woolly-minded philanthropists.

Granville Sharp was very conscious of the part he had played in creating these same 'Poor Blacks'. Had he overlooked it, there were ill-wishers in plenty to remind him of what Francklyn called his 'indiscreet zeal' which by depriving the slaves of their masters' protection without substituting any other had exposed them to 'the extremities of cold and hunger' (p. 165). His opponents described it as the inevitable outcome of his 'wild and dangerous' attempt to abolish the slave trade, which, said Boswell, 'must have been crushed at once, had not the insignificance of the zealots who vainly took the lead in it, made the vast body of planters, merchants and others, whose immense properties are involved in that trade, reasonably enough suppose that there could be no danger' (Boswell's *Johnson* II, 391). It was confirmation too of Ramsay's dictum that it would be inhuman and impolitic to free a slave who could not earn an honest living for himself. From every point of view, it was incumbent on Granville Sharp to take the problem of the 'Poor Blacks' in hand and find some remedy. What he had in mind was to restore them to Africa where under proper supervision and good government they might form a centre of civilization for the benefit of their fellow-countrymen, and a source of wealth for England by promoting legitimate trade with the native tribes. The difficulties in the way of his scheme were very great, but were sensibly diminished by his junction with the Quakers who could offer more money and a wider experience than Granville Sharp could hope to provide by himself.

His efforts were at once more successful than he could have hoped and less successful than he deserved. With the help of his committee he acquired from the Timni Chief, Nembana, an area of some twenty miles square in Sierra Leone; and with the assistance of the Government he dispatched four hundred negroes to become the first settlers. The venture was to prove unlucky, but even without the element of ill-luck, it would have been surprising if it had succeeded. Granville Sharp had been more hopeful than wise. The four hundred whom he had collected were among the dregs of the ex-slaves, the least trustworthy, the most lazy. They had moreover been domestic slaves and as such unused to agriculture, which they despised and detested. Their status had always been superior to that of their brethren on the plantations, and to be sent from the house to the fields had always been regarded as the worst form of punishment. As free men they were not disposed to sink in the only social scale of which they had knowledge. They were, in short, ashamed to dig, and at the same time had no experience of trading, and no other means of gaining a livelihood. Nor were they a balanced society. They had few or no womenfolk of their own, and such women as went with them were scarcely a help. Negroes, it is well known, possess a fascination for the more unstable and abandoned types of white women, and some sixty prostitutes from the slums of London were sufficiently attracted to throw in their lot with them. Prostitutes are not normally good settlers, nor is an excess of men likely to improve their quality.

Arrived in Sierra Leone, the colony prospered, or at least remained

peaceful, so long as the only work required of the settlers was to con-
sume the provisions which had been sent out with them; but there was
trouble directly the provisions were finished and the need for labour
loomed large. The prospect of success, never bright, was extinguished
two years later when in 1789 the colony was attacked and destroyed by
a neighbouring chief who cherished a grudge against the white slavers
and anything connected with them.

The set-back was serious and in the case of other men might well
have proved fatal; but Sharp was not to be discouraged. He began all
over again and by 1791 had succeeded, with the help of Henry Thornton, a wealthy banker, a Member of Parliament and a man of wide
experience, in obtaining an Act of Parliament for the incorporation of a
new company whose object was, as the preamble said, to promote
'general trade and commerce from these Kingdoms to and with the
coast of Africa, and from thence to and with the several interior
Kingdoms and countries of that continent'. He took the further precaution of vesting the territory in the Crown, so that it became British
territory in the fullest sense. An able governor of the name of Dawes
was sent out, with a still more able second-in-command, the youthful
Zachary Macaulay, destined to become the father of the historian, who
stepped into Dawes's shoes some two years later. The wretched rem-
nants of the first settlement were collected together and reinforced by
eleven hundred ex-slave refugees from the revolted American colonies; and a new capital, gratefully and hopefully christened Freetown,
was soon in process of building.

But alas for their hopes! In 1793 war broke out between England
and France, and the next year an embittered American slave-trader,
whose victims had occasionally escaped to the new settlement and
there found refuge, avenged himself by guiding a French revolutionary
squadron to the spot, where the exponents of liberty manifested the
fruits of their faith by burning Freetown and making themselves
drunk on looted spirits and ridiculous in stolen feminine finery.
Macaulay was left with nothing but a heap of ruins, but like Sharp he
was not to be discouraged. He was determined to succeed, and he did.
The settlement grew up again and prospered, and when in 1808 it was
taken over by the Government as a Crown Colony, it was already a
shining light in the Dark Continent. Its fortunes had been, and were
still to be, chequered; but fifty years later Sharp's justification was pronounced by Fowell Buxton when he wrote: 'with all its defects, if
anything has anywhere been done for the benefit of western Africa, it

has been there. The only glimmers of civilization; the only attempt at
legitimate commerce; the only prosecution, however faint, of agriculture, are to be found at Sierra Leone. . . . And there alone the Slave
Trade has been in any degree arrested' (Buxton. *The African Slave
Trade and its Remedy*, p. 365).

III

But in 1787, that was still in the future. The new committee had
other work to do beside assisting the young colony. Indeed they were
not much concerned with the 'Poor Blacks', and if it had not been for
Sharp, who reluctantly and against his will, had been elected to the
chair, might have ignored them altogether. Their eyes were fixed on a
different goal which, as they had hitherto been moved by sentiment
rather than reason, was at first a little vague and misty. They detested
slavery, which they looked on as sin; but they soon found that slavery
was a word of wide connotations. At their first meeting they agreed,
without difficulty or discussion, that the slave trade was both unjust
and impolitic, and that they must procure and publish such information
and evidence as might tend to its abolition. But clearly greater precision was needed, and at their third meeting, held early in June, they
addressed themselves to the point.

It soon appeared that there was a cleavage of opinion, which sprang
from a difference of approach. The majority, being sound men of
business and perhaps a little unimaginative, kept strictly to that part of
the subject of which they had some knowledge—the slave trade: it
must be abolished. They were strongly supported by Clarkson, who
had less knowledge and no more imagination, but much more lively
emotions. He had never met a slave face to face, and in view of Mansfield's judgment was never likely to; his knowledge had come from
books and had been concerned almost entirely with the details of the
trade and its accompanying abuses; his researches, equally, had
brought him into contact not with slaves but slavers, and his emotions,
always lurking close beneath the surface, had been heightened by the
sensations he had felt on the deck of the first and only slave ship he had
ever so far boarded. In his own words: 'the sight of the rooms below
and of the gratings above and of the barricado across the deck, and the
explanation of the uses of all these filled me with both melancholy and
horror. I found soon afterwards a fire of indignation kindling within
me' (Clarkson I, 238). It was only to be expected that he should

re-echo and emphasize the views of the majority—the slave trade must be abolished.

Sharp did not dispute the necessity, but he was a man of greater imagination and more human sympathies. For him, the trade was merely an instrument; that it must go was self-evident, but it must go as part of a wholesale clearance. The sum and substance of the evil was not the slave-trader or the slave-ship, but slavery itself; it was not enough to dam one particular source of supply, or to feel a fire of indignation against mere agents; the first step must be to succour the victims. It was natural for Sharp to take this view, for his interest had been roused originally, not by books nor by the sight of a slaver, but by the misery and wrongs of a living, palpitating human being, whom he had met face to face, mutilated and scarred with the visible marks of cruelty. From that moment his one object had been to set slaves free— singly, if he could do no better; by battalions, if he could move the legislature or found a successful colony in Sierra Leone; but best of all by a full and final emancipation of every sufferer, if the work of the new committee could only effect it. His ambition was to open the gates of freedom to a whole continent, and be able, like the prophet of old, to proclaim that 'the people who walked in darkness have seen a great light . . . for thou hast broken the yoke of his bondage, the rod of his oppressor'.

At that third meeting Sharp put forward his views, but the committee were reluctant to adopt them. Their hesitation is easy to understand. Sharp was a single-minded enthusiast, ready to put all to the hazard; the others were hard-headed business men uncomfortably conscious of the magnitude and pitfalls of the task. There were so many and such influential persons interested in maintaining slavery—the traders, the planters, the merchants, the city bankers, and all, in fact, connected in any way with the vast commerce to and from the West Indies. To antagonize them unnecessarily was not only foolish, but might so easily jeopardize the whole movement. It was, of course, essential to win popular support and while doing so they were bound to make enemies as well as friends, but they were naturally anxious to limit the number of their adversaries. It is not, therefore, surprising that, in their eagerness to deprecate opposition, they tended to twist logic, not deliberately but by an intuitive self-deception. They persuaded themselves that slavery and the slave trade were two separate evils, quite distinct the one from the other, and decided that it was too much to hope that they could overthrow both. If they aimed too high, they might well lose all, and therefore they must be content to grapple with one alone. But which? Clearly the one most likely to appeal to the public at large, the one of which the facts were most easily to be obtained, the one which might be expected to arouse the least opposition—in a word, the slave trade. The public already had some knowledge of it and more distaste; their sympathy was probable. The facts could be obtained in England as easily, perhaps more easily than elsewhere.

And as for opposition, to attack slavery in its full extent would consolidate all their opponents of every sort, the planters in the colonies as well as the merchants in England and the traders in Africa; but if they attacked the trade alone, they had a reasonable prospect of dividing their enemies. They could promise the planters that they had no intention of meddling with their property or depriving them of their slaves either now or hereafter; their existing slaves would remain untouched, and they could make sure of future supplies by adopting a system of breeding recruits at home instead of importing them from abroad. If only they would realize the fact, that was a cheaper and better method; it would cut out the cost of the barracoons on the African coast; it would do away with the losses of the middle passage; it would end the risk, inseparable from public auctions, of finding that the slaves they had purchased were suffering from hidden diseases; it would simplify the process and reduce the waste of 'seasoning'. That surely was an argument which should appeal to the planters and perhaps no less to the city bankers. If so, the number of their opponents would be sensibly reduced.

Whatever its effect on others, the argument satisfied the committee. It went further, inducing them to believe that by abolishing the trade, they would benefit the negroes; for if a planter had to depend on the offspring of his present slaves, he would indubitably encourage them to marry and make decent homes, and would no less indubitably feed at least the mothers-to-be on something approaching a sufficient scale. The whole status of slavery would be automatically raised and brought nearer to a condition in which freedom could be safely granted.

It was in vain for Sharp to point out that the same and even better results would flow from the abolition of slavery. The committee agreed; they admitted that so far as the object in view was concerned, it did not much matter which evil they attacked; 'the same end would be produced in either case' (Clarkson I, 286); but they maintained that the path to the one was much easier than the path to the other. An attempt to abolish slavery would not only be a direct interference with the planters' property, but an encroachment on the rights of the colonial legislatures, whereas the abolition of the trade was a matter within the jurisdiction of the English Parliament which was admittedly entitled to regulate commerce within the Empire, and could enforce its decisions through the navy and the customs officials. If the same end could be reached by either route, the choice must be governed by the practical difficulties, and the practical difficulties all pointed in one direction. The committee's premises were unsound and their logic weak, but they had their way, and in order that there might be no mistake, decided that for the future they should be known officially as 'The Committee instituted in June 1787 for effecting the Abolition of the Slave Trade'.

The committee were sincere and earnest, and according to Clarkson their decision was not only wise but contributed greatly to 'their success. 'I am persuaded', he wrote in 1808 when the abolition was at last a fact, 'that, if they had adopted the other object, they could not for years to come, if ever, have succeeded in their attempt' (Clarkson I, 289). It may be so; yet, as will appear, their decision was a constant source of difficulty, continually tripping them up and giving their opponents a handle against them. And as for the lapse of time, it took the reformers twenty years to get rid of the trade—and then only in law, not in practice—and a further twenty-five years to complete their work by freeing the slaves. Would they have taken more than forty-five years, had they from the first followed Sharp's advice? It may well be doubted.

XIV. Wilberforce

I

RAMSAY'S *Essay* had been published in 1784, Clarkson's in 1786. Between those two dates there had occurred in the life of William Wilberforce one of those spiritual upheavals which, working through an individual, may sometimes influence the whole world, but must always have a revolutionary effect on the individual himself. In 1785 he experienced that adventure of the soul known as conversion. He went into it a gay young man with a bright political future full of alluring hopes; he came out of it still a gay young man, even if the gaiety was tinged with a deeper and more serious hue, but with a wholly different outlook on his career, the full impact of which he neither could nor would evade. He had surrendered political for moral issues; he had dedicated himself to spiritual instead of material ends; he had preferred the quiet approval of a good conscience to the glamour and glory of the honours list. What he needed to make his calling and election sure was a knowledge of the exact task which Providence had assigned to him.

At the time Wilberforce was twenty-six years old. He had been born at Hull on the 24th August, 1759, the son of a rich merchant, who died when he was eight. From birth he had been a delicate and in his degree an Ariel-like being, with a frail body but a gay spirit, with poor eyesight but a witty tongue, with a round-shouldered stoop but a most melodious voice. To his other qualities was added that natural charm which is unable to make enemies and cannot avoid making friends. After his father's death, he had been pampered by a loving and anxious mother, proud of his gifts and full of worldly ambition for him. She had put him to school at Putney, but hearing that the aunt, in whose charge he had been placed, was tainted with the new evangelical doctrines, so potent among the poor and so unfashionable among the rich, had promptly recalled him to Hull and perseveringly obliterated any tendency towards 'enthusiasm', as it was called, by a never-ending round of gaiety. 'No pious parent', said Wilberforce in later years, 'ever laboured more to impress a beloved child with sentiments of religion than my friends did to give me a taste for the world and its diversions.' They were not unsuccessful. Wilberforce went up from Hull to Cambridge, and came down from Cambridge to London, full of the *joie de vivre*, delighting in dinners and dancing, fond of theatres and club life, a master of sparkling conversation, enjoying picnics by day and excursions by night, and sipping happily all the pleasures which London society so plentifully afforded. If the influence of the unfashionable aunt persisted, it showed itself rather in the innocent character of his amusements than in any inclination towards a life of devotion.

At Cambridge he had become acquainted with the young William Pitt. They were not of the same college nor of the same year, for Pitt, as a precocious scholar, had gone up ridiculously early; but they were

I

of the same age, and there must have been, from the first, some mutual attraction, for the acquaintance begun in those youthful days was destined to ripen into a lifelong and deeply-felt friendship. Pitt, having gone up earlier, came down earlier, and though nominally reading law in Lincoln's Inn, spent the greater part of his days in the gallery of the House of Commons, waiting till the laggard steps of time should bring him to his majority and give him the right to stand for Parliament. For Pitt's career had long since been settled both by his father's hopes and his own wishes—he was to be Prime Minister.

What lay before Wilberforce was not so clear. There was a family business waiting for him at Hull, if he chose to adopt it; but business rarely holds out great attractions for a rich young man in the heyday of his popularity. Wilberforce meant to follow the fashion, and the fashion for wealthy youngsters of good birth and broad acres was to engage in politics. So Wilberforce, like Pitt, had to fill in the time until he could stand for Parliament; and, like Pitt, he spent long hours in the gallery of the House, serving a silent apprenticeship. In those fresh surroundings the two young men renewed the acquaintance begun at Cambridge, spending most of their days at Westminster and most of their nights in cheerful dinners and dances or in the more exciting atmosphere of political clubs. Pitt was fascinated by Wilberforce's charm, and Wilberforce was swept off his feet by Pitt's dominating personality and the lustre of his father's name. It was as certain as anything could be that when they entered Parliament together, as they meant to do, Wilberforce would be the fidus Achates of his brilliant companion.

II

Pitt reached his majority in May 1780 and Wilberforce three months later. The times were anxious, and, for Pitt at least, a challenge in their confirmation of his father's worst fears. When the year began, England was at war with America, France and Spain, and when it ended, with Holland as well; while the Northern Powers, including Russia, had entered into a league of armed neutrality aimed at her naval supremacy. If foreign affairs were threatening, there was little encouragement at home; Ireland was demanding legislative independence, and in England itself the popular discontent flared up during June into the Gordon Riots, when religious fanaticism whipped the mob into a six-days' orgy of tumult and destruction. The inevitable reaction, when violence had subsided in shame, emboldened North, the Prime Minister, to dissolve Parliament in the hope of being returned to power with an enhanced majority. The general election, thus sprung on the country, took place in September (1780) and Wilberforce, who the month before had returned home to celebrate his coming of age and was already hailed as the local candidate for the future, was triumphantly and unexpectedly early elected the member for Hull. Pitt was not quite so lucky. He had hoped to represent his university, but, unlike Wilberforce, had not been on the spot at the crucial moment enveloped in a rosy haze of congratulations and rejoicing. Cambridge rejected him, but the check was temporary; before the year was out, Sir James Lowther, at the instance of the Duke of Rutland, had placed his pocket borough of Appleby at Pitt's disposal.

The two friends entered Parliament on the verge of a political crisis. During 1780 there had been a series of victories over the colonists in America, but they had merely gone to show how right Pitt's father had been in declaring that it was impossible for England to conquer America by force of arms. English generals might overthrow colonial troops, but they could not overcome the vast spaces of a continent, or for that matter counteract the feebleness of a government which had lost command of the seas. By the end of 1781 Cornwallis, with a French fleet at his back and illimitable miles of unconquerable territory in front, had been starved into surrender at Yorktown, and the war was virtually at an end. It was inevitable that North must go, and in March 1782 Pitt, whose reputation was already made, staked out his claim to office by declaring boldly that if invited to join a new administration, he would not accept a subordinate post. A fortnight later North had resigned, to be succeeded first by Rockingham, and on his death three months later, by Shelburne (July 1782), who maintained a precarious hold on power until April 1783, when he was ousted by a coalition of Fox and North under the nominal premiership of the Duke of Portland, the same Duke of Portland before whom Granville Sharp was in vain to display his shorthand notes of the *Zong* trial.

Rockingham had offered Pitt a subordinate post which, in accordance with his warning, he had refused. Shelburne, with greater perspicacity, had made him Chancellor of the Exchequer. The coalition were eager to win him to their side, but Pitt was too wise to take part in a ministry which, besides being unpopular in the country, bore in itself the obvious seeds of decay. No coalition between a dissolute young Whig and a discredited old Tory could hope to last. Pitt rejected their advances, and being now relieved of office, spent the autumn in a carefree tour on the Continent, with Wilberforce as a companion. Shortly after their return, the coalition was dismissed by the King, and on the 19th of December, 1783, Pitt, still only twenty-four years of age, became Prime Minister. It was a marvellous achievement, but for all his success his position seemed to be hopeless. Not only was he guilty, as his father had been before him, of 'the atrocious crime of being a young man', but with his lack of years and equally evident lack of experience, he had to confront a world of enemies abroad with nothing to help him but a defeated army, a decayed navy and an empty treasury; while at home he had ranged against him an angry and disdainful opposition which enjoyed a large majority, and included in its ranks almost all the eloquence and ministerial ability in the House. His overthrow seemed certain; but relying partly on the King and partly on what he believed to be the popular will, he clung doggedly to office, ignoring one parliamentary defeat after another, until in March 1784 he deemed the time ripe for an appeal to the country. The election succeeded beyond his highest expectations; he was returned with a triumphant majority, to remain in office, with one short interval, until his death some twenty-two years later.

III

During the anxious months preceding the election Wilberforce had been Pitt's mainstay and help; his silvery tongue had been his most powerful support in the House; his loyal devotion a never-failing comfort and beacon of hope. In a very real sense he was Pitt's lieutenant. The country recognized the fact, and as they were determined to elevate Pitt, so they were disposed to honour his lieutenant. At the election, Hull had not seemed sufficiently important. By general acclaim Wilberforce had been chosen to represent the county, and he came back to the House one of the members for Yorkshire, the largest and most powerful county constituency in the kingdom. He was now not only Pitt's close and acknowledged friend, but a marked man in his own right, a rising star in the political firmament. It is easy to understand why the Quaker Committee were so much impressed when Clarkson told them that he was in touch with Wilberforce. If Clarkson could persuade Wilberforce, the personal friend of the Prime Minister, one of the members for Yorkshire, and the obvious choice for future honours and high ministerial rank, to interest himself in the question of slavery, then Clarkson was an acquisition which they could not afford to lose.

But while the committee were in one sense wholly right, in another sense they were happily misled. Wilberforce had returned to Parliament with all the honours and all the reputation which the committee imagined; but, perhaps unknown to himself, his prospects and even his wishes were changing—not of his own volition, nor of the volition of the country, but at the will of fate. There was a subtle psychological difference, one of those differences which can be felt by a sensitive soul but can rarely be explained. Before the election, Pitt's supporters had been few in number, and Wilberforce in throwing himself into the fight on his behalf had been swayed by a feeling of chivalry as well as of friendship. He had experienced the thrill which comes from battling against odds in a just cause. But there was something more; Pitt had not only been a loved comrade, he had also presented the appealing figure of a good man struggling with adversity, and Wilberforce had responded with a double portion of loyal enthusiasm. But Pitt at the head of a triumphant majority presented a different figure altogether, making no demands on chivalry and no appeal from weakness. Wilberforce could not react in quite the same way, nor could he hold quite his former position as Pitt's leading champion; he must now share Pitt with others; he must now take a comparatively back seat, commensurate with his youth and inexperience. That Wilberforce fully appreciated the change is improbable; but there can be little doubt that his enthusiasm did not glow with entirely so white a heat after the election as before, and that very fact gave him a greater measure of freedom to pursue his own destiny.

Into this changed atmosphere there came almost at once, and with ever-increasing intensity the shadow of his coming spiritual conflict. Shortly after his twenty-fifth birthday, in the August of the election year, he happened to run across a certain Isaac Milner who had once been his schoolmaster and since those days had become a distinguished mathematician and a Cambridge don. Wilberforce in his schooldays had admired Milner and now, somewhat older, but with the same warm heart and ineradicable friendliness, he renewed the acquaintance gladly, inviting Milner to join him in a second tour on the Continent which he was busily arranging, this time without Pitt. Milner accepted, and during the winter of 1784 and again in the summer of 1785 he and Wilberforce were constantly together, and as Milner was a deeply religious man, they were as constantly discussing religion. 'By

degrees', Wilberforce wrote long afterwards, 'I imbibed his sentiments, though I must confess with shame that they long remained
merely an opinion assented to by my understanding but not influencing
my heart.' Yet in spite of his later self-reproach, the influence was not
so very tardy. It soon came to oppress and torment him with a feeling
of guilt and sinfulness, as a result of which he passed through several
months of severe mental and spiritual conflict. At last, in December
1785, he turned for help and advice to John Newton, the rector of St.
Mary Woolnoth, and through his ministration was led into the
evangelical fold, there to find rest and that abiding peace which springs
from the assurance of spiritual rebirth. Wilberforce was a new man,
and the career of politics, which had once appeared so dazzling, now
seemed almost a hindrance, distracting him from his preordained work;
for assuredly some task had been allotted to him, a task which he must
discover for himself.

It may have been chance which led Wilberforce to Newton—chance,
Fate's maid-of-all-work—but the chance was significant. Newton was
a tough and rough old character who had tasted life at many points,
and more particularly in the slave trade. After a stormy, and very
unsavoury youth, Newton had found himself captain of a slave ship
and had followed his trade with high enjoyment and good success.
Then had come his conversion. It had opened his heart at once to the
consolations of religion, but had been slow in opening his eyes to the
enormity of his calling. For a time he continued to enslave negroes
with as much zest as he preached to the members of his crew; but
enlightenment came at last, and thereafter he regretted, with robust
sorrow and lurid confessions, his career as an 'old African blasphemer',
and in his eagerness to win souls had thrown up his employment to
become a parson. This was the man who brought balm to Wilberforce's tortured soul, and mere gratitude would have deepened
Wilberforce's interest in all that affected him—his present work and
past life, including those details of his past in which the slave trade
bulked so largely. Inevitably Wilberforce was being guided to his preordained task.

The next step was painful. Wilberforce had to inform not only
sceptical friends but Pitt, that Parliament had no longer the same
attraction; that he felt it incumbent upon him to withdraw from public
life at least until his mind was more settled; and that even if he subse-
quently returned, he could never again be 'so much of a party man'
as he had been before; his outlook must in future be governed by

higher and holier principles. The news worried Pitt; for though he was no longer struggling against a hostile majority, he numbered few men of genius among his supporters, and could ill afford to spare one of his brightest debaters, one of his most persuasive orators. He was more than anxious to keep Wilberforce at his side, and used all his influence to that end. At first, as Wilberforce recorded, 'he tried to reason me out of my convictions'. When that failed, he looked round for some means of harnessing Wilberforce's convictions to a parliamentary end, so that at least he would remain in the House, where he might be expected to give Pitt active support from time to time. An opening was soon offered by Wilberforce himself. Newton's stories and his own earnest but vague aspirations had stirred him up to take an interest in the slave trade; he began to make inquiries into the charges that were being bandied about, inviting to his house anyone who seemed to have first-hand knowledge or could give him reliable information. The setting up of the Quaker Committee lent an element of urgency, and Wilberforce began to discuss the matter with Pitt. That astute states-man saw his chance, and in Wilberforce's own words: 'Pitt recom-mended me to undertake its conduct as a subject suited to my character and talents. At length I well remember, after a conversation in the open air, at the root of an old tree at Holwood, just above the steep descent into the Vale of Keston, I resolved to give notice, on a fit occasion, in the House of Commons, of my intention to bring the matter forward.' The die had been cast.

XV. Conflicting Evidence

I

WHEN PROMISING to help the Quaker Committee, Wilberforce had laid down two conditions—first, that he should retire if a better advocate could be found, and secondly that he must be properly briefed. Pitt had satisfied him on the first point. After the celebrated conversation in Holwood Park, it would have been false modesty to have doubted any longer. But the second point remained. On that it was for the committee to satisfy him, and one would have thought that his obvious course was to become one of their number, so that he could attend their meetings and not only benefit from their deliberations but also guide them by his own parliamentary knowledge. He preferred, however, not to join them. His aloofness was the outcome of a reluctance to burn his boats. Nor was it unreasonable. It could very plausibly be argued that from the purely parliamentary point of view his advocacy would carry greater weight if he appeared to act as an independent man speaking from the heart rather than as the representative of a society speaking to a brief. Possibly also Pitt had some influence. It was of importance to him that Wilberforce should not become too absorbed in the work of outside bodies, which might in the end lure him away from politics altogether—a consummation which Pitt did not care to contemplate. Whatever the reason, Wilberforce held himself apart, looking to the committee for information rather than for inspiration. The committee were content; and on the understanding that he was to be their mouthpiece rather than their direct representative in Parliament, set themselves to consider what exactly they wished him to advocate. As already recorded, they came to the conclusion that there were 'two evils quite distinct from each other', slavery and the slave trade, and that it was expedient for them to attack the latter alone. Their decision was certainly wrong. So far from being distinct, the two evils were vitally interconnected, and of the two slavery was by far the more important. Without slavery, the trade must inevitably die; but so long as slavery existed, the trade could not be abolished; it would continue in one form or another, if only as a flourishing black market. The decision was not only wrong in fact, but at variance with the committee's fundamental aim; and certainly it embarrassed Wilberforce's advocacy.

II

But whether right or wrong, the decision had one advantage. Wilberforce needed powder and shot, and in England it would clearly be easier to track down the shortcomings of the trader than to unveil the evils of slavery; the trade had its headquarters in London, Bristol and Liverpool, while slavery could be studied at first hand only in Africa and America.

The task of collecting the evidence was entrusted to Clarkson. The choice was excellent; Clarkson was as eager as he was indefatigable. But he had his drawbacks. There were two in particular, his excessive emotionalism and a flaw in his sense of proportion which led him to waste too much time on matters of lesser importance. He set out on his travels in June 1787, and did not return till the following November. In those five months he covered the whole western side of England, visiting all the big towns and cities from Bristol to Liverpool, as well as Manchester and Birmingham in the Midlands. He had no difficulty in getting information of sorts. Bristol and Liverpool in particular were full of gossip about the trade on which they battened. But the inhabitants were less disposed to give incriminating details than to gloat over the rising prosperity of their towns, though they could also enlarge on particular complaints of their friends and relations. Clarkson found that their gossip was either hearsay or irrelevant; solid, first-hand evidence of the type he required was singularly hard to obtain.

Worse still, such information as he could get, lured him into by-paths which he was too ready to regard as highways. Almost from the start he found himself investigating, not the slave trade, but the treatment of the sailors engaged in it. They were often very shockingly treated, and Clarkson was correspondingly distressed. He began to delve into their conditions of service, and by a laborious examination of muster-rolls, discovered that the rates of death and desertion among the crews of slave ships were much the highest of any class of merchant vessel. Here, Clarkson felt, was a complete answer to the statement sometimes made that the slave trade was an excellent nursery for seamen. So far from being an excellent nursery, the figures made it only too clear that, possibly the nature of the trade and certainly the epidemics which swept through the overcrowded decks, led to an excessive and wholly unnecessary wastage of England's maritime population. Whatever the explanation—and on that point Clarkson made no inquiry—there was no disputing the fact; and as it was his own discovery, Clarkson became absorbed in it. During his five-months' tour, he traced the fortunes of no less than twenty thousand seamen, a work of manifest supererogation.

In his researches, he penetrated into all the low haunts where sailors were in the habit of congregating, and watched with horror the various processes by which incautious young men were entrapped. He listened with pained sympathy to any sailorman with a tale of harsh treatment, and from time to time was so moved that he instituted proceedings against a captain or mate on behalf of the oppressed victim—proceedings which the captain or mate generally avoided by a voluntary payment of damages. It is not surprising that he became an object of dislike to masters and of suspicion to owners, and that promising sources of information had a curious habit of suddenly running dry. Nor could he complain if opponents such as Francklyn wrote disparagingly of 'the reverend author who, in the different masks of an African sailor and a pettifogging attorney, is said to have visited the alehouses and brothels of Liverpool, to find out witnesses to the enormities committed by the masters of Guinea ships' (Francklyn, p. IX); for that after all was what had mostly engaged his attention.

He uncovered a multiplicity of abuses, and heard numerous stories of violence, swindling and cruelty—how young men were decoyed by prostitutes and rascally publicans; how they were carried off dead drunk to the ships, and bounced into signing articles of agreement without reading them; how they were offered seemingly attractive wages, only to be defrauded by payment in foreign currency; how they were flogged unmercifully on board; and how they were sometimes done to death. The stories harrowed his over-sensitive feelings, and indeed were sad enough as pictures of human depravity; but they had little to do with the slave trade as such. Similar stories could be told of other merchant ships or, for that matter, of the Royal Navy itself with its press-gangs and crimps. The sea in all its features was a hard and brutal mistress in the eighteenth century, and if the slave trade stood pre-eminent in devilish practices, its pre-eminence was still only a matter of degree. So far as the fortunes of the crews were concerned, the true answer to their distresses was not to abolish the slave trade, but to humanize the conditions.

The same conclusion was largely true of Clarkson's other discoveries. When he managed to turn his mind from the crews to the slaves, he proceeded with the same meticulous care, measuring the space allotted to the slave cargo in individual ships and examining the records to discover the numbers actually carried. From these figures he was able to prove that the overcrowding was at least at times wholly iniquitous; the slaves were barely able to lie down and often could only sit in a crouching position. The picture was horrifying enough, and Clarkson did his best to enhance the horror by collecting specimens of the shackles, handcuffs and thumb-screws used in the ships, which added a visual and sinister meaning to his array of statistics.

But here again, while he was certainly providing material to condemn the methods, he failed to prove that there was any essential connection between the methods and the trade. Reform was clearly desirable; but need it go as far as abolition? The link was missing between what was done and what it was necessary to do; for the overcrowding, even if usual, was not universal. Nor was sufficient thought given to the reasons for the brutalities. However much they might be to the perverted taste of individual captains, they had their roots in the fact that the cargoes consisted of slaves who were kicking against captivity and eager to escape. Hence the shackles and bolts! Hence the rigorous confinement! The captain was taking proper care of his cargo. Had the slaves been willing emigrants, the harshness would have been unnecessary and might have been expected to vanish. It was not the trade, but the status which needed abolition. The trade, after all, was no more than a shipping agency, while the status was, or should have been, a slur on humanity. Clarkson overlooked the fact, and in his anxiety to abide by his committee's ruling, almost went out of his way to assure more thoughtful inquirers that emancipation was no part of his plan (Clarkson I, 347).

But if he thus deliberately shut his eyes to the glaring iniquity of slavery, he never forgot the merchants or their claims, both moral and financial, and tried to placate, if not convert them by providing alternative uses for their ships. He conceived the idea of substituting an honest trade in goods for the dishonest traffic in slaves, and with that in view spent much time and effort in collecting specimens of African products—gums, cotton, indigo, musk, pepper, mahogany, cloth and dyes. It was very well meant, but unfortunately his zeal was divorced from experience. The specimens he collected added nothing to the merchants' knowledge; he discovered no type of trade that was not already established, nor could he show any means by which it might be increased. His efforts were well-meaning but infructuous.

Yet if the evidence which Clarkson collected was more voluminous than valuable, he had not been wasting his time. In the course of his travels he had done one thing of quite outstanding importance, one thing which if rightly handled might well have resulted in immediate and overwhelming victory. He had been supremely successful as a propagandist, rousing the inhabitants of the towns and great cities through which he had passed. They were now taking a decisive interest in the question of slavery; associations for the abolition of the trade were springing up all over the country, and petitions were beginning to flow into Parliament. The measure of Clarkson's success is to be seen in the growing fears of the opposition. At the outset they had, after the fashion of Boswell, smiled contemptuously at what they regarded as the fuss made by a few negligible fanatics; but now they were alarmed in earnest. They began to gather their forces together for a counter-attack, very conscious of the need for a strong and effective propaganda on their own behalf. Clarkson had undoubtedly roused the country.

III

The mounting public interest made it clear that the time had come to raise the question in Parliament. Clarkson was summoned back to London, and in November (1787) laid the results of his efforts before the committee, and especially before Wilberforce and Pitt. He did so in great detail, and being kindly treated, was disposed to think that he had briefed them well and truly. They were grateful for his work from which, indeed, they profited; but they also realized that it was insufficient. Much more would be wanted, if the attack in Parliament was to be successful. 'We begin', wrote Wilberforce sadly, 'to perceive more difficulties in the way than we had hoped there would be.' The opponents were mustering in all the strength which money and vested interests can provide, while the reformers could not but feel that, even with Pitt's support, their ranks were sadly lacking in weight. The three protagonists—Clarkson, Wilberforce and Pitt—were all still in their twenties. How could they hope to overcome an evil so enormous and so deeply entrenched? Youth, if it be well-intentioned, is a time of generous enthusiasms, but it can also be timid and hesitating, and in this case youth had shown itself more cautious than age.

The only one of the committee to advocate emancipation in the widest sense was Granville Sharp, the 'father' of the movement, while Clarkson, Wilberforce and Pitt confined themselves deliberately to the smaller issue of the trade.

Pitt and Wilberforce were no doubt influenced by considerations of a public nature—the duties of their position, their responsibilities to their constituents, their knowledge of Parliament's likely reaction. Clarkson had no such curbs; in his case there seems to have been a trace of inherent weakness which at times sapped his resolution. No doubt the adventures which he met with in the course of his travels and which he relates with modest satisfaction, were more daunting than any to be met with in parliamentary debates; but even amongst friends he did not always present a very bold front. Sarah Fox, that calm and clear-eyed lady, has left in her diaries a revealing picture of him among the Quakers of Bristol: 'The beginning of this month', she wrote, 'we had a visit from Clarkson. . . . His person was agreeable, his address modest and manly, neither eager to talk nor affectedly silent. Yet I thought he seemed oppressed with the weight of the good work which now brought him to Bristol. At the entrance of a person whom he believed to be no friend to the Abolition, he was almost wholly silent' (*Diary*, Vol. II, p. 5).

It was no doubt in part this natural timidity which induced him to emphasize the committee's decision not to touch the question of emancipation; but it was a pity, because it confirmed him in a wrong decision, and was wholly unnecessary for his purpose. The people at large drew no distinction between abolition and emancipation. When they spoke of abolishing the slave trade, they meant, quite simply, abolishing slavery. The method and the difficulties were not present to their mind. 'To me,' wrote Sarah Fox, 'the subject of the slave trade is attended with effects which make great inroads on my peace, and even on my rest; yet I trust the time is not far distant when the same gracious Power who has been pleased to employ so many instruments in their service, will enable them to accomplish the glorious work of their deliverance'; and by deliverance she most certainly meant something more than the suppression of the slave merchant.

Wilberforce and Pitt were more analytical, though when it came to arguments in debate, they were as apt as Sarah Fox to confuse the status and the trade. In these early days, however, they kept the two well apart, and they both recognized that the evidence which Clarkson had collected, excellent and conclusive as it was in its own limited sphere, was not sufficient for their purpose. The opposition in Parliament would take their stand on wider issues of national importance. They would undoubtedly argue that slaves were essential for the prosperity of the West Indies; and if there must be slaves, then there must also be a slave trade. Parliament could control that trade only in part, and to abolish England's share in it would merely throw the door wide open to foreign ships and foreign merchants. The negroes would be no better treated; the brutalities would probably be worse; the profits would certainly go abroad; and beyond doubt the cost of slaves would rise. The prosperity of the West Indies was at stake. If they were ruined, it was impossible to foretell the effect on England, on the City, on the thriving towns of Bristol and Liverpool, on the many industries that went to create and sustain the merchant marine; and not least on the supply of rum for the navy, and sugar for the ordinary citizen. There would be a tidal wave of disaster, overthrowing so much that was now prosperous and happy, and sending out ripples to disturb and agitate unnumbered and unknown creeks and backwaters. The whole country from one end to the other would suffer.

Pitt recognized the force which such an argument would have in Parliament. It would carry tremendous weight, especially at a time when the loss of the American colonies was fresh in men's minds, and when Canada was in the turmoil of absorbing and re-settling the dispossessed loyalists streaming up from the States. If on top of these losses and problems, disaster were to fall on the islands, England's prospects in the New World would be poor indeed. Any step which threatened their stability must be examined with more than ordinary care, and the claims and arguments of the planters treated with a circumspection commensurate with their importance. Unless they could be convincingly refuted, they must be, and they would be, accepted as final and conclusive.

Pitt was being driven from a moral to a material standpoint, perhaps against his will, for it was at this very moment that he wrote 'if the principle of humanity and justice on which the whole rests, is in any degree compromised, the cause is in a manner given up' (Pitt to Eden, 7th January, 1788. Auckland Correspondence I, 304). Yet the line of attack which had been chosen was driving both him and Wilberforce irresistibly along the path of material values. They were becoming entangled in a web of details which were contradictory in themselves, open to refutation, often irrelevant, and certain to breed doubts. The further they plunged into this quagmire of conflicting evidence, the more they were in danger of losing touch with the common people, whose massive support was founded entirely on moral grounds, and who responded far more readily to tales of cruelty than to economic theories. Yet this change of emphasis on Pitt's part was inevitable if the fight was to be over the slave trade and not the slave. Trade meant facts and figures; slavery meant bodies and souls.

IV

When Clarkson's contribution had proved insufficient, Pitt turned for help to Ramsay, that other warm advocate for the slaves. Ramsay, who was an honest, an able, and in many ways a moderate man, had much to tell him from first-hand knowledge, but it was couched in a form extremely irritating to the planters. He recognized, and said, that many of them were kindly masters, and that the brutalities were more often than not the work of agents, particularly young agents. But he also declared roundly that the planters did not know their own business or what was good for them. 'Never', he said, 'was national property more absurdly laid out' (Questions, etc. Ramsay Papers, p. 41 ff. Rhodes House Collection), and it was from this absurdity that most of the evils arose.

He offered them advice on the whole range of their activities, advice which was no doubt sound enough, but which was made unpalatable by his open contempt for their capacity. The existing practice, he said, 'has been long established, and requires an effort to break through it of which I know few planters capable' (Observations, etc. Ramsay Papers, p. 34). According to him, 'almost every small plantation, and perhaps more than half of all the sugar plantations do not support themselves and pay the interest money now due upon them'. Their bankrupt condition sprang partly out of the method of cultivation and partly out of the number and cost of the slaves. 'If', he wrote, 'planters will turn their useless domestics into the field, will buy up the slaves of poor white people, will throw out of culture all such cane land as pays not for the tillage, which . . . is above a quarter of the whole; if instead of pretending to feed their slaves with grain purchased from North America or Europe, they will cultivate island provisions for them; if they will supply their cattle with artificial grass, then half the present number of slaves may send more than the present produce to market' (Questions, etc. Ramsay Papers).

The planters could hardly be expected to change their methods so completely and so immediately on the advice of a man who had never been a planter himself. Nor were they likely to accept his financial arguments. Ramsay was rash enough to indulge in figures, and proved to his own satisfaction that the purchase of slaves was uneconomic. His estimates purported to show that on the purchase of six slaves, the annual loss, after 'seasoning', was £99. Even he was staggered at what he had proved. 'I am well aware', he admitted, 'that a person not acquainted with the West Indies will with difficulty be brought to believe in such a calculation. I cannot help it,' he added as he hurried on to his remedy. The planters, he argued, should not buy slaves but breed them. There was nothing to prevent such a course but the disproportion of the sexes, which was not inevitable but sprang out of the avarice and inhumanity of the planters, who thought it cheaper and easier to buy the ready-made article from the dealer and work it to death, than to undertake the toil and expense of raising and training a brood of children on their own estates. Whether or not such evidence was likely to convince the House, it was certainly calculated to annoy the planters. They were far more bitter against Ramsay than they had ever been against Clarkson; for Clarkson had stressed their cruelties but Ramsay their absurdities, and it is more hurtful to be called a fool than a villain.

What from Pitt's angle was more disturbing was that Ramsay's evidence did not altogether tally with Clarkson's. Clarkson had harped on the overcrowding of the ships; so had the committee; the most telling piece of propaganda which they ever produced was a pictured plan purporting to show how the slaves were stowed between the decks: 'the print', said Clarkson, 'seemed to make an instantaneous impression of horror upon all who saw it' (Clarkson II, 111). But Ramsay was by no means consenting. He agreed that in general the ships were fitted out for excessive numbers, but went on to say that the number actually carried depended on what the ships found when they arrived in Africa. The barracoons were not necessarily full; the raids were not necessarily successful; the dealers might be short of stock and the captains unwilling, for whatever reason, to loiter off the coast long enough to complete their cargo. So long as the trade was brisk and slaves were offered in great numbers, overcrowding undoubtedly did take place, but at other times overcrowding was by no means general; on the contrary it was quite common for slave ships to carry fewer than their allotted numbers (Ramsay Papers, p. 66).

Clarkson, again, laid great emphasis on the deaths and desertions among the crews and the harsh treatment they received; the trade, according to him, was unhealthy and a dead loss to the maritime population. Ramsay's picture was different. He pointed out that slave ships carried more hands than other vessels. In addition to the crew, they signed on men whose only job it was to round up the slaves. These were the men who mainly suffered in health since in their search for their prey they had to row in open boats at night on malarial rivers and pestilential swamps. But as soon as the slaves had been rounded up and safely stowed on board, their work was done and they became supernumeraries. The captain was eager to get rid of them 'by any means in his power, ill-treatment, picking a quarrel, giving opportunities for desertion'. In other respects 'the trade was not remarkably unhealthy' (Ramsay Papers, p. 26). So said Ramsay. Not that he wished to weaken Clarkson's evidence, but that, in spite of his protestations, what lay nearest to his heart was emancipation not abolition, and he was a little afraid of the outcome of a campaign for abolition alone. He uttered a much-needed warning: 'great caution', he said, 'will be necessary in wording the bill, lest while attempting to improve the state of slaves, the legislature acquiesce in, and acknowledge, slavery' (Note for Lord Hawkesbury. Ramsay Papers, p. 27). He, like the people at large, wanted to free the slave, not merely to suppress the trade.

It is not surprising that Pitt grew cautious. He knew that his Cabinet were not unanimous in support and that the King was on the whole opposed. For that reason, if no other, he could not make abolition a Government measure; and if it was to be left to an open vote, some more positive evidence was essential. Pitt believed, or at least hoped, that it could be obtained, and for that purpose early in 1788 instructed the Privy Council to inquire into, and report upon, the conditions of British commercial intercourse with Africa. At the same time he told Wilberforce that he must hold his hand.

XVI. The Struggle in Parliament

I

WILBERFORCE, being more concerned with morals than politics, had hoped to introduce a motion into Parliament early in 1788, but when Pitt assured him that nothing could be done until the Privy Council had made their report, he agreed to hold his hand—reluctantly, one must suppose; for it was one more step in the wrong direction, a step towards the arid argumentation of Parliament and away from the instinctive reaction of public opinion. As though Fate meant to emphasize his mistake, Wilberforce had no sooner agreed to delay than his health began to fail. Throughout February and March he grew weaker and weaker from intestinal troubles, and the doctors more helpless and hopeless. They expected him to die, and wishing to avoid responsibility, ordered him to Bath to drink the waters. In no way deceived by their manœuvre, and imagining that he was going to his last home, Wilberforce solemnly bequeathed his mission to Pitt, entreating him to move the motion which he was himself no longer capable of doing, and to carry on to victory the cause which filled his heart and mind. Pitt promised, and buoyed up by that promise,

Wilberforce went down to Bath—to die, as he thought; to be snatched from death, as it proved, by doses of opium, which he swallowed with reluctant horror as smacking too much of sin, too little of medicine.

Pitt had promised and no doubt meant to abide by his word, but the 'cause' was already showing signs of being 'bound in shallows'. The report of the Privy Council was slow in arriving; and it soon became obvious to Pitt, as he told the impatient Granville Sharp, that no effective action could be taken till the next year. The best he could do at the moment was to exact a promise from the House that at least they would consider the matter early in the next session. He did so on the 9th May (1788) in a short and deliberately tepid speech, reserving his opinion as he said for the full debate. The House promised, as he wished, but the delay was doubly unfortunate; it allowed time for the ferment in the country to subside; it allowed time for the trade to consolidate its opposition; it allowed time for the slaves, on rumours of what was happening in England, to grow restive and menacing and so breed doubts in English minds; and perhaps worst of all, it allowed time for the cause to be prejudiced by the actions of well-meaning but short-sighted supporters.

Among the Members of Parliament who had been profoundly moved by what they had heard, was Sir William Dolben, member for Oxford University. He boarded one of the slave ships to see for himself, and was so horrified at what he saw that he was not content to wait till the next session; he must strike a blow at once, and accordingly introduced a Bill into Parliament under which the number of slaves who could be carried in a ship was to be proportioned to the tonnage. Though the bill was only of temporary application, the trade naturally opposed it; they had no wish to be regulated in any way or for any period; but they were not seriously perturbed. As Ramsay had pointed out, overcrowding was by no means universal, and some slight restriction on the numbers would probably have little or no effect on the profits. What they must do was to see that the proportion allowed was as high as they could get it. Although, therefore, the trade made a fuss and in doing so stirred Pitt up to a vigorous denunciation, the Bill was passed without trouble. The results, however, were not so happy, for while the benefit to the slaves was small and the curb on the traders slight, the effect on public opinion was harmful. The people at large had petitioned Parliament, and Parliament had responded. Whether the steps they had taken were right or wrong, sufficient or insufficient, was hardly a matter for the man in the street; he was not an expert; he was not master of the facts. Presumably Parliament had done what was needed, and now that action had been taken by the authorities, the man in the street could put the matter out of his mind. The more thoughtful and the more compassionate might still have had doubts, but in general Dolben's Bill tended to water down the effects of Clarkson's propaganda.

II

On the 9th of May (1788), Pitt had been studiously non-committal, feeling himself bound for political and parliamentary reasons to confine himself to the trade. Others had felt freer, and basing themselves on moral grounds had urged that Parliament ought to go further and abolish slavery as well as the trade. With a generous disdain for half measures, Fox argued that 'a cold-hearted policy was folly when it opposed the great principles of humanity and justice'; and Burke, treading close on his heels, declared that not only was the slave trade directly contrary to the spirit of the British Constitution, but that 'the state of slavery which followed it, however mitigated, was a state so improper, so degrading, and so ruinous to the feelings and capacities of human nature, that it ought not to be suffered to exist'. They were expressing the sentiments of the common people. 'What compensation', cried a back-bencher, 'could be made to the slaves for being torn from their nearest relations and from everything that was dearest to them in life?' That same feeling was predominant when, the next month, Dolben introduced his Bill.

The demand for emancipation was a natural, an inevitable, extension of the abolition of the trade, and indeed it represented the object which the Quaker Committee had originally had in mind. It frightened the trade far more than Dolben's Bill, more even than the threat of abolition—for abolition after all could be reversed; but there was a finality about emancipation which precluded the hope of revival. Yet, frightened as they were, they thought, on reflection, that they might snatch an advantage out of this apparent cleavage of opinion and confuse the issue by driving a wedge between the abolitionists and the emancipators. With this in view they accused the Quaker Committee of a secret design to abolish slavery, declaring that, unlike Fox and his more extravagant followers, the committee were not being honest and were libelling the trade, not because the trade was bad, but in order to further a disruptive policy which would ruin the West Indies; the whole question must be examined, not in the light of nonsensical stories about cruelties in Africa and the horrors of the middle passage, but of the prosperity and even the continued existence of the West Indian colonies.

The committee fell into the trap so cunningly laid; they felt it incumbent on them to make some answer, yet were embarrassed to know what they could honestly say. In the end they issued a public notice repudiating the design with which they were charged. Their repudiation was in accord with the assurances that Clarkson had given freely and Ramsay with hesitation, but in essence it was at least a *suggestio falsi*. Worse still, it served to diminish the popular interest; for the people's object was to put an end to slavery, and they could only feel confused at what seemed to them to be fine-drawn distinctions without much meaning. They were disappointed, too, at Pitt's tepid speech on the 9th of May, believing that if he had moved for the immediate abolition of the trade, he would have carried his point with acclaim. Inevitably their interest dwindled. The traders had won a distinct victory, and pressed on exultantly with their preparations to win a further and final victory when the matter next came before Parliament.

III

In the face of their onslaught and in the absence of Wilberforce, the reformers were discouraged and hesitant, but in October (1788) Wilberforce returned from Bath to infuse fresh life into the campaign. Though no one could call him robust, he had recovered some measure of health, and he was ready and willing to squander that measure in promoting the good of the cause, but he had to await the appearance of the Privy Council's Report. When it was published, in April 1789, it proved to be a factual document, making no recommendations and adding little or nothing to the existing body of knowledge; but with its appearance Wilberforce felt able to introduce his motion, which he did on the 12th of May (1789).

His speech of three-and-a-half-hours, was at once a reasoned indictment of the trade, based on the evidence given before the Privy Council, and an eloquent appeal to the hearts and consciences of his hearers, demanding the total abolition of the trade in the name of humanity, morals and religion. The speech was highly praised—indeed it deserved praise—and was weightily supported by Burke, Pitt and Fox.

But it came too late; the fatal delay of over a year had given the trade too long a start. Their representatives in the House were well primed, and the other members, anxious to do right but bemused by propaganda and without government guidance, were uneasy and uncertain; there was so much conflicting evidence on either side; so great a risk to the empire; so troublesome a doubt about the economic consequences; so obvious a possibility of doing injustice to the planters. In their perplexity they jumped at a way of escape offered by one of the members who asked whether it was not a surrender of their privileges to accept evidence given before the Privy Council which should have been given direct to Parliament. The point was purely technical and not good even at that; but it did offer a way of escape, and the House with genuine relief decided to preserve their privileges intact, and to hear the evidence for themselves early in the next session. So the matter was shelved for another year; and in a burst of relief, and perhaps to quiet uneasy consciences, the members passed without further ado a Bill presented by Dolben to amend and continue his temporary act of the year before.

IV

Though Wilberforce had not succeeded, his efforts had not been entirely wasted; he had learnt something of the opposition's arguments, which he now set to work to counter. One of their strongest points had been the possibility, which they magnified into an undeniable fact, that if England withdrew from the trade, other nations would take it up. Both Wilberforce and Pitt had long foreseen this argument and as early as November 1787 had taken some steps to arm themselves against it. They had asked William Eden, our Ambassador at Paris, to sound the French Government on 'the idea of the two nations agreeing to discontinue the villainous traffic now carried on in Africa' (Pitt to Eden, 2nd November, 1787. Auckland Papers I, 266). But the reply had not been encouraging; the French Government, like the English, preferred to hold itself aloof. The Government, however, did not speak for the whole nation; there were high-minded Frenchmen who were inclined to sympathize, and indeed took some active steps. Early in 1788 a number of influential persons founded La Société des Amis des Noirs, with the avowed object of abolishing, not merely the slave trade, but slavery itself. If they thus differed from the English committee in the extent of their aims, they differed also in the motives which impelled them to action. They were infected with that enthusiasm for humanity which in the first flush of the French Revolution swept, bright and dazzling, over the whole country, intent on discarding the past and making all things new, but which, in the gruelling test of reality, too soon fell from its lofty ideals into a quagmire of cruelty and self-seeking. The aspirations of Les Amis rested on too frail a foundation; they had no prospect of passing from wishes to fulfilment. It was different with the English committee. They were inspired, not by the lure of novel and nebulous abstractions, but by the spirit of Christianity which had endured for eighteen hundred years, and had taught them to love, not humanity, but their neighbour. Its foundations might be overlaid, but could never be shaken.

Wilberforce, rebuffed but not discouraged, now decided to try again; and as soon as the House had risen, sent Clarkson over to France, in the hope that he might succeed where Eden had failed. But Clarkson, the big, blundering Clarkson, so noble in his intentions, so laborious in his efforts, was destined to raise difficulties rather than allay them. For a time he enjoyed a pleasant feeling of importance while he was being invited into great houses and petted by the ladies of high society, and still more when the King showed an interest in his mission by graciously accepting copies of his pamphlets. But France in the second half of 1789 was a dangerous place; the ferment of the revolution was stirring, and it needed a less simple soul than Clarkson's to ride the coming storm. Clarkson was temperamentally a wishful thinker, too easily misled by appearance. He believed, because he wanted to believe, that the National Assembly meant what they said when they declared the French colonial slaves to be free; and had no doubt that they would receive into their ranks the deputies, all coloured freed men, who had come from San Domingo to demand equality with the whites for themselves, and some present amelioration in the status of slaves.

But all went awry. Clarkson's approach to the National Assembly, discreet as it was, merely roused the enmity of the French planters; and his open friendship with the coloured deputies bred ugly suspicions. The rumour went round, no doubt deliberately inspired, that he was an English agent, endeavouring, under a cloak of humanity, to increase England's share of the slave trade at the expense of France. France should not allow herself to be deceived, but should draw the right conclusion from the fact that in spite of all her highfalutin talk about the righteousness and morality of abolition, England had not herself taken the smallest step to advance it. As ever, France must beware of *perfide Albion*. The attitude of the National Assembly stiffened towards both Clarkson, the deputies and the slaves; and Clarkson was told brusquely that if England wanted France to abolish the trade, she must first give unequivocal proof of her own intentions. As Pitt felt unable to make abolition a Government measure, no such proof was forthcoming. The Assembly regarded their suspicions as justified, and any hope there might have been of a change of heart was dashed when the coloured deputies, returning angry and frustrated to their own country, gave vent to their wrath by precipitating a servile rebellion. Clarkson's mission was more than a failure in France, and soon proved to be a source of offence in England; for on returning, he forgot his rebuff and remembered only the heart-warming slogans of liberty, equality and fraternity, and by harping upon them laid both himself and the 'cause' open to a charge of Jacobinism at the very moment when England was turning with horror and loathing from the excesses across the Channel. However undeserved the charge, it was a godsend to the planters.

v

Towards the end of 1789 Parliament began to hear through its own ears the evidence it had already heard through the report of the Privy Council. But the process was slow and laborious and no one could have been surprised if the 'cause' had been lost through sheer boredom. So indeed the opposition hoped; for delay was now their policy. Before long, however, Wilberforce, alive to the danger, persuaded the House to transfer the taking of evidence to a Select Committee, sitting continuously and open to any member who cared to attend.

Yet in spite of everything, progress continued to be desperately slow. The evidence for the trade was well organized and voluminous, though flat to a degree. They had no wish to make it flamboyant, designing it less to give enlightenment than to smother in advance any possible reform. The witnesses were marshalled in groups, each hammering at its own particular point, with monotonous and uniform regularity. The governors of the 'forts' dealt with the African at home. One after another they declared that he was uncivilized, indolent and lazy, and had no calling he could follow with benefit to himself or the world, except slavery. In Africa slaves were to be found everywhere; they were the only merchandise, the only currency; they passed from owner to owner, and on their own admission preferred a white to a black master. How they became slaves, who could tell? No one had penetrated more than a few miles from the coast, but it was generally accepted that they were criminals or debtors or prisoners of war.

The governors were followed by the captains and surgeons of slave ships who spoke of the middle passage. The slaves were brought on board, generally in irons, by native traders; they were treated well, they were given plenty of food, they were allowed exercise and reasonable amusement. Maybe at times their quarters were overcrowded, but they preferred to lie close together in order to keep warm. On the whole their health was good, though, of course, in such a mass of degraded humanity some were bound to be diseased; and epidemics could occasionally break out, especially if the ships were held up on a fever-laden coast. When any fell ill, every attention was paid to them; they were given special food, and even wine, and lodged in the captain's cabin by way of a sick-bay. As for the crews, the greatest mortality occurred among the landsmen who were signed on simply to look after the slaves; they were not themselves sailors, nor seasoned to the climate; on the contrary they were often 'the very dregs and outcasts of the community' (*Observations on the Project of abolishing the Slave Trade*, p. 19). No one need be surprised if their record of health was indifferent. It was true that seamen also were occasionally lost, but more usually in the West Indies than on the voyage. In the islands they were exposed to all manner of temptations, and in particular were lured by the prospect of higher pay to desert the African for the West India ship on the run home.

After the captains came an impressive group of admirals, who, remarkably, had never seen any sign of the ill-treatment of slaves while they had been on the West India station; on the contrary, with striking unanimity, they declared that they had often envied the slaves their carefree happy existence. Beside this testimonial to the humanity of the planters and the advantages of slavery, the admirals expressed, with some vehemence, their belief that the trade was of the utmost import-ance to the country as a nursery for seamen and a source of recruits for the Royal Navy, which had only too often to operate in West Indian waters.

Hitherto the witnesses had been weighty rather for their numbers and rank than for their facts and figures. But there was at least one witness of a different calibre. George Hibbert was a London merchant, engaged in the West India trade, and well qualified to voice the alarm and uncertainty felt in the City. Had his firm, he said, ever imagined that the slave trade would be abolished, they would certainly not have made the great advances to planters which in fact they had made. So far from expecting abolition, the City had looked on the trade as particularly safe, sanctioned as it had been by a long and impressive series of Acts of Parliament. He enumerated fifteen such Acts extending from the time of Charles II to the time of George III, the central feature of which had been a determination to support and encourage the sugar colonies as highly advantageous to England. Nor was that attitude surprising when the figures were considered. In the last year for which returns were available, the value of imports from the West Indies to Great Britain had amounted to nearly five and a half million pounds, while the value of exports from Great Britain to the West Indies had been over a million and a half. All that weight of trade had been built up on a foundation of slavery. If it was to be retained and expanded, there must be an average annual import of slaves to the number of fifteen or sixteen thousand, who at £35 a head represented well over half a million pounds.

Nor was that all; the trade which provided the slaves gave employment to a total of twenty-one thousand seamen, serving in 1,815 vessels of a capacity of 242,000 tons. The grand total of England's interest in the trade was in the neighbourhood of seven million pounds. So far as the City was concerned, abolition could only result in shaking the credit of those merchants, by no means a small number, who had engaged at all deeply in the West India trade; they would be obliged, however unwillingly, to press their debtors in the colonies and even to foreclose on mortgages. Plantations would have to be sold, and their value would be adversely affected by the amount of property thus thrown on the market. The flourishing trade which had been built up over so many years and had brought so much wealth to England's coffers would run a serious risk of decay and extinction.

From the national point of view the evidence of the City and the admirals was impressive, and was given additional weight by warnings that other nations—France in particular—were watching with undisguised interest the progress of the campaign in England; they were anticipating the recession of England's share of the trade, and were already preparing to extend their own commitments. Mingled with these semi-patriotic pleas were various titbits of information intended to checkmate in advance any possible plans for reform. Breeding, which the reformers advocated with such confidence, had been tried and had failed; it was ruled out, as a scheme of general application, by a disproportion of the sexes, due, not to any unwillingness on the part of the planters to buy female slaves, but to the fact that they were in short supply, no doubt owing to the polygamy practised in Africa. A further, and possibly more compelling, reason was the licentiousness of the female slaves, their proneness to venereal disease and their indifference to their children, which together with the prevalence of 'jaw-fall' and other tropical maladies led to a high rate of infant mortality. Even if, contrary to expectations, breeding could keep up existing numbers, it could not supply the labour required for new plantations, nor could it be expected to repair the sudden and heavy losses occasioned by the not uncommon incidence of epidemics and physical calamities. What, too, of the gap while the children were growing to manhood? During that interval, the older slaves would be dying off in the course of nature, and either the plantations would fall out of cultivation or a dwindling group of slaves would be worked harder than ever. It was only too probable that they would rise in despair at the prospect, and would massacre the whites. There had been rebellions for lesser causes.

Against this weight of testimony, what could Wilberforce offer? Of himself of course, nothing; he looked to the committee, who looked to Clarkson. That indefatigable man, suddenly recalled from France, set to work at once and was able to trace a number of persons who could and did tell him tales of horror; but, unfortunately, they told their tales in private and were very reluctant to repeat them in public. Nor was it surprising. Captains and mates were not anxious to quarrel with what had been, and might again be, their bread and butter, nor did they like telling tales out of school. Surgeons, equally, had no wish to annoy their clients, often their best clients—the rich West India merchants or the shipowners living in the big mansions of Liverpool and Bristol. As for the common sailors, they could be hurried away to sea by the traders and even when available did not carry much weight. It was on this occasion that Clarkson performed his best-known feat, that of tracking down a naval rating without knowing his name, address or whereabouts. The only clues he had were a hint that the man was serving in a ship laid up 'in ordinary' somewhere on the south coast, and that he had once been heard to say that he had accompanied a native expedition on a raid to collect slaves. That was enough for Clarkson; too little was known for certain about these raids, and here was a man who seemed to have first-hand knowledge; he must be found. Armed with a permit to board naval vessels which he obtained from Sir Charles Middleton (afterwards Lord Barham), Clarkson started at Deptford and worked through all the ports as far as Plymouth. There in the 317th ship which he had visited, he found the man for whom he was looking. The trouble he took is eloquent of his thoroughness, but perhaps still more eloquent of the paucity of useful evidence which he was able to secure.

VI

At last the evidence on both sides was completed, and on the 18th of April, 1791, Wilberforce moved for leave to bring in his Bill for the immediate abolition of the slave trade. He spoke earnestly and eloquently, basing his arguments on the evidence which the House had been hearing for so many months, and denouncing with vigour and deep feeling the cruelties in Africa and the horrors of the middle passage. But, being hampered by the decision to press only for the abolition of the trade, he had to touch with a lighter hand on the miseries which the slaves endured in the plantations. True, he dwelt on their unhappy fate and the degradation which, he said, must result from a system of slavery; but he was precluded from drawing the obvious conclusion. Instead, he had to emphasize that emancipation was not his aim, admitting that the slaves were not yet ripe for freedom, and tacitly refusing to look forward to a time when they might become so. Following the same line of thought, he denied any wish to hurt the planters; their prosperity was a matter of concern to him; and it was out of real conviction that he urged them to adopt the solution put forward by the Quaker Committee, the solution which, he declared, would give both them and him all that they wanted. By the simple and natural means of breeding their slaves at home, the trade could be safely abolished, their own requirements met, and the conditions of existing slaves improved without loss or trouble.

But whatever Wilberforce might wish, or say, or think, the debate inevitably revolved, not round the trade, but round slavery itself. The trade was a mere means to an end, and all eyes were fixed on that end, all thoughts on the possible or probable results of emancipation. No one attempted to deny that there were individual cases of cruelty at every stage, or that the condition of slaves could be improved; but the planters insisted that all such matters could and should be dealt with by regulations. It was the duty of the local assemblies to look into the problem, and in fact they had recently introduced laws to remedy abuses and would no doubt continue to do so. But slavery must be maintained and with it the trade. The point at issue was nothing less that the prosperity of the sugar colonies, and all that their prosperity meant to England herself. The House should keep well in mind the unchallenged evidence of the admirals that the trade was essential to England's naval supremacy, and the equally unchallenged evidence from the City of the effect which its abolition would have on our own financial stability. Nor, for that matter, should the House forget that the planters had their rights; it was contrary to every instinct of British justice that they should be deprived of their property and their means of livelihood without at least full compensation—a matter running into tens of millions of pounds.

The Parliament of 1791 may have been unreformed, but it was none the less composed of Englishmen who, whatever their political allegiance, were swayed by an Englishman's love of his country and an Englishman's respect for the rights of private property. The members were angered and shocked by the stories of cruelty and would gladly have done what they could to prevent them in future, but they could not bring themselves to believe that the aberrations of individuals would justify them in doing anything which might shake the foundations of England's greatness. Wilberforce was bound to lose his motion so long as he based his argument not on moral grounds but on what he called 'every principle of sound policy'. From the evidence, sound policy appeared, if anything, to point in the opposite direction. Worse still, Wilberforce seemed to be holding something back. His obvious course was to take the high moral line and denounce slavery for what it was—the denial of every right and every virtue for the attainment of which humanity had toiled and suffered since the days of Eden. Englishmen can respond to ideals, if they are open and generous, but not if there is any suspicion of concealment or half-heartedness. No one accused Wilberforce of insincerity, but for the majority abolition without emancipation was a half-baked measure which did not convince. The House weighed the matter in the scales of 'sound policy', and came to the conclusion that the manner in which Africans treated Africans in the heart of their own continent was a matter for the African conscience; and that the evidence of a few seamen, possibly disgruntled or over-sensitive, on the horrors of the middle passage, could not overthrow the more weighty and reliable evidence of the captains and surgeons. Sound policy in short did not require the abolition of a trade which the City and the naval authorities regarded as one of the foundations of our prosperity. They refused leave to introduce the Bill by 188 to 163.

Wilberforce was not dismayed; he had anticipated defeat. The House might honestly doubt the expediency of abolishing the trade; they could certainly refuse to act; but there was a power more vast and more potent than the House—the moral conviction of the country. Wilberforce warned the House that 'whatever they might do, the people of Great Britain would abolish the Slave Trade when, as would now soon happen, its injustice and cruelty should be fairly laid before them'. It was to the common people that he was looking, not to Parliament; and, as it proved, the common people were willing and ready to give him not only the abolition of the trade for which he was asking, but also the emancipation of the slaves for which he was restrained from asking. But the struggle in Parliament was to be long and severe.

VII

Wilberforce meant what he said when he spoke of enlightening the people. He had a year in which to act before he could raise the question again in the House, and it was his earnest intention that during that year the country's enthusiasm should be renewed. It had once been bright and glowing, but had become, not so much cold, as lost in perplexity and doubt. People were asking troubled questions. Were the horrors and cruelties all they were represented to be? Had Parliament failed in its duty? Could the arguments of the trade be brushed lightly aside? And above all, did abolition threaten the country's prosperity? The doubts were real, but Wilberforce, convinced that slavery was odious in English eyes and cruelty abhorrent to the English character, was certain that the people would respond as before, when once they had been reassured. But if their interest was to be revived, he must follow the example set by the trade, and push ahead vigorously with a new and powerful campaign.

He lost no time; Clarkson was sent once more on his tours; corresponding societies were established in one town after another and public meetings were arranged throughout the country. Fervour was soon rising, and help came from unexpected quarters. The poets got busy, and Cowper, in particular, who had early shown a practical interest, now redoubled his efforts, writing a new poem, 'The Negro's Lament', which was circulated far and wide, and, set to music, was sung in drawing-rooms and whistled in the streets. Wedgwood, the master potter, made a similar contribution from his art, with perhaps an even wider appeal. He produced a cameo depicting on a white background a negro pleading for pity. It caught the popular imagination, and was used as a decoration on snuff-boxes, bracelets, hatpins and gewgaws. As the campaign progressed, feelings grew stronger, and a movement sprang up spontaneously to boycott the use of West India sugar. It spread with startling rapidity, somewhat to the dismay of Wilberforce, whose gentle nature shrank from inflicting loss on planters or dealers. Far more to his taste were the petitions to Parliament demanding abolition. They came in an ever-growing flood from all quarters of England, Scotland and Wales, so that when on the 2nd April, 1792, Wilberforce rose to renew his well-known motion, he was almost literally bulwarked by a pile of five hundred and seventeen petitions lying on the table, with two more still to come.

The campaign had not been without its effect on Wilberforce himself, and it coloured his speech. Though he still gave instances of cruelty as the basis of his argument, his outlook was subtly different. The appeal was less to the lacerated feelings of pity and more to the high claims of justice and morality. The end to which he looked, passed for the first time beyond the mere abolition of the trade and turned, however timidly, towards the goal of emancipation. He did not ask for it at once, admitting that in their present degraded state the slaves were not fit for it, but he could not deny that he wished it for them, nor that he hoped for the coming of a time when the soil would have been prepared for that plant of celestial growth, full and complete liberty. The higher, unwritten, law was constantly in his mind, obliterating the details of the trade and proving all palliatives to be inadequate. It was not cruelty that condemned slavery, but the system itself. Whoever bought a slave, be he kind or cruel, was buying arbitrary power, and arbitrary power was an evil thing in whatever manner it was wielded. Nor did the higher law admit that regulations could ever be sufficient to right the wrong. Regulations might lessen the physical ills, but they could never cure a broken heart, they could never legislate for the affections, they could never bind the passions and feelings of the mind, and until they could, their labour would be vain. Slavery was the worst of evils; for in contradistinction to all others, it gave no scope for a concomitant good. It robbed war of its generosity; it deprived peace of its security; it displayed the vices of polished society without its knowledge or its comforts; and the evils of barbarism without its simplicity. It was 'pure, unmixed, unsophisticated wickedness'. Justice, morality, religion, all demanded the abolition of the trade. So did the people, who had expressed their wishes beyond cavil or doubt by presenting a far larger number of petitions than they had ever done on any other subject. The representatives of the nation must not show themselves less just than the people they represented.

The exalted tone which Wilberforce adopted was amply sustained by Fox and Pitt, but of far greater moment than eloquence was the unmistakable expression of the people's will—all the more emphatic because of the efforts of the trade to influence it. During the year the trade had been as active as Wilberforce and their propaganda had been underlined by events abroad. In the autumn of 1791 there had been a fresh outbreak in San Domingo, when the maddened slaves had massacred two thousand whites, had destroyed a thousand plantations and reduced to penury the families of twelve hundred planters. Their rebellion had spread to Martinique, and more ominous still to the English colony of Dominica. The traders had been prompt to point the moral. If the mere talk of abolition could produce such horrors, what would be the effect of abolition itself? All the calamities which the planters had foretold were in process of fulfilment before their eyes. Ruin, murder and disaster were the inevitable harvest springing from the reformers' ignorant interference with a long-established and successful system. So the planters had dinned into the ears of the people.

But neither revolts in the West Indies nor the growing tumults across the Channel had been able to stem the flood of petitions. The traders were obliged to bend before the storm. They retired grudgingly, keeping their eyes open for any chance of a respite, and when one was offered, they seized it eagerly. Barely a fortnight before the debate, the King of Denmark had signed an edict proclaiming that Danish participation in the slave trade was to cease in eleven years time— from the beginning of 1803. The King must be given all credit for his action, but the fact remains that Danish participation was trifling and its abolition involved no hardship. There was no real comparison between what the Danish King had done and what Wilberforce was demanding. But the trade saw their opportunity. Dundas, on their behalf, argued that the wise decision of the Danes to hasten slowly, was one which England would do well to follow. By all means let the slave trade be abolished, but not precipitately. Let it be done gradually, giving time for fresh arrangements to be made, for female slaves now in short supply to be bought, for depleted establishments to be renewed, for fresh plantations to be stocked. So the transition could be made harmlessly and by natural degrees. It seemed a reasonable compromise, and though Wilberforce resisted, Dundas carried the day. Gradual abolition, to end the trade by 1796, was approved by 230 votes to 85.

The Commons had spoken, clearly if not so decisively as Wilberforce had wished. The fact that they had not been more definite gave the trade a hope that something further might be gained in the Lords. In that hope their representatives suggested that the Lords should follow the example of the Commons and hear the evidence for themselves. They agreed. Witnesses were duly summoned, and as in the case of the Commons, the session ended before the evidence was completed. All was postponed again; and before the hearing could be renewed, war had broken out with France. In the turmoil of war, no one had time to think of reforms, nor any desire; sterner matters were afoot. Wilberforce seemed to have lost his chance, and slavery seemed more firmly entrenched than ever.

VIII

So in one sense it was. To all appearance interest in the subject was dead. The hearing of witnesses by the Lords was neither continued nor brought to an end; it simply petered out. In the Commons, Wilberforce renewed his motion year after year, with so little success that at last, in 1800, he gave up the attempt, waiting for the destined time, which, with unquenchable faith, he believed would come, to carry him on to victory. In the country the fervour had apparently died, and Clarkson, sent to rekindle it, was forced by ill-health to give up the mission. Yet hopeless as the struggle seemed and barren the years, there was undeniable progress. On the moral plane, the victory was already won. Nobody now attempted to uphold slavery on any ground but expediency; nobody any longer denied the vicious cruelty of the trade or the inherent degradation of the system. Some opponents even began to think of a compromise—the suspension of the trade for a few years—but were overborne by their more fanatical brethren. There were other matters, some quite extraneous, which were not without influence. The war, which shattered Wilberforce's hopes, also curtailed the trade. Slaves could no longer be transported so freely as before, so that in three years the numbers coming from Africa fell by nearly three-quarters. The consequent shortage compelled the planters to revise their opinions on a number of points, and not least on the possibility and prospects of breeding. Not that they consciously weakened in their attitude, but that unconsciously the atmosphere was changing. Then again, the war, which was so unsuccessful on the Continent, was prosperous in the West Indies. The French sugar colonies fell to England, and being far less exhausted by over-cultivation at once became serious competitors of the older English islands. The planters watched them with anxious eyes, and began to think it might be no bad thing if their supply of slaves could be cut short. It was also during these seemingly empty years that Sierra Leone passed through its preliminary troubles, and, reaching stability, held out a genuine hope that trade with Africa might be based on something less revolting than slavery. Last but not least, in 1801 the union with Ireland brought an influx of Irish members into Parliament—members, with no mandate from the trade and no preconceived ideas, who were naturally inclined to feel a generous and humane sympathy with an oppressed people.

Under these changed conditions Wilberforce felt encouraged in 1804 to make a further effort. His motion that the trade should be abolished forthwith was passed, to his joy, by a majority of 75; and within a few weeks he had presented and carried the necessary Bill through all its stages in the Commons. At long last victory seemed to be assured. But alas! the evil he was fighting was too big to be overthrown by a single assault. When the Bill was sent up to the Lords at the end of June, they declared that there was not sufficient time for dealing with the matter that session and that it must be deferred to the next. Wilberforce felt disappointed but nothing more; and in 1805 with a light and almost insouciant heart, so sure was he of success, he reintroduced his Bill—only to suffer the bitterest blow of his life. On second reading the Bill was thrown out by 77 votes to 70. 'I never felt so much on any parliamentary occasion', was his dejected comment; and a few days later he confessed that 'from the fatal moment of our defeat on Thursday evening, I have had a damp struck into my heart. I could not sleep either on Thursday or Friday without dreaming of scenes of depredation and cruelty on the injured shores of Africa'.

Yet depression could not be allowed the final word. There was still a minor concession which might be secured, a concession which would have been unnecessary if the Bill had gone through, but now that the Bill had been lost, would stand as a pledge for the future. England had lately taken Guiana from the Dutch; the form of its government, pending the treaty of peace, was to be settled by Orders in Council which required no law and no appeal to Parliament. Wilberforce begged Pitt to include a provision forbidding the importation of slaves into colonies conquered from the Dutch. From the first Pitt had been a staunch, if embarrassed, supporter—staunch, not only because of his friendship but also of his convictions; embarrassed, because of the presence of so many anti-abolitionists in his Cabinet. But he could not refuse so earnest a request, especially as the proposal was not altogether repugnant to the planters; and so in September 1805 he took the first effective step towards abolition by making the Order in Council for which Wilberforce was pressing. He made it only just in time; for four months later he was dead.

In the strange battle for abolition where apparent success was too often the prelude to defeat, the death of Pitt seemed at first sight to be the final blow, but proved in fact to be the harbinger of victory. Having lost Pitt, Wilberforce turned of necessity to Pitt's successor, Fox, and found to his relief that Fox was 'quite rampant' on the subject, and ready to throw himself into the cause more heartily even than Pitt. Without any delay he and Wilberforce agreed to test the parliamentary climate by introducing a Bill to extend and complete the work which Pitt's Order in Council had begun. The House, perhaps ashamed of its lapse the year before, perhaps now, in spite of its unreformed character, more ready to respond to the people's wishes, passed a Bill to prohibit the importation of slaves in British ships not only into Guiana but into any colony conquered by Britain during the war, and at the same time forbade the outfitting of foreign slavers in British ports.

Encouraged by this further success, Fox himself, on the 10th June, moved the resolution for immediate abolition which Wilberforce had moved so often and so vainly over the years. Though the debate was protracted, there was a new spirit abroad which would not be gainsaid. The resolution was carried by 114 votes to 15, and a fortnight later a similar resolution was carried in the Lords. It was by then too late to take the final step that session, but Wilberforce looked forward to the coming session with a prophetic confidence quite unjustified by his past experience; and lest the trade should take advantage of the interval to boost their traffic while they had the chance, rushed through a short Bill to prohibit the use of any ships in the slave trade which had not been so used before.

Yet for all Wilberforce's confidence, the abolition of slavery was not to be obtained without constant alarms. It almost seemed to demand human sacrifices, for as Pitt's death had followed the first tentative step, so now Fox's death followed the second. He had been suffering from dropsy when he moved the resolution in June, and three months later he was dead (13th September). All seemed once more thrown into the melting-pot, but Wilberforce refused to be dismayed. He was certain that the next session would see his efforts crowned with success; and hurrying down to Lyme as soon as Parliament rose, he spent the winter preparing and publishing his final treatise on the subject, which he entitled *A Letter on the Abolition of the Slave Trade addressed to the Freeholders and other inhabitants of Yorkshire*—a letter which in his exuberance he extended to 396 printed pages! Before it had reached the persons to whom it was addressed, the Bill for the abolition of the slave trade had been introduced into the House of Lords and received its first reading on the 2nd January, 1807. It had a quick and uneventful passage, for the steady work of the abolitionists and the pressure of public opinion had done their work thoroughly. Though there was some show of opposition, it had no heart, and on the 10th of February the Bill was read a third time and sent to the Commons.

There, the sense of expectation was greater. When the Bill came up for its second reading on the 23rd of February, the House was crowded. Members came flocking in, not to listen to the opposition, but to atone for past sins, to join in the tardy triumph of virtue, and above all to acclaim Wilberforce without whose faith and patient perseverance the cause had never been won. Tributes were offered in plenty but the noblest was paid by Romilly who in glowing and never-to-be-forgotten words compared Wilberforce with Napoleon—Napoleon haunted by the thought of the blood he had spilt and the oppressions he had committed, Wilberforce serene in the knowledge that he had preserved for life and happiness so many millions of his fellow-creatures. The ovation which followed was too much for Wilberforce; he was suffused in tears, but they were tears of joy and gratitude and thanksgiving.

The second reading was carried by 283 votes to 16, and thereafter the Bill went forward by easy stages to its final conclusion on the 25th March. It laid down that no vessel was to clear for slaves from any port within the British dominions after 1st May, 1807, or land a slave in the colonies after 1st March, 1808. The trade was at an end.

XVII. Patchwork

I

THE TASK which the Quaker Committee had entrusted to Wilberforce had been to secure 'the abolition of the Slave-Trade, and not of the slavery which sprang from it' (Clarkson I, 288). Faithfully he had pursued that task, never once deviating from his brief for hard on twenty years. Indeed, on the very eve of victory, he opposed a motion made by Earl Percy that a date should be fixed after which children born of slaves should be free, and in doing so went out of his way to affirm that he was glad the suggestion had been made, because it enabled him to show that, as he was no advocate of emancipation himself, so he would oppose it when advocated by others (Mathieson. *British Slavery and its Abolition*, p. 20). Wilberforce, in short, had done what he had been asked to do; he had secured the abolition of the trade. The question, however, remained whether the committee's original decision had been right. Was it sufficient to do away with the trade? Would abolition produce the results which the committee had expected? Would it lead, however slowly, to better conditions on the plantations, to rising standards of life among the slaves, and the prospect of eventual freedom? All too soon there was reason to doubt. The expected results did not follow; the committee appeared to have been over-optimistic; no one seemed to benefit.

Indeed, a new position was arising, which could not be defended in logic or tolerated in fact. In logic, so long as slavery was permitted, the trade was clearly as legitimate as it was necessary; no fault could be found with it in itself, but only in its methods. If it was right and moral to enslave a baby at birth, it could not be wrong or immoral to enslave him at an older age. Hence the planters and merchants did not regard indiscriminate abolition as reasonable; they were not disposed to give it their assent; nor would they hesitate to circumvent it if they could. They were soon given the chance. The disappearance of the English ships handed the trade over to foreigners, just as the merchants had foretold, and the suppression of the legitimate market inevitably gave rise to a black one. Slaves were needed, or so the planters believed, and the gap left by the English traders was promptly filled by the

French, the Portuguese, the Spaniards, and above all the Americans. The new-comers profited greatly; for the drop in demand reduced the price of slaves on the African coast while the absence of a steady supply enhanced their price in the islands. The dispossessed English traders looked on with envious eyes. They were jealous of all their successors, but they found the presence of the Americans a particularly bitter pill, for Congress had passed an abolition act at almost the same moment as Parliament; and by dealing in slaves the Americans were flouting their own laws, as well as purloining a trade which the merchants regarded as their own. Worse still, though nominally the Americans were supplying Cuba alone, actually they were carrying on a lucrative though clandestine traffic with the British islands. The example was too inviting and the lure of the black market too overpowering. Ships began to sail from England intent on smuggling, and their owners found, to their satisfaction, that if they were successful in one venture out of three, they were amply repaid.

As for the slaves themselves, some owners perhaps cherished them more carefully, but the majority went on much as before. Except for one thing. They had never much cared for releasing their slaves until they became too old to work; now, with the lack of a free market, they became bitterly hostile to any suggestion of manumission. The slaves, in short, were more firmly enslaved than ever.

As the position developed, three things gradually became clear, one after the other; first, that the Abolition Act must be tightened up if the black market was to be suppressed; secondly, that some method must be devised for curbing the activities of foreigners; and thirdly, that no remedy could be found for the ills of slavery short of complete emancipation.

II

Pending growth of the conviction that emancipation was inevitable, Parliament and the reformers put their trust in amendments to the Abolition Act. When the evasion of its provisions had become notorious, their first idea was to increase the penalties. It was a policy of despair, for the Act, as originally passed, had imposed penalties that should have been sufficiently crushing. The ship and cargo were to be confiscated and a fine levied of £100 for each slave carried. The larger the cargo, the greater the loss, and as informers were offered half the fine, the risk seemed altogether excessive. Yet the merchants were not discouraged, so huge were the possible profits. The illicit trade grew steadily. Ships cleared out in apparent innocence from Liverpool or Bristol, to be fitted with the necessary trappings—the platforms and bulkheads, the nets and partitions—at sea or in a foreign port, while at London they were soon being equipped in the Thames itself. One such ship was detected in 1810, barely three years after the passing of the Act, complete with its quota of padlocks and handcuffs, of shackles and chains, and prepared for a cargo which, it was estimated, would return a net profit of £60,000. It was the last straw. Everyone agreed that something must be done and in the next session Parliament made slave-trading a felony punishable by transportation.

Yet the prizes were still too alluring, and by 1815 illicit importations had become so prevalent that Wilberforce felt obliged to attempt a remedy which should be, not merely a punishment imposed after the event and dependent on discovery, but a deterrent in advance. He proposed that each colony should be required to keep a register of slaves and to carry out a census from time to time, the returns from which should be compared with the register, thus making evasion clear and discovery inevitable. The planters resisted this effort to close their black market with all their might, complaining with well-simulated indignation that they were being charged with complicity in the foreign slave trade without a shred of evidence. Owing partly to their opposition and partly to the lateness of the session, the Bill was dropped. But the evil continued, and so clearly contravened the popular wish that in 1824, as a final effort, Parliament passed a further Act making the trade piracy, and so punishable by death. But by that date even the unreformed House of Commons was becoming convinced of the truth, which had been axiomatic with the people from the first, that the only way of suppressing the trade was to put an end to slavery itself. The battle was taking a new turn.

III

So much for the enforcement of the Act. The brake on the activities of foreigners was a different affair. The interest which Pitt and Wilberforce had shown, at the end of 1787 (see p. 149), in the French slave trade had been a matter of tactics rather than morals. They had hoped, by carrying the French Government with them, to mollify the British traders, or at least to deprive them of an obvious argument. Their failure was a cause for regret rather than a disaster. Equally as a matter of tactics Wilberforce had hoped in 1801 to infuse abolition into the negotiations leading to the Treaty of Amiens, but had been frustrated by the Minister's lack of enthusiasm. When, however, abolition had been carried in England without the support of France, the position altered. It was no longer necessary to woo France as a matter of tactics, and it would not have been surprising or unnatural if the approach to her had been dropped; France was clearly unwilling and her help of no further consequence. But after her own long-drawn-out struggle, England had convinced herself that slavery, or at least the slave trade, was not merely a blot to be erased from the English escutcheon, but one of the major sins of the world against which all good Christians must unite. The conviction grew as public opinion in England passed almost imperceptibly from horror at the slave trade to detestation of slavery. England and her Ministers began to feel the compulsion of a missionary spirit; it was no longer sufficient to abolish the English part of the trade, the whole traffic must be swept from the face of the earth.

During the Napoleonic wars little could be done to influence other nations; they had too much to think about at home; but the people of England never lost sight of their goal, and in the negotiations which followed Napoleon's downfall, their representatives were given much clearer and more emphatic instructions on the need for abolition than on any other point. 'There is hardly a village', Castlereagh wrote, 'that has not petitioned on this subject; both Houses of Parliament are pledged to press it; and the Ministers must make it the basis of their policy' (Quoted. Rose. *The Revolutionary and Napoleonic Era*, p. 327). At Paris, where the powers assembled in May 1814 to banish Napoleon to Elba and settle the terms on which the Bourbons should be restored, the Abolitionists, represented by Zachary Macaulay, urged that no colonies should be returned to France unless she first promised not to import slaves into them. Castlereagh did his best, but France was not disposed to go so far or so fast; she demanded and obtained a pause of five years in which to make arrangements. 'The French', Wilberforce was told by Lord Liverpool, the Prime Minister, 'took the matter up in a high tone, and resented our dictating to them, believing that all our pleas of having abolished ourselves, or urging them to abolish, on grounds of religion justice and humanity, were all moonshine—mere hypocrisy' (Quoted, Klingberg, p. 139). Wilberforce would gladly have redeemed the five years by the cession of Mauritius, St. Lucia and other British conquests, and in the House expressed his lively fear that the Treaty of Paris (30 May, 1814) in which the moratorium had been granted, would prove to be 'the death warrant of a multitude of innocent victims, men, women and children, whom I had fondly indulged the hope of having myself rescued from destruction'.

Yet the treaty had not been without its positive side. It had introduced the nations of Europe to the problem of abolition as a matter of international interest and the common concern of humanity. For the most part they had never thought about it before, and were both puzzled and suspicious at England's insistence on its importance. In general they needed time to become familiar with the idea; but two nations, Sweden and Holland, were sufficiently impressed to accept immediate and unqualified abolition as the basis of their policy. It was no doubt easier for them than for others, seeing that their participation in the trade was small; but a breach had been made in the ranks of the slave-owning nations which offered hope for the future.

IV

When the people of England realized that the Treaty of Paris did not provide for abolition on the scale and at the speed they had expected, they were stirred to their depths. For more years than they cared to remember they had been fighting France for the freedom of the world, and now that they had at last gained the upper hand they were not disposed to leave the vast African continent outside the pale. Spontaneously, they poured in petitions to the House of Commons, seven hundred and seventy-two in the space of five weeks, signed by nearly a million of England's thirteen million inhabitants. It was with that massive backing that Castlereagh went in the following November to the Congress of Vienna, where the object of the nations was to carve up Europe as they thought appropriate, but where England included the further object of ending the trade in negroes.

While the nations were arguing, Napoleon escaped from Elba, and with a measure of political adroitness which one may hope was not merely cynical, attempted to placate England by ceding the point on which she was so curiously insistent. By a decree of the 28th March, 1815, he abolished the French slave trade. It may be that he had learnt his lesson and that his offers of peace were as genuine as his abolition of the slave trade; but the allies were taking no risks. He was hunted down and dismissed to captivity at St. Helena. But his decree remained. Castlereagh used it as a lever to coerce Louis XVIII, and by a second Treaty of Paris (20th November, 1815) Great Britain and France agreed mutually to spare no effort to ensure 'the most effectual measures for the entire and definitive abolition of a commerce so odious and so strongly condemned by the laws of religion and of nature'. It was a notable achievement for, after Great Britain, the only slave-trading nations of any importance were France, Spain, Portugal and the United States.

Having dealt with France, England turned to the other three. At about this moment, her strange little war of 1812 with the United States came to an end, and she managed to insert into the treaty of peace the same provisions regarding the slave trade as she had agreed with France. But while France ended, or at least lessened her share of the traffic, the States took no effective action. On the contrary they assumed for themselves the place in the trade which Great Britain had abandoned, thereby not only losing a great chance but ensuring fifty years of troubled existence ending in a civil war.

Portugal and Spain proved less stubborn, though by no means accommodating. They gave vague promises of abolishing the trade in eight years' time. Portugal also agreed, in return for a payment of £300,000 and the outstanding balance of a loan, to confine her activities during the interim to the area south of the Equator. Two years later (September 1817) Spain agreed to somewhat similar restrictions in return for a payment of £400,000.

Abolition was becoming a costly pursuit, and its enforcement was still more expensive. Treaties were of no value unless the traders were kept under control, and the only country with a navy sufficiently large to carry out the work was England. The others were content to leave it to her, but were not so ready to give her the necessary authority. For years England was negotiating with the continental powers and with the States to secure a reciprocal right of search and the setting up of international commissions through which captured slave ships could be condemned. Progress was extremely slow, but England persevered. The continental powers came to a final agreement with her in 1842, but not the States. They held out until, as it has been said, 'the American slave-trade finally came to be carried on principally by United States capital, in United States ships, officered by United States citizens, and under the United States Flag' (Du Bois. *Suppression of the Slave Trade*. Quoted, Klingberg, p. 170). Until the States conformed to the views of the civilized world, there could be no final conclusion; but in the meantime England could, and did, continue to lead the way.

XVIII. Freedom

I

THE PEOPLE had been convinced from the first that emancipation alone could cure the ills of slavery, but the reformers, too conscious perhaps of the practical difficulties, had been slow to accept that view. But accept it they had to, finally. In the end Wilberforce admitted that the reformers had been wrong in the line which they had previously adopted. 'When the public attention', he wrote, 'has been attracted to this subject, it has been unadvisedly turned to particular instances of cruelty, rather than to the system in general, and to those essential and incurable vices which will invariably exist whenever the power of man over man is unlimited.' The abolitionists, in their eagerness, had been 'led to dwell too much and too exclusively, perhaps, on the slaves being underfed and overworked, and on the want of due medical care and medical comforts'. Such physical shortcomings were natural to the system, but only as accompaniments; they must sink into insignificance beside the inherent moral evils, and especially that evil 'which runs through the whole of the various and cruel circumstances of the negro slave's condition, and is at once the effect of his wrongs and sufferings, their bitter aggravation, and the pretext for their continuance—his extreme degradation in the intellectual and moral scale of being, and in the estimation of his white oppressors' (*An Appeal*, etc).

These words were written in 1823, but they were the culmination of a long period of thought and preparation. Two years earlier (May 1821) Wilberforce had told a fellow Member of Parliament, Thomas Fowell Buxton, that for many years he had been watching and waiting for 'a proper time and suitable circumstances of the country to raise the question of how best to provide for the moral and social improvement of the slaves, and ultimately for their advancement to the rank of a free peasantry'. The time, though it had not yet come, seemed to be approaching, and he therefore invited Buxton to form an alliance with him, that might 'truly be termed holy', to prosecute this new war, and if need be to carry it on to victory by himself, should Wilberforce, who was now sixty-two and in failing health, be compelled through age or infirmity to retire (Buxton's *Memoirs*, p. 104). Buxton was slow in making up his mind—he was much engaged on other works of reform—but in the autumn of 1822 he agreed.

Thereafter events moved quickly. The following January an Anti-Slavery Society was founded with the avowed object of procuring immediate improvement and eventual emancipation. How greatly the atmosphere had changed in high quarters was shown by the fact that though, as in 1787, the Quakers were once again well to the fore, they were by no means alone; the Society had a royal duke for its president, and numbered five peers and fourteen Members of Parliament among its vice-presidents. Early in March Wilberforce gave the new crusade a flying start by publishing '*An Appeal to the Religion, Justice and Humanity of the Inhabitants of the British Empire in behalf of the Negro Slaves in the West Indies*'; and the inhabitants at any rate of Great Britain responded exactly as they had done before. Later that same month he presented to the House the first public petition for emancipation, one drawn up by the Quakers, but made no attempt to base any motion upon it, feeling himself too old and too infirm to play any longer a leading part.

The motion which was to open the campaign was left to Buxton, who moved it on the 15th May, 1823. 'The object', he said, 'at which we aim is the extinction of slavery—nothing less than the extinction of slavery, in nothing less than the whole of the British dominions.' Yet even now the days of procrastination were not over. The terms of Buxton's motion were that 'slavery ought to be abolished throughout the British Colonies with as much expedition as may be found consistent with a due regard to the well-being of the parties concerned'. The terms were no doubt unexceptionable; but they were lacking in any sense of urgency; moderation seemed to be the burden of a song which demanded a full-throated crescendo if hesitations were to be swept away. When Buxton came down to details, it was evident that he had paid too much regard to the well-being of the planters, too little to that of the slaves. One might have supposed that so vast a change in the established order must entail some sacrifice, however slight, on the part of the owners—some reparation to the slaves for the hardships of the past, some atonement for the drabness of their stunted lives, some reward for their hitherto unrequited labours. Yet the owners were to suffer no loss, nor any real inconvenience beyond an unspecified check to arbitrary actions in which they should never have indulged.

If the owners were to suffer no loss, the benefits to the slaves were niggardly. Their greatest advantage was that henceforth they were to be attached to the land, and so spared the heartbreak of being sold away from their homes and perhaps their families to meet the debts of a bankrupt, or to satisfy the greed of an avaricious, master. In addition they were to be assured, as a right instead of as a favour, of one day a week for themselves as well as the Sunday. They were also to be allowed to marry, to receive religious instruction and to be accepted as witnesses. But of freedom there was no mention, except that masters who were disposed to manumit a slave were not to be hindered, and any slave who was able to purchase his own freedom was to be allowed to do so by instalments. Apart from that, no prospect of liberty was held out to existing slaves. The vaunted extinction was to be brought about, not by immediate or even delayed emancipation, but by the method which Earl Percy had proposed and Wilberforce had rejected in 1807, by regarding as free the children of slaves born after a certain date. By that means, slavery would not be abolished but rather, as Buxton said, would expire, would, as it were, burn itself down to its socket and go out.

In view of the popular feeling throughout the country, the Government could not oppose the underlying object of the motion, nor did it wish to do so, but in view of the excessive weight which the West India party could exert in Parliament it was anxious to avoid positive enactments. Canning, therefore, the Leader of the House, criticized Buxton's methods rather than his aims. He argued, truly enough, that to give freedom to the offspring of slaves was 'at once the least efficient and the most hazardous' mode of emancipation. Slavery receding slowly before a rising tide of freedom would become intolerable, especially after Parliament had pronounced slavery to be contrary to Christianity and the British Constitution. It would be better by measures of amelioration to fit the slaves for freedom, so that in due course it could be granted to them without danger to the owners, to private property or to the slaves. Such a policy could best be carried out by the colonies themselves, to whom it should be left. He therefore proposed that Parliament should proceed by way of recommendations, urging the local assemblies to embark of their own accord on plans of amelioration. Only if the local assemblies were contumacious should the House consider sterner measures. So it was decided, with the consent of the emancipators who buoyed themselves up with the thought that the Government had approved their motion in principle, and by implication had promised to coerce the colonies if the need should arise.

But timidity had its usual effect. The colonial assemblies received the Government recommendations with angry defiance. The only result was unrest among the slaves. Being given no information and grasping eagerly at vague rumours, they jumped to the conclusion that the King had granted them their freedom and that their masters were suppressing his edict. By turns they were hopeful, anxious, perturbed and restless; and in Demerara, in particular, took part in a species of strike which, though singularly free from violence, the planters were pleased to call insurrection and put down with hideous ferocity. Among other things they arrested a missionary, Smith by name, who in fact had used his influence to restrain the slaves, but was charged with complicity and after a farcical court martial was condemned to death. As it happened he was consumptive, and his illness being aggravated by his treatment, he died before the sentence could be carried out. But he was none the less a martyr and his martyrdom was not to be in vain.

The assemblies had undoubtedly been contumacious and there was little likelihood of a change of heart. They were confirmed in their attitude partly by their ingrained, though unacknowledged, fear of the blacks, partly by a genuine belief that emancipation meant economic disaster, and partly by an erroneous conviction of their own importance to the Empire. They were under the impression that the West Indies were still, as they had been a hundred years earlier, one of the corner-stones of England's commerce and wealth. Overlooking the fact that the industrial revolution had entirely altered their economic significance, the colonists were apt to suppose that, following the example of the United States, they could threaten to secede and that any such threat would at once bring Parliament to heel. It was a fantastic supposition, as they mustered barely one hundred thousand whites, scattered over a number of island communities, not one of which was, in modern parlance, viable. This heady conceit however made them obstinate, and on this occasion they supported their defiance by magnifying the disturbances—the so-called insurrection of Demerara, one or two risings in Jamaica, destructive of property, but otherwise mainly abortive, and a few riots in Barbados—which, though in no sense serious, made excellent propaganda.

As exploited by the planters they undoubtedly shook the Government, who in consequence were reluctant to respond when reminded of their promise to take sterner measures. Possibly they would have taken no action at all, if it had not been for the furore created by the treatment which Smith had endured and the belief that it had hastened his death. The public were horrified and would not be appeased. Their petitions which in 1823 had numbered two hundred and twenty-five rose to six hundred in 1824. Government could not ignore them; they must take some action, but the method they chose was too timorous to be effective. Of the West Indian possessions four—Trinidad, St. Lucia, Demerara and Berbice—were recent captures still under colonial office administration, and, unlike the others, without legislative assemblies. Government now decided that if coercion must be employed, it should be exercised against these four Crown Colonies. Officials were more amenable than assemblies, and recent conquests must put up with whatever treatment they received. The Government's recommendations, in short, were to be tried on the colonial equivalent of the dog, in the hope that the other islands, seeing them to be beneficial or at least innocuous, might adopt them of their own accord. Accordingly the Government's model system of slavery was embodied in an Order in Council, and imposed willynilly on Trinidad. Though the benefits were not very striking, the system did result in some mitigation of slavery, and a few islands, mainly the smaller ones, were induced to adopt one or other though not all of its provisions. In general, however, the colonists were stubbornly unresponsive and their intransigent attitude roused the people against them. Public pressure was continually mounting. Even so convinced a supporter of slavery as Lord Dudley and Ward was forced to admit that the cry of indignation which came 'from every corner of the kingdom, from every city, corporation, town and village' had made the views of the people clear and was too powerful to be wholly disregarded (Mathieson. *British Slavery and its Abolition*, p. 170). Certainly the Government could not disregard it; and in 1826, driven to make a further effort, they drew up heads of a bill embodying the provisions of the Trinidad Order in Council and sent them to the various assemblies with a request that they should adopt them in Bills of their own drafting. But in vain. The local legislatures at best prevaricated, at worst were sullenly obstinate.

The rejection of their proposals placed the Government in a dilemma. Their policy of action through the assemblies was not merely administrative caution, nor yet simply the wish to avoid antagonizing the West India party. Lurking at the back of their mind was a very real fear that if the planters were deprived of their slaves by government action, they would not merely claim but would be entitled to compensation. What that compensation would amount to, they did not know; but be it large or small, they doubted whether the country would consider it for a moment. Canning half admitted the difficulty by trying to avoid the obligation. The Government's proposals, he argued, did not deprive the masters of their slaves. On the contrary, by improving their moral status, the proposals would add to their value and so be in the interests of the masters. Compensation, therefore, was clearly inappropriate. It had no place in any system of amelioration. In so far as it might have any justification, it must be sought in the provisions allowing slaves to purchase their freedom. Those provisions included regulations for settling the price, and the masters might dislike this element of compulsion and even regard it as unfair; but it was intended to meet the masters' reasonable claims and at least assured them of what the Government considered a just and fair price. The Government proposals, in short, whether the planters realized it or not, absolved Parliament from the need to pay compensation and placed it squarely on the slaves themselves; they were not to be granted, but to buy, emancipation. It was a policy which could satisfy no one. Whatever might be true of individuals, the slaves as a whole had no prospect of raising the money; the planters had neither security of tenure nor certainty of compensation; the reformers saw no end to their labours; and the Government no method of redeeming their promises. It was fortunate for them that before the planters had finally rejected their proposals, Canning's Government had been brought to an end by Canning's death.

II

For the next few years England was absorbed in her own internal reforms. The whole of the legal, economic and parliamentary systems of the country were undergoing a radical overhaul. It was now that the criminal law was revised on humane lines, the police force instituted, the Catholics emancipated and trade unionism founded; while towering over all was an insistent demand for the reform of Parliament and the reorganization of the electorate. In the midst of such wholesale movements, the case of the slaves was momentarily overlaid but not forgotten; rather, it was absorbed into, and became part of, the general advance towards a new ideal of equal justice and ordered liberty. Indeed, it was in one sense the parent stem from which all the others sprang. Being founded on the Christian belief in the brotherhood of man, and actuated by the demands of Christian charity, it had offered for forty years an example which compelled respect even if it could not command success, and in the end had turned the thoughts of those less interested in the distant and unseen evils of slavery to the only-too-abundant and only-too-obvious evils at home. Thanks to the example which the abolitionists had set, there was now a spirit of reform abroad, and their specialized efforts were caught up in and might be proud to conform to the general pattern. It was as well; for much as they had accomplished under the old conditions, when the Members of Parliament represented private interests rather than the public good, it may be doubted whether they could have succeeded finally until, in a new reformed House, the members really represented the electorate and had accepted the doctrine that in the last resort their own opinions must defer to the expressed wishes of the people.

While the prospects of parliamentary reform were growing, the Anti-Slavery Society was steadily coming to the conclusion that the Government's plan was founded on a fallacy. It was impracticable for slaves, so long as they remained slaves, to be fitted for freedom by any process of education; the two conditions were too utterly incompatible. It followed that emancipation could not be introduced by degrees; it must be given immediately or not at all. As Buxton put it: 'under the most mitigated system, slavery is still labour obtained by force; and if by force, I know not how it is possible to stop short of that degree of force which is necessary to extort involuntary exertion. A motive there must be, and it comes at last to this; inducement or compulsion; wages or the whip' (Klingberg, p. 250). There was no alternative to immediate emancipation, and if that led to troubles, they must be endured patiently as the inevitable consequence of past sins. In this conviction the Society prepared itself for a fresh campaign on new lines, but for the next two years was held up by the great struggle for parliamentary reform. One general election followed another and there were constant changes of ministry; nor did the ferment end till the Reform Bill received the royal assent in June 1832. With that out of the way, the ground was cleared for the final battle and the Anti-Slavery Society at once set on foot a nation-wide campaign. Lectures, addresses, pamphlets, posters were employed with a profusion never yet attempted in England, and the success of these efforts was strikingly evident; the number of affiliated societies in the provinces rose by leaps and bounds from two hundred to thirteen hundred, and over a million and a half signatures were rapidly obtained to petitions. The country once again, made its wishes clear beyond a doubt, nor was it in any degree deflected from its course by the vehement counter propaganda of the planters.

Yet that propaganda had its effect. The planters had by now given up hope of maintaining slavery as a system, and were concentrating on two points—the retention of their existing slaves for as long as possible, and a demand for compensation. At first sight the latter demand seemed hopeless. During the passage of the parliamentary Reform Bill the people had scouted the idea of compensating the owners of rotten boroughs, who in their opinion had suffered no genuine loss. If anything they were receivers of stolen property, filched from the public, and it was right that they should be forced to disgorge their illegal gains. It was natural to expect that the people would display the same uncompromising spirit in the case of the slaves, whose treatment by the planters roused their indignation and whose plight their sympathy; but, perhaps as the result of the planters' propaganda, their feelings took an entirely different turn. They recognized that slavery had been condoned, and more than condoned —encouraged—by many parliaments over many years, and they felt that what Parliament had deliberately given should not be lightly taken away. Slavery they abhorred and were determined to end, but if it could not honestly be abolished without injustice to the masters, then, in Heaven's name, let the masters receive their price. It was better for England to lighten her pocket by however large a sum, if by so doing she could equally lighten her conscience.

It is strange but true that the Government did not appreciate the views of either the reformers or the public. As against the reformers, they could not bring themselves to believe that emancipation must or even could be granted immediately; such a course was dangerous; and unnecessary, since in their opinion it was not impossible for a slave to be half bond and half free and in that intermediate state to be educated up to complete emancipation. That therefore was the proper method to adopt; any other could only lead to trouble. And as against the planters, they shied from the idea of paying compensation, clinging to their view that the owners need be put to no loss if only they would act reasonably, mollifying public opinion by an immediate change of tactics, and protecting their own interests by an orderly system of gradual amelioration.

This three-cornered battle swayed to and fro with varying success, but the end was inevitable. The massive force of popular wishes could not be checked or resisted. The final and decisive thrust was given in

April 1833 when a deputation, unprecedented at the time, of three hundred delegates from all parts of the country carried a petition to the Prime Minister himself in Downing Street. Government began to give way in the usual grudging and gradual manner. The next month they produced their Bill; slavery was to be totally abolished from the 1st August, 1834; but existing slaves were for twelve years to be placed in a state of apprenticeship, working for their masters during three-quarters of the day and for the other quarter receiving wages out of which they were to purchase their freedom; and in order to enable the planters to pay the wages, Government were prepared to advance to them, as a temporary interest-bearing loan, the sum of fifteen million pounds.

The scheme was an effort at compromise which had little to commend it. The reformers saw no virtue in apprenticeship which was simply the discarded system of education under a thin disguise; and in any event would not agree to so long a period. The planters saw no advantage in a loan which they would have to repay; it was no more than a device to throw the cost of emancipation on to their shoulders and to deny them any redress. Meanwhile the public at large were impatient for an end to be made. They had expressed their wishes; they were in no mood to deny the means or to haggle over the cost. Whatever was necessary to be done, should be done at once.

In such an atmosphere, Government was forced to retreat from the attitude they had taken up, an attitude moulded by a sense of economy which satisfied no one. What then were the new conditions to be? The planters were clamouring for compensation, and the people were prepared to give it. The Government therefore, yielding to popular opinion, promptly changed the loan of fifteen million pounds to a free gift. They were so prompt that the planters were taken by surprise, but realizing that they had little time left and that fortune must be taken at the flood, as promptly offered to support the Government's Bill if the fifteen million were increased to twenty. There was a spirit of mixed pity and remorse abroad which was almost reckless in its determination to do justice to all parties, securing freedom for the slaves and flinging down with scorn the uttermost farthing of compensation. The Government therefore could afford to give way, declaring with what in the circumstances might be thought a cynical brazenness that after all twenty million pounds was not too great a sum.

Over against the traders stood the reformers. They also had their demands to make, pressing for immediate emancipation, or at least a substantial reduction in the period of apprenticeship. Their demands embarrassed the Government, since the twelve years' apprenticeship had been agreed as part of the compensation promised to the planters. They were bound therefore to propose the whole period. The House, however, was under no pledge, and when Buxton, feeling that he had the people behind him, moved for a reduction, the House consented by a large majority to cut down the period to seven years in the case of plantation slaves and five in the case of domestic slaves. Nor were they moved by the planters' complaint that they were being deprived of their promised compensation. Parliament was prepared to do every justice to the planters which could be done at the cost of the nation, but had never promised and never would promise to benefit them at the expense of the slaves. The planters bowed to the inevitable and so the battle ended. On the 28th August, 1833, the Bill which emancipated all slaves in all British dominions received the royal assent.

Wilberforce had died a month earlier, but he had lived long enough to know that his object had been attained. England by freeing her own slaves had begun the process of 'pulling away the corner-stone of slavery throughout the world' (Buxton to Clarkson, 22nd Sept. 1833. Buxton's *Memoirs*, p. 283); but the world has been in no hurry to complete the work. Slavery is not yet dead. The example, however, remains, and though Englishmen have largely forgotten their own good deed, there are times when foreigners remember it. Let Dr. Channing of the United States be their spokesman:

'Other nations have won imperishable honours by heroic struggles for their own rights. But there was wanting the example of a nation, espousing with disinterestedness, and amidst great obstacles, the rights of those who had no claim but that of a common humanity—the rights of the most fallen of the race. Great Britain, loaded with an unprecedented debt and with a grinding taxation, contracted a new debt of a hundred million dollars, to give freedom, not to Englishmen, but to the degraded Africans. This was not an act of policy, not a work of statesmen. Parliament but registered the edict of the people. The English nation, with one heart and one voice, under a strong Christian impulse, and without distinction of rank, sex, party or religious names, decreed freedom to the slaves. I know not that history records a national act so disinterested, so sublime' (Channing. A letter on the Annexation of Texas. 1839).

Postscript

I

IN 1833 England embarked on a great act of faith. Hopes were high, but the issue was still obscure. The apprenticeship through which freedom was to come differed in itself little from the old slavery. Its success would depend on the response given by the planters who had always been reluctant and often contumacious. Would they continue in their old ways? Channing, in slave-ridden America, thought they would. When the scheme was but a few months old, he declared that the masters 'have done much to exasperate the slaves whose freedom they could not prevent; have done nothing to prepare them for liberty; have met them with gloom on their countenances, and with evil auguries on their lips' (*Slavery*, p. 129). But Channing was too fearful, and faith was justified. The new spirit which had swept through England, spread to the colonies; and the first irritable reaction, quickly subsiding, gave way to a more gracious attitude. In less than three years, Lord Glenelg, the Secretary for the Colonies, found that apprenticeship had brought about 'an improvement in society and an accession to human happiness of which history furnished no previous example'. It had proved, as the Governor of British Guiana said, 'a complete and triumphant success'. Nor were its benefits confined to the slaves. Channing, in repentant mood, wrote, 'I have heard that a West Indian planter residing in this country, who was strenuously opposed to the act of emancipation, speaks now of his estate as more productive than formerly' (ibid., p. 184); and the City of London was soon rejoicing at an unprecedented, if temporary, rise in the volume of West Indian trade. The planters were not slow to recognize the change or to grasp its reason. They began to look with quickened interest beyond apprenticeship. Antigua and Bermuda, indeed, never introduced it, jumping straight to emancipation; and in spite of some natural hesitations and some kicking against the pricks, all the islands had renounced it by the 1st of August, 1838. On and from that date the last vestige of slavery had disappeared from the English colonies. All the slaves were free.

II

But the reformers were not content. Two problems still remained to be tackled—the problem of the other nations, and the problem of Africa itself. For the moment, nothing could be done about the other nations. Hitherto they had regarded England's actions either with cynical indifference or with selfish hopes. They were willing enough that England should ease her own conscience, but they were not disposed to let her ease theirs, which were not in fact troubling them. Nor would they willingly surrender the opportunities which her conduct had opened up. It was hardly within the compass of the reformers to alter that attitude; treaties with other nations were matters of public, not private, concern; and all the reformers could do was to urge on the Government the desirability, if not the duty, of bringing diplomatic pressure to bear.

Africa, however, was another story. The conviction that her inhabitants had been shamefully treated was a reason for taking an interest in the country itself. It dawned on the reformers, and indeed on others, that Africa had been neglected from the beginning; denied her share in the slow upward progress of civilization, and left without help or support to struggle in primitive darkness. She ought to be redeemed; she ought to be given her rightful place in the comity of continents. It could hardly be doubted that, properly handled, she had a contribution to make to the sum of human prosperity, and she ought to be allowed to make it.

In that belief, Buxton set his heart on a new approach to Africa. The abolition of slavery, however good in itself, was purely negative. So, in essence, was the system of naval patrols set up to suppress the trade. How much better if the magnificent labour force, now released from alien bondage, could be taught to cultivate the soil of Africa! How much more beneficial, if naval patrols could give place to merchant vessels and legitimate trade! How much happier if African natives could be led from the darkness and terrors of witchcraft to the light and liberty of Christianity! It seemed to him that with the aid of Government it should be possible to induce native chieftains, not only to discard the slave trade altogether, but to grant concessions for agricultural, commercial and religious settlements, through which the blessings of European civilization could be introduced.

He urged his views on the Government with such vigour and such success that in 1841 an expedition set out, under Government auspices, to explore the Niger, conciliate the natives and enter into agreements with their rulers. It began well, but within a few months ended in disaster. The failure greatly depressed Buxton and undoubtedly hastened his death. Yet it was not without its lesson, nor without its promise. The want of success had not been due to opposition from the native chiefs, who had shown themselves interested and willing; it had been caused by the climate and the ravages of malarial fever. Of the one hundred and ninety-three European members of the expedition forty-one had died and most of the others had been laid low. Clearly matters had been rushed; clearly much exploratory work was needed. The Government drew back, but volunteers pressed in, attracted by the mystery and excitement of a new country. They were fascinated by the unknown and eager for adventure, whether it were tracking the Nile to its source, or simply indulging in big-game hunting. Whatever their object, they were penetrating unexplored lands; and they sent back news of what they found—accounts of the splendid marvels of nature; stories of the grim horrors of savagery. Interest was inevitably quickened, and hard on the heels of the explorers—indeed, often ahead of them—came the missionaries. Africa began to yield her secrets, and among the first and most daunting was the discovery that the slave trade which had been put down with such trouble in the west, had sprung to new life in the east.

III

For centuries Arabs had been in the habit of raiding Africa for slaves; but the practice had become extensive and highly organized only when the Sultan of Muscat towards the middle of the nineteenth century, established a suzerainty over the island of Zanzibar and a large tract of the neighbouring mainland. Slave-trading was the principal source of wealth for this new kingdom and became as easy as it was profitable when the Arabs acquired fire-arms and were financed by Indian merchants. Fortified by these advantages, the Arabs were growing ruthless, penetrating ever more deeply into the continent and systematically depopulating wider and wider areas in their search for prey. It was estimated that from forty thousand to forty-five thousand slaves were passing annually through the markets of Zanzibar. The east-bound traffic was bidding fair to rival the old traffic to America, not only in numbers but in wanton waste of life. Livingstone thought that ten were sacrificed for every slave sold. It was his first-hand account of the atrocities which helped to rekindle and turn in this new direction the sentiments of his countrymen which had swept slavery out of the colonies. England determined that East Africa also must be rescued. But how to do it was not so clear. It was no longer a matter of internal reform where public opinion could be decisive; it was a matter for external action which neither government nor officialdom was anxious to take. England was on good terms with the Sultan; she recognized that however sympathetic he might be to reform, he was hampered by financial considerations and perhaps still more by the deeply-rooted customs of the country. It was hard to coerce him, and perhaps unwise. Nor could it be overlooked that Zanzibar was full of Indian merchants who had sunk large sums in the trade. As British subjects they expected to be helped rather than hindered in what, after all, was a legitimate business in Zanzibar.

Yet the factors, which at first sight seemed unfavourable, might easily be turned to advantage if the right man could be found. The friendly relations with the Sultan were based on confidence in England's good faith. Having experienced England's help and being satisfied that she had no ulterior motives, the Sultan was disposed to listen to her advice and anxious to meet her wishes. His co-operation could, within limits, be expected. And as for the Indian merchants, they must accept the limitations as well as the advantages of British citizenship. All that was needed was the right man on the spot, and it so happened that the cause of freedom was powerfully assisted by a series of able men—Hamerton, Rigby, and Kirk—who held appointments as Consuls at Zanzibar one after the other. Hamerton, who had accompanied the Sultan on his original voyage from Oman, secured a treaty in 1845 under which the Sultan agreed to prohibit the export of slaves from Africa, except to his Asiatic possessions. Hamerton was followed by Rigby, who took strong action against the Indian merchants, emancipating, on his own authority, large numbers of their slaves, on the ground that, as British subjects, they had no right to possess them. He began operations in February 1859, and in 1861 recorded in his diary: 'before I left Zanzibar I had the satisfaction of giving liberty to upwards of 8,000 African slaves, who but for my interference would have passed all their lives in bondage' (Russell, p. 95). At a later date, when Kirk was Consul, two treaties were signed; the first, in 1873, prohibited all traffic in slaves by sea; the second, in 1876, prohibited the trade by land as well. But the country was wild and unsettled; slavery was a deeply-rooted institution and the trade was one which could too easily be disguised. In spite of treaties it continued to flourish and indeed from about 1884 was said to be on the increase.

But by 1884 other issues were beginning to arise. It was becoming increasingly evident that Africa would not, and perhaps could not, be left isolated from the rest of the world to develop in her own way. Some outside influence would certainly mould her future, and the urgent question was what that influence was to be. There were two possibilities already existent in her borders—the one strong, organized and forceful; the other intermittent, uncertain and in a real sense unwilling. On the one hand were the Arabs who in pursuit of slaves were penetrating decisively into the heart of Africa. They were forming settlements to promote their trade; and as they found it convenient to profess loyalty to the Sultan of Zanzibar, they were beyond doubt creating an embryo Moslem empire, stretching out from the coast on the east and coming down from Egypt in the north—an empire of slavery and suppression, of cruelty and dark ignorance. Over against them stood a trickle of explorers, a few devoted missionaries, one or two enlightened Consuls, and here and there a man of inspired genius. These had no idea of empire; their main objects were to end the slave trade, and to humanize and enlighten the natives. They had little enough encouragement from the Government, but their own burning conviction, their large humanity, and their compelling religion were sufficient to curb the Arab infiltration, though not to solve the problem of Africa's future.

What the upshot would have been had these two forces been left to their one-sided duel is a nice question for academic theory; but they were not left to themselves. The other nations of Europe—Belgium, Portugal, France, Italy and Germany—suddenly awoke to the fact that Africa was being opened up, and was proving to be a no-man's-land of immense potentialities. There it lay, unoccupied, unappropriated for anyone to grab. The nations set on foot a deliberate movement to carve out colonies for themselves. Before long the trend was obvious and England reluctantly found herself involved. Africa as a consequence was divided into spheres of European influence, and slavery became an international problem.

IV

The slaves' position was not necessarily affected by the manœuvres of the nations, but it was morally desirable that in the carving-up of

Africa some voice should be raised on their behalf. The duty fell inevitably to England, since the other nations were too interested or too indifferent. Some, like France, Spain and Portugal, were deeply involved in the trade from Zanzibar ('The French have commenced the slave trade all along the coast on an immense scale'—Rigby to Miles, July 1858. Russell, p. 72: 'The activity of the Spanish slave trade and the open support given to it by the French Consul and the French naval officers gave me great trouble and anxiety'—Rigby's *Diary*, 29th August, 1860. ibid., p. 88: 'In September (1859) Rigby sent both to Bombay and to the Foreign Office dispatches to the effect that an extensive slave trade was going on with the full knowledge and connivance of the Portuguese authorities'—ibid., p. 149). Others, like Belgium, were too eager in their pursuit of annexation, or like Germany, too ruthless. The United States were ruled out, partly by distance and still more by lack of authority; it was not long (1865) since they had abolished their own slavery, less out of principle than to end a civil war, and at the same time were responsible in Liberia for a system which showed all the vices and none of the virtues of the worst type of colonialism. England alone had the experience and the will and the moral right. Through her exertions, the Conference of Berlin (1885) laid some restraint on Belgium's freedom of action in the Congo by requiring the signatory powers 'to help in suppressing slavery and especially the slave trade'. Following upon that first tentative step, and again on England's initiative, a Conference held at Brussels in 1890, laid it down that the suppression of the slave trade must be regarded as the main justification for annexing colonies, and drew up elaborate measures for its abolition. It was no doubt because politicians rarely learn from the past that in 1890, as in 1787, the reformers concerned themselves with the trade instead of the status, striving to abate the symptoms rather than to eradicate the cause. None the less, under the supervision of a specially appointed Slavery Board and with the active help of the British Navy, the two Conventions of 1885 and 1890 had much to their credit in the years leading to the First World War.

After that war it was natural that the problem should be handed over to the League of Nations, and in 1922 the necessary resolution was moved by Sir Arthur Steel-Maitland. But Leagues, like Conventions, move slowly; the constituent members when asked for information proved exceedingly coy; and the reason became clear when, at last, hopeless of concerted action, the assembly set up a Committee of

Experts to investigate and report. The committee found that slavery, which the civilized world was apt to think of as having been killed by Wilberforce, still existed, here and there, and especially in Moslem countries, even in its crudest form; but that a greater threat to human freedom lay in the fact that slavery was tending to hide itself under apparently innocent or even meritorious disguises; girls were bought by the payment of what was euphemistically called 'dowries'; children were 'adopted' by rich foster-parents with a view to eventual enslavement; debtors were reduced to bondage which was said to be temporary but in fact held no prospect of release and even descended to a second generation; and in many countries individuals were subjected to forced labour in one form or another. It was clear that these conditions were 'analogous to slavery' and must be fought and overthrown no less than slavery proper.

When the report was issued, England drafted a new Convention which, with certain amendments, the League adopted in 1936. It was notable as containing the first definition of slavery ever to be introduced into an international document. But, though the definition was thought to be wide enough to cover the various systems 'analogous to slavery', its effectiveness was greatly lessened by the League's decision to allow forced labour for 'public purposes', thus condoning in advance the concentration camps of Germany and the labour camps of Soviet Russia. But worse was to follow. As originally conceived the Convention offered adequate machinery for the suppression of the trade, but the sting was taken out of its provisions, first by the rejection of England's proposal to regard the transport of slaves by sea as piracy, and secondly by the League's failure to reappoint the Slavery Board or any other executive body. It was not until 1934 that a permanent committee was set up, and then only in an advisory capacity. Yet in spite of this handicap it was instrumental during its short life in stirring national consciences and securing better international cooperation. It might have gone far, had not its activities been cut short by the Second World War.

With the renewal of peace there was much lip service to the cause of freedom, including the Universal Declaration of Human Rights, by which in December 1948 the United Nations laid down that 'no one shall be held in slavery or servitude; slavery and the slave trade shall be prohibited in all their forms'. Again a committee was set up to investigate, and again it reported on much the same lines as before. The facts might vary in detail from time to time, but the problem was always the same—how to secure a general and genuine determination to end the evil. On this occasion the committee found that except in a few backward areas crude slavery was dying out and the trade was decreasing; where it existed, it had gone underground. But it had been succeeded by 'analogous forms' which, the committee said, affected a much larger number of people than had been affected by 'slavery of the classical kind'; and that to meet this new threat the Convention of 1926 must be strengthened. Brought face to face with the facts, the constituent members tended once more to be coy; progress was desperately slow and frequently interrupted. Once again England had to take the lead. She drafted a Supplementary Convention, in which the definition of slavery was expanded to make sure that all 'analogous forms' were covered, and the provision making the trade piracy was re-inserted. This had become the more important as evidence was accumulating that the vast new wealth from oil revenues was reviving the old Arab longing for slaves, so that the trade was increasing rapidly in and around the Red Sea and the Persian Gulf. But it was in vain. The United Nations, at the instance of Egypt, India and the Soviet Union, rejected the piracy clause in favour of milder provisions. Forced reluctantly to accept the amendment, the British representative hoped that 'other delegates will realize that we are inspired by a spirit of compromise and by the desire to prevent misunderstanding in their minds' (*Times* Report, 29th August, 1956). In September 1956 the Supplementary Convention was adopted, and came into operation on the 30th April, 1957, but as yet no executive body has been appointed to supervise its working. So the matter rests.

v

Slavery has existed from the beginning and will last in one form or another so long as men lust after power. It has resulted in more misery, more murder, more degradation, more sadness, suffering and sin than any other human institution. It crushes individuals; it blights communities; it sours all human intercourse, for its sign-manual is fear— fear which possesses both master and man, both ruler and ruled. It has dealt viciously with the past, and perhaps more viciously with the present; for in its modern forms slavery if less obvious is more widespread and its fear more pervasive. The fear of a servile rising among its satellites haunts the Soviet Praesidium; the fear of a servile fate heightens the tension between East and West; the fear of a servile revenge broods in South Africa and overshadows the States; the fear of servile indignities, brain-washing, torture and sudden death, cows vast multitudes throughout the world. That is the modern contribution, and it treads hard on the heels of the old crude slavery now rising again in the Middle East, of the sham adoption of children (Mui Tsai) in China, of the peonage of South America, of the sale of women under the pretence of marriage, and of the various forms of debt-bondage and forced labour. All are still alive and claim their victims, not by ones or twos but by the hundred thousand. What can be done to end it? In all history the only power which has ever faced and overcome slavery is Christianity, which affirmed and, amid the compromises of united nations and the squabbles of disunited churches, still affirms, that God is love and that perfect love casts out fear. It remains now as before the slave's only hope.

Nor is the hope vain, for the spirit of Christianity, though it moves slowly, moves surely, and by simple ways not always obvious at first glance. The slavery of the Old World died on that moment when St. Paul proclaimed that in the eyes of God there was neither bond nor free, but only human beings, dear to the Creator. So, too, in the English colonies of the New World, slavery received its death-blow when the Quakers denied the right of any man to usurp the dominion over his fellows which God had reserved for Himself. And surely in these last times there has been thrown down a challenge, positive and full of promise, which cannot be ignored. For two hundred years and more the British Empire, too easily condemned because too little understood, has, over wide areas of the world, raised backward peoples from potential or actual slavery, to a higher concept of their duty to God and their fellow-men, till now they stand, in the pride or prospect of full nationhood, members of a Commonwealth where law controls and freedom reigns. In their onward march, they will make mistakes, as we have made them; there will be follies and failures, backslidings and faults, but the Commonwealth, if it remains true to its Christian traditions, will stand as a beacon in a dark world, and an example, however imperfect, of that brotherhood of man to which, if there is to be lasting peace and prosperity, the world must surely come.

BIBLIOGRAPHY

Abridgement of the Minutes of Evidence taken before a Committee of the whole House, 1789

Anti-Slavery Reporter, Various issues.

ARISTOTLE, *Politics*, translated by J. E. C. Welldon, 1905

BANCROFT, G., *History of the United States*, 3 Vols, 1853

BOOTH, C., *Zachary Macaulay*

BURY, J. H., *A History of the Roman Empire*, 6th Impression, 1913

BUXTON, Sir T. F., *The African Slave Trade and its Remedy*, 1840
Memoirs, Edited by C. Buxton, 3rd Edition, 1849

CLARKSON, T., *An Essay on the Slavery and Commerce of the Human Species particularly the African*, 1786
The Abolition of the African Slave Trade, 2 Vols, 1808

COUPLAND, Sir R., *Wilberforce*, 1923

DE TOCQUEVILLE, A., *Democracy in America*, 2 Vols, 1875

DICKSON, W., *Letters on Slavery*, 1789

ELIOT, E., *Christianity and Slavery*, 1833

Essay on the Abolition of Slavery throughout the British Dominions without injury to the master or his property (Anon), 1833

FOX, Sarah, *Diaries* (MSS)

FRANCKLYN, G., *An Answer to the Rev. Mr. Clarkson's Essay*, 1789

FROUDE, J. A. *Elizabeth*, 5 Vols (Everyman)
English Seamen in the Sixteenth Century, 1895

GARDINER, S. R., *History of the Commonwealth*, 4 Vols, 1903

GREENIDGE, A. H. J., *Greek Constitutional History*, 1902
A History of Rome, 1904
Roman Public Life, 1901

GRIGGS, E. L., *Thomas Clarkson*, 1936

GROTE, G., *A History of Greece*, 1907

HAKLUYT, R., *The Principal Voyages of the English Nation*, 7 Vols (Everyman)

HARRIS, Rex, *Jazz* (Penguin Books), 1957

HELPS, Sir Arthur, *The Spanish Conquest in America*, 4 Vols, 1900–4

HENDERSON, B. W., *The Life and Principate of the Emperor Nero*, 1905
HENSON, Josiah, *Uncle Tom's Story of His Life*, 1877
INGRAM, J. K., *A History of Slavery and Serfdom*
IRVING, W., *Life of Columbus*, 4 Vols, 1828
Jamaica, As it was, as it is, and as it may be (Anon), 1835
JOHNSON, T. L., *Twenty-eight years a Slave*, 7th Edition, 1909
JOHNSTON, Sir H., *The Negro in the New World*, 1910
KLINGBERG, F. J., *The Anti-Slavery Movement in England*, 1926
LASCELLES, E., *Granville Sharp*, 1928
LECKY, W. E. H., *History of England in the 18th Century*, 8 Vols, 1883
LIVINGSTONE, D., *Missionary Travels and Researches in South Africa*, 1857
LUCAS, C. P., *Historical Geography of the British Colonies*, Vol. II. *The West Indies*, Second Edition, 1905
MacINNES, C. M., *Bristol and the Slave Trade* (*The West in English History*), 1949
    England and Slavery, 1934
MACKENZIE-GRIEVE, A., *The Last Years of the English Slave Trade*, 1941
MacMUNN, Sir G., *Slavery through the Ages*, 1938
MADDEN, R. R., The Island of Cuba, 1849
MARTIN, Sir H. W., *A Counter Appeal*, 1823
MATHIESON, W. L., *British Slave Emancipation*, 1932
    British Slavery and its Abolition, 1823–38, 1926
    Great Britain and the Slave Trade, 1929
    Memoirs of a Monticello Slave, 1951
MOMMSEN, T., *The History of Rome*, 4 Vols, 1862
NEWTON, John., *An authentic narrative of some remarkable and interesting particulars in the life of John Newton*, Fifth Edition, 1782
    Thoughts on the African Slave Trade, Second Edition, 1788
NICKOLLS, R. B., *A Letter to the Treasurer of the Society instituted for the purpose of effecting the abolition of the Slave Trade*, 1787
NUGENT, Lady, *Journal*, Edited by F. Cundall, 1939
Observations on the Project for Abolishing the Slave Trade (Anon), 1790
OWEN, N., *Journal of a Slave Dealer*, 1930
PITT, W., *Parliamentary Speeches*, 3 Vols, 1808
PRESCOTT, W. H., *Conquest of Mexico*
    Ferdinand and Isabella, 3 Vols, 1857
RAMSAY, J., *An Essay on the Treatment and Conversion of African Slaves in the British Sugar Colonies*, 1784
    A letter to James Tobin Esq., 1787

Objections to the Abolition of the Slave Trade with Answers, 1788

Papers (MSS) (Rhodes House Library)

A Reply to Personal Invectives, 1785

Report of the Debate on a Motion for the Abolition of the Slave Trade in the House of Commons on Monday and Tuesday, April 18th and 19th, 1791

ROBERTSON, W., *Historical Works*, 8 Vols, 1840

RUSSELL, C. E. B., *General Rigby, Zanzibar and the Slave Trade*, 1935

SHUCKBURGH, E. S., *A History of Rome*, 1896

SIMON, Kathleen, *Slavery*, 1930

STANHOPE, *Life of William Pitt*, 4 Vols

STEVENS, W., *The Slave in History*, 1904

STOWE, Harriet Beecher, *A Key to Uncle Tom's Cabin*, 1853
Uncle Tom's Cabin, 1892

TACITUS, *On Britain and Germany*, translated by H. Mattingly (Penguin Classics), 1954

THISTLEWOOD, Thomas, Mss Journals in the Lincoln Archives

THUCYDIDES, *History*, translated by B. Jowett, 2nd Ed., 2 Vols, 1900

TREVELYAN, Sir G. M., *The Peace and the Protestant Succession*, 1934

TREVELYAN, Sir G. O., *Life and Letters of Lord Macaulay*, 1876

WESLEY, John, *Thoughts upon Slavery*, 1774

WILBERFORCE, W., *An Appeal to the Religion, Justice and Humanity of the Inhabitants of the British Empire in behalf of the Negro Slaves in the West Indies*, New Edition, 1823
A Letter on the Abolition of the Slave Trade addressed to the Freeholders and other Inhabitants of Yorkshire, 1807

WOODWARD, W. H., *The Expansion of the British Empire*, 1907

INDEX

Accabah (a slave), 92
Africa, 24, 25, 36, 48, 53, 57, 58, 59,
  69, 71, 79, 88, 121, 123, 124,
  127, 136, 144, 145, 148, 151,
  154, 155, 160, 161, 165, 168,
  179, 182, 183, 184, 185, 186
Alarm, 110
Albuquerque, 29
Alexander VI, 40
Algiers, 24
Allen, Mr. 87, 94
Alva, Duke of, 39
America, 24, 26, 29, 30, 41, 42,
  43, 44, 57, 66, 67, 68, 69, 77, 78,
  79, 101, 111, 112, 130, 131,
  136
Amiens, Treaty of, 167
Amis des Noirs, La Société des, 149,
  150
Andalusia, 24
Anne, Queen, 50
Anne and Mary, 110
Antigua, 83, 100, 181
Antilles, 76
Appleby, 131
Arabs, the, 183, 185, 188
Aristotle, 12, 13, 15, 25, 28
Ashanti, 60
Assiento, 50, 52, 54, 57
Athens, 13, 14, 16, 20
Attica, 14, 15
"Attorneys", 78
Azores, 40

Bahamas, 83
Bancroft, George, 36, 41, 42, 112
Bank of England, 50
Barbados, 49, 78, 79, 82, 99, 100,
  107, 173
Barbary, 24, 43

Barham, Lord, 155. *See also* Middle-
  ton, Sir Charles.
Barracoons, 26, 61, 62, 127, 144
Barton, Mr., 92
Bath, 103, 145, 146, 148
Baxter, Richard, 99
Belgium, 185, 186
Belsen, 35
Benezet, Anthony, 111, 112
Benin, 61
Berbice, 174
Berlin, Conference of, 186
Bermuda, 46, 83, 100, 181
Bimba Back, 88
Birmingham, 137
Black River, 87
Blackstone, Dr. 108
Bobadilla, 31
Bombay, 186
Boswell, James, 122, 139
Bourbons, the, 167
Bowditch, 60
Bridgwater, 114
Bristol, 47, 48, 55, 105, 136, 140, 141,
  154, 166
Brussels, 186
Burke, Edmund, 147, 148
Buxton, Sir T. F., 61, 84, 124, 170,
  171, 176, 179, 182, 183

Cambridge, 117, 119, 129, 130, 131,
  133
Canaan, 13, 97
Canada, 75, 142
Canary Islands, 37
Canning, George, 172, 175
Cape of Good Hope, 43, 77
Caribbean Sea, 43
Carthage, 23
Carthagena, 65

Cary, Colonel, 68
Cary, John, 54
Cassius, Caius, 20
Castile, 26
Castlereagh, Robert Stewart, Viscount, 167, 168
Catholicism, 26, 28
Cavell, Nurse, 54
Cecil, Sir William, Lord Burghley, 37
Channing, Dr. 179, 181
Charles V, 33, 36, 40, 97, 100
China, 189
Christianity, origin, 21;
    impact on slavery, 22–4;
    and the Negroes, 25, 84, 100–102,
    115, 150, 172, 175, 179, 182,
    189
Clarkson, Thomas, 118–121, 125,
    128, 132, 133, 154, 157, 160
    and collection of evidence, 136–
    140, 141, 142, 144–7, 148;
    in France, 150–1
Code Noir, 76
Coffee (a slave), 89
"Coffles", 62
Colbert, Jean Baptiste, 76
Collgrove, Mr. 87, 94
Columbus, Christopher, 24, 26, 28,
    29, 30, 31, 41, 42, 43
Congo, The, 186
Congress, American, 12, 112, 165
Constantinople, 44
Cope, Mr. 85, 93
Cornwallis, Lord, 131
Corsairs, 24
Cowper, William, 103, 106, 157
Crimea, 44
Cromwell, 47
Cuba, 33, 43, 165
"Customs", 59
Cyrus (a slave), 91

Darien, Bishop of, 34
Dawes, Governor, 124
Decelea, 14
Declaration of Independence, 12
Defoe, Daniel, 106
Delos, 20

Demerara, 173, 174
Denmark, 66, 76, 159
Deptford, 155
Derby (a slave), 92
Dick (a slave), 92
Dolben, Sir W., 146, 147, 149
Dominica, 159
Dorril, Mr., 90
Dudley, Lord, 174
Dundas, Henry, Viscount Melville,
    159, 160

East India Company, 48
Eden, William, Lord Auckland, 149,
    150
Egypt, 13, 185, 188
Elba, 167, 168
Eliot, E., 59, 84
Elizabeth I, 37, 38, 39, 40
England, connection with slavery, 11;
    and Hawkins, 36;
    trade with Africa, 37, 38, 40, 41,
    42, 44, 45, 47, 48;
    and slave trade, 51–4;
    slaves in English colonies, 77–85;
    and abolition of slave trade, 97;
    religion in England, 98;
    in 1780, 130–1;
    other references, 57, 66, 76, 101–
    103, 104, 105, 106, 107, 109, 110,
    112, 113, 114, 116, 124, 127, 141,
    146, 149, 150, 151, 153, 156, 158,
    160, 165, 167, 168, 169, 173, 175,
    177, 179, 181, 182, 184, 186, 187,
    188
English (a slave), 89
Ephors, 16
Epicureans, 21
Ergastulum, 17
Estebez, 36

Fenchurch Street, 108
Ferdinand, King, 29, 30, 32, 97, 100
Flanders, 33, 39
Fox, Charles James, 131, 147, 148,
    159, 162, 163
Fox, George, 99, 100
Fox, Sarah, 140, 141

France, 41, 44, 50, 66, 75, 76, 98, 124, 130, 137, 149, 150, 151, 153, 154, 160, 161, 165, 166, 167, 168, 169, 185, 186
Francklyn, G., 79, 118, 119, 122, 138
Freetown, 124
Fullerswood, 89

Gambia, 41
Gardiner, S. R., 52
Gaza, 13
Genoese, 33, 48
George, Boy, 92
Germany, 12, 48, 185, 186, 187
Gibeon, 13
Glenelg, Lord, 181
Godwin, Rev. Morgan, 59, 80
Gold Coast, 79
Gooding, George, 89
Gordon Riots, 130
Granada, 24
Greece, 13, 20, 23, 67, 69
Guiana, 76, 161, 162, 181
Guinea Coast, 26, 36, 37, 40, 43, 46

Haiti, 26. See also Hispaniola
Hakluyt, R., 37
Ham, 25
Hamerton, Colonel, 184
Hardwicke, Earl of, 105, 109. See also Yorke, Philip
Harley, Robert, Earl of Oxford, 50
Hawkins, Sir John, 36, 37, 38, 39, 40 48, 51
Hayden, Lewis, 68
Hebrews, 20
Hellas, 15
Helots, 15, 16, 28
Henson, Josiah, 93
Hertfordshire, 119
Hibbert, George, 152
Hispaniola, 26, 27, 29, 30, 31, 32, 36, 37, 43, 52
Holt, Lord Chief Justice, 104, 108
Holwood Park, 135
Hottentots, 77, 80
Hull, 129, 130, 131, 132
Humphrey (a slave), 92, 93

Iberian Peninsula, 24
Independence, War of, 112
India, 42, 188
Indians, West, 28, 29, 31, 32, 44
Inquisition, Spanish, 30, 34
Insurrections, servile, 18
"Interlopers", 49, 50
Ireland, 130, 161
Isabella, Queen, 26, 27, 28, 29, 30, 31, 44, 74, 87, 100
Israelites, 13
Italy, 18, 24, 185

Jackson, Mr., 87
Jamaica, 33, 83, 85, 93, 108, 110, 113, 122, 173
James, River, 41
Jamestown, 45, 77
Jefferson, Thomas, 68
Jerusalem, 21
Jervis, John, 110, 111. See also St. Vincent, Earl of,
Jobson, Captain, 41, 52, 77
Johnson, Dr., 106
Johnson, Thomas, 90
Joshua, 13
"Jumpers", 72

Kent, 115
Kentucky, 68
Kerr, John, 108
Keston, 135
Kirk, Sir John, 184
Kite, Sir R., 108
Knight, Joseph, 112
Koromantis, 79, 80
Kumassi, 60

Lacedaemonia, 15, 28
Las Casas, 24, 30, 31–3, 34, 35, 74, 100
Lay, Benjamin, 101
League of Nations, 186, 187
Lecky, W. E. H., 52
Leeward Islands, 83
Leo X, 52, 97
Lexington, 68
Liberia, 186

Lincoln, 85
Lincoln's Inn, 130
Lisle, David, 107, 108
Liverpool, 55, 105, 113, 136, 141, 154, 166
Liverpool, Lord, 167
Livingstone, David, 63, 183
Locke, John, 106
Lok, John, 36, 37, 54
London, 37, 48, 55, 101, 103, 105, 106, 107, 108, 111, 120, 122, 129, 136, 140, 152, 166, 181
Long Pond Piece, 92
Louis XIV, 76
Louis XVIII, 168
Lowther, Sir James, 131
Lyme, 163

Macaulay, Zachary, 124, 167
Madrid, 31, 32
Manchester, 137
Mano, 57
Mansfield, Lord, 82, 110, 111, 112, 114, 121, 122, 125
Martin, Sir Henry, 79
Martinique, 159
Maryland, 93
Mauritius, 167
Mediterranean, 23, 110
"Meeting for Sufferings", 115
Mexico, 39, 43
Mexico, Gulf of, 43
Middleham, Dean of, 84
"Middle Passage", 53, 58, 62–6, 70, 127, 148, 152, 155, 156
Middleton, Sir Charles, 155. See also Barham, Lord
Milner, Isaac, 133
Molyneux, Mr., 117
Montesquieu, Charles de Secondat, 106
Moors, the, 23, 35
Moses, 20, 99
Moslems, 24, 185, 187
Muscat, 183

Napoleon, 163, 167, 168
National Assembly, 150, 151

Navigation Acts, 47
Negroes, 24, 25, 32, 35, 38
  numbers allowed to be imported, 41
  and Portugal, 42, 44
  in Bermuda, 46
  and the Assiento, 50
  European doubts regarding, 59
  on the "middle Passage", 63
  in Spanish colonies, 75
  in French colonies, 75
  in Danish colonies, 76
  in English colonies, 77–85
  on sugar plantations, 78
  in Barbados, 78
  how kept in submission, 90
  attitude of Quakers towards, 102
  in England, 103
  in Sierra Leone, 123
  physical and moral conditions, 170
Nembana, 123
Nero (a slave), 91
Nevis, 100
New England, 47
Newton, John, 81, 134, 135
Niger, River, 183
Nile, 183
Noah, 97
North, Lord, 100, 111, 131
Nugent, Lady, 122

Obeah, 59
Oman, 184
Orange, Prince of, 39
Ovando, Nicolas de, 31
Owen, Nicholas, 54, 55, 56, 57

Padstow, 38
Paris, 149, 167
Paris, Treaty of, 167, 168
Peckard, Dr., 117
Peloponnesian War, 14
Pennsylvania, 101
Percy, Earl of, 164, 172
Pericles, 15
Persian Gulf, 188
Phibbah, 86

Philip II of Spain, 37, 38, 40
Pitt, William, 129–132, 133, 134, 135, 136, 140, 141, 142, 144, 145, 146, 147, 148, 149, 151, 159, 162, 163, 166
Plaister, Mr., 87
Plato, 14, 20
Plymouth, 37, 155
Pope, Alexander, 106
Pope, the, 37, 40, 46, 98, 100
Portland, Duke of, 114, 131
Porto Rico, 33
Portugal, 24, 25, 26, 35, 40, 42, 43, 46, 58, 66, 98, 165, 169, 185, 186
Potter, Captain, 56
Predial Slavery, 15, 25,
Privy Council, 145, 146, 148, 149, 151
Purchas, Samuel, 61
Putney, 129

Quakers, 99, 100, 101, 102, 106, 111, 112, 114, 115, 117, 120, 121, 123, 132, 135, 140, 147, 155, 164, 171, 189

Ramsay, James, 70, 71, 78, 83, 115–117, 120, 123, 128
  and Pitt, 142–5, 146, 148
Randolph, Thomas Mann, 68
Red Sea, 188
Religion, 21, 22, 25, 74–6, 133–4
  attitude of Church to slavery, 83–85
  attitude towards abolition, 98 ff
"Repartimientos", 26, 28, 31
Ridolfi Plot, 40
Rigby, General, 184, 186
Robertson, Dr., 113
Rockingham, Lord, 131
Roger (a slave), 94
Rome, 16, 19, 20, 21, 67, 68, 69
Romilly, Sir S., 163
Rousseau, Jean-Jacques, 12
Russia, 45, 130, 187, 188
Rutland, Duke of, 131
St. Bartholomew's Hospital, 108

St. Helena, 168
St. James, 84
St. John de Ullua, 39
St. Kitts, 70, 115
St. Lucia, 167, 174
St. Paul, 22, 23, 94, 189
St. Thomas Island, 113
St. Vincent, Earl of, 110
Salt Savannah, 89
Salter, James, 93
Sambo (a slave), 91
Samson, 13
San Domingo, 150, 159
Scotland, 112, 158
"Scramble", 67
"Seasoning", 69–71, 80, 127, 143
Sekwebu, 63
Seneca, 20
Serfdom, 23, 28
Sharp, Granville, 106, 111, 112, 114, 117, 119, 120, 128, 131, 140, 146
  and Jonathan Strong, 107–8
  and James Somerset, 109–10
  and the "Poor Blacks", 121–4
  views on slavery, 126
Sharp, William, 107, 108
Shelburne, Earl of, 131
Sherborow River, 54
Siberia, 35
Sicily, 24
Sierra Leone, 38, 64, 123, 125, 126, 161
Slavery, two stages, 11
  the penalty of weakness, 12
  predial slavery, 15
  in Rome, 16–20
  and Christianity, 22
  in Middle Ages, 23
  changing characteristics, 25
  slave market in America, 29
  and Las Casas, 31
  under Cromwell, 47
  and England, 51–4
  Cary's views, 54
  sale arrangements, 57
  sources of supply, 59
  two types, 67
  and the whip, 72

five forms of negro slavery, 74
Spanish slavery, 75
statistics, 78–9
and sugar, 79
British slavery, 77–85
the attitude of the Law, 81–3
Mansfield's judgment, 110
and Quakers, 115
Ramsay's views, 115–7
the Quaker Committee, 125
Sharp's views, 126
and Burke, 147
emancipation, 178, 181
and the United Nations, 187
Slave Trade organisation, 54, 55, 62
Slaves, "Natural" slaves, 12, 25, 34
as "nationalised" labour, 13
in Athens, 14, 15
in Sparta, 15
plantation slaves at Rome, 18
town slaves at Rome, 19
and Christianity, 23
negro slaves introduced into Europe, 24
and Portugal, 26
and "repartimientos", 26
Indian slaves in Hispaniola, 27
demand for slave labour in Barbados, 49
and the Assiento, 50
bids for freedom, 56–7
on the "Middle Passage" 63–6
auctioned, 67
domestic slaves, 68–9
plantation slaves, 69–71
type preferred by British planters, 79
and the Law, 81
Thistlewood, 87 ff
bitterness against runaway slaves, 89
dominated by hunger, 90 ff
brought to England, 102
status in England, 108
evidence regarding, 151–2
Buxton's proposals for, 171–2

and apprenticeship, 178
Smith, Adam, 113
Smith of Demerara, 173, 174
Smith of Virginia, 44, 45, 77
Smollett, T., 65
Somerset, James, 109, 110, 112
"Soul Driver", 67
South Africa, 189
South America, 189
South Carolina, 42
South Sea Company, 50
Sparta, 14, 16, 18, 20
Spain, 24, 26, 27, 28, 29, 31, 35, 37, 39, 40, 43, 44, 46, 47, 48, 50, 74, 81, 98, 130, 165, 169, 186
Spanish Inquisition, 30
Steel-Maitland, Sir A., 186
Stewart, Charles, 109, 110
Stoics, 21
Stowe, Harriet Beecher, 36, 90
Strong, Jonathan, 107, 108, 109
Stuart, Mary, 37, 40
Subject Populations, 12
Sugar Plantations, 78–9
Sweden, 48, 168

Tacitus, 13
Talbot, Charles, 104
Teston, 115, 120
Thames, the, 166
Thistlewood, John, 88, 89, 93
Thistlewood, Thomas, 85–94
Thornton, Henry, 124
Thucydides, 15
Tom (a slave), 91
Tony (a slave), 92
Trinidad, 174
Tripoli, 24
Tunis, 24
Tymor, 45

Uncle Tom's Cabin, 36, 93
United Nations, 187, 188
United States, 142, 165, 169, 179, 181, 186
Universal Declaration of Human Rights, 187
Utrecht, Treaty of, 50, 52

Venice, 42, 43
Vienna, 168
Virginia, 41, 42, 44, 45, 46, 48, 68, 77, 109

Wades Mill, 119
Wales, 158
Walsingham, Sir Francis, 37
Wanicher, 88, 92
Wapping, 107
Wedgwood, Josiah, 158
Wesley, John, 113
West Indies, 31, 39, 40, 41, 43, 46, 66, 67, 68, 69, 75, 76, 79, 84, 104, 105, 108, 115, 116, 119, 126, 141, 143, 147, 152, 153, 159, 161, 173
Wilberforce, William, 62, 63, 64, 66, 79, 80, 121, 136, 140, 141, 142, 145, 146, 149, 150, 151, 154 156,

157, 164, 167, 170, 171, 172, 179, 187
his youth, 128–35;
introduces first motion, 148;
and his first Bill, 155;
changing outlook, 158;
acclaimed, 163;
and register of slaves, 166;
Will (a slave), 92
William and Mary, 104
Woolman, John, 101

Ximenes, Cardinal, 32

Yorke, Philip, 104. See also Hardwicke, Earl of
Yorkshire County, 132
Yorktown, 131

Zanzibar, 183, 184, 185, 186
Zong case, 82, 113, 114, 131